MONDAYS AT 3

MONDAYS AT 3

A story for managers learning to lead

Greg Giesen

Greg Giesen & Associates, Denver, Colorado

A GGA, Inc. Publishers Publication
© 2007, 2011 by Greg Giesen & Associates, Inc. All rights reserved.
First edition 2006. Second impression 2006.
Second printing, 2007.

Printed and bound in the USA by
GGA, Inc. Publishers
Highlands Ranch, CO 80126
Phone: 1-866-322-7868
www.GregGiesen.com

ISBN-10: 0-9788555-9-0 (previously ISBN 0-9788555-0-7)
ISBN-13: 978-0-9788555-9-8

Second Edition
(Formerly *Ask Dr. Mac: Take the Journey to Authentic Leadership*)

Cataloging in Publication Data is on file with the Library of Congress

Book Cover Design by Creative Visions

In Memory of Dr. Mac

Thank you for everything that you did
to make this world a better place.

Contents

Contents

Contents

Contents

Acknowledgments

I MUST BEGIN BY ACKNOWLEDGING my two biggest fans, my mother and father, who believed in me from the start and have showered me with encouragement all the way to completion of this book.

Next, I'd like to acknowledge my wife, Tanya, who always supported my writing and my vision for this project. Without her constant encouragement during the tough times, I may not have finished writing this book.

I'd also like to thank my extended family—Cindy, Mel, Katie, Charlie, John, Jay, Helen, Megan, Nick, Amy, Mike, Lee Ann, David, Christal, Brian, Colleen, Michelle, David, Ginger, Taylor, Will, Claire, Tommy, Lori, Steve, and grandma Bobbie— for their support, curiosity, and for allowing me to use their names as characters in the book.

I must recognize all the University of Denver graduate students who patiently allowed me to read various chapters to them over the past two years. I'd like to especially thank the following DU students for providing an initial review of my first draft: Ehab Abushmais, Craig Albers, Carla Campbell, Santhosh Chavakula, Steve Chucker, Chris Claggett, Michael

Holton, David Lindenmuth, Tom Rankin, Sanjay Rathore, and Melissa Risteff.

Susannah Ortego was my primary editor. Rarely have I ever had the pleasure of working with someone who edited my work in such a substantive way, while maintaining such a noncritical and supportive manner.

Other supporters that have played a significant role in the evolution of this book include Ann Moore, Jo Ellen Snell, and Ray Herr, MD.

Finally, I want to acknowledge my friend and colleague, Garry Shelp. Although he may no longer be with us in body, he certainly is in spirit. I'm so glad that he was a part of my life.

MONDAYS AT 3

Introduction

Managing is as much about *how* you manage as it is about *what* you manage. I know. I learned it the hard way. My first management experience ended in a dismissal—mine! Oh sure, I've got plenty of excuses and can point fingers with the best of them, but I refuse to go there. The truth is, I could have chosen to make my situation different but I didn't. As it turned out, getting fired was the wakeup call that changed my life.

Fast-forward to today, twenty years later. I am now a successful management consultant, graduate school professor, author, and keynote speaker. Ironically, I specialize in helping supervisors and managers manage more effectively. Talk about coming full circle! Boy, if I only knew then what I know now.

They say in my profession that we teach what we most need to learn. Perhaps that's why I do what I'm doing. Nevertheless, these past twenty years have taught me a tremendous amount about management—so much, in fact, that this book practically wrote itself. And truthfully, it's only the tip of the iceberg. I hope there will be more books to come. But for now, it's my pleasure to introduce you to *Mondays at 3: A story for managers learning to lead.*

Like Justin, our protagonist, the story itself is fictional, but I can tell you that the situations that occur within this story are nothing but real. Certainly some of the scenarios have come from my direct experiences in *being* a manager, but most have been drawn from my work *with* managers, as a management coach and consultant. In many cases, I was called in to help a company fix a group dynamics problem that, more often than not, involved a manager and his or her employees. What I usually discovered was that the problem had something to do with poor management skills. In other words, the manager didn't know how to manage people. But does that really surprise you? It didn't surprise me. Too many managers are still being promoted today based on their knowledge and expertise in a particular area without much consideration given to their ability to lead others. But the problem doesn't stop there. The manager's manager has to assume responsibility for providing the necessary support and resources needed to develop the new manager's leadership skills. As you can see, rarely is it just about one person. And addressing this issue will require more than just this book...but at least it's a start.

I wrote *Mondays at 3* primarily for all new supervisors and managers who could use a little more support, empathy, and guidance in becoming better *people managers*. But honestly, I have yet to meet anyone in the management ranks who wouldn't benefit by the story you are about to read. After all, isn't learning to lead others a lifelong process? It is to me. And to assist you with that process, I've incorporated many of the insights and lessons learned from this tale into fourteen individual journal entries that appear throughout the book. A complete list of all the journal entries can also be found in the back of the book.

Finally, you'll find some "Dear Dr. Mac" letters in the back of the book as well, designed primarily to help you get started in becoming the leader you were meant to be.

That's it for now. It's time for you to start your journey with Justin and Dr. Mac. I hope you enjoy reading the book as much as I enjoyed writing it.

—GREG GIESEN

Part One

Life Is Good

It's all about the game

"SO WHAT ABOUT IT?" mumbled Justin, a bit annoyed that Megan was talking to him while he was watching his football game.

"I think you should read it, that's all," she said, as she threw the business section of the Sunday paper at him rather forcefully. "There's a column in there that talks about problem employees. Don't you still have that woman at work who talks on the phone with her friends all day?"

The newspaper fell to the carpet near Justin's feet, completely unnoticed by him. Feeling ignored, Megan shook her head in frustration and stormed out of the living room.

It was Sunday afternoon and Justin refused to let any thoughts about work seep into his consciousness. The kickoff between the Chicago Bears and Minnesota Vikings was about six commercials away, just enough time for Justin to call his next play. It went something like this: *Spring to the bathroom, then cut back through the kitchen, around the fridge, grab a beer and dart through the pantry just in time to heist the open bag of white powdered donuts, and be back at the couch—all within four minutes. Ready, set, go!*

Justin was the kind of person who easily entertained himself, and often preferred it that way. He certainly could be very social and turn on the charm whenever the situation called for it, but his natural tendency was to keep to himself. It was the world in which he felt most comfortable. Megan, on the other hand, was quite the opposite. She was much more extraverted and very involved in the lives of her friends. She preferred to be around people and drew a tremendous amount of energy from her social interactions.

Unfortunately, personality differences and Justin's football obsession were two distinctly different animals, at least from Megan's perspective. Yet, despite her growing frustration, she also knew full well what she was getting herself into when they married more than eleven years ago. Justin was just as much of a football junkie then as he was now and he never professed to be any different. Why, they even met playing intramural football against each other on the campus of Northwestern University. Of course back then Megan was sure that he would grow out of his football fanaticism, especially once they started a family. Instead, it had expanded to the kids. Even their five-year-old son Tommy looked forward to playing tackle with his father during the television commercials each Sunday. And Michelle, at only eight, could already throw a spiral with the football better than most of the boys in her class.

Needless to say, Justin couldn't be happier. Football was quickly becoming a family bonding event—at least for the majority of the family.

Family 2 bonding

"**D**ID YOU READ IT YET?" Megan yelled from the laundry room.

"Oh yeah," Justin yelled back, "it was great!"—not remembering what it was he was supposed to have read. He was having a hard time shifting away from the game. It was halftime and the Bears were already down by fourteen points. Justin was feeling edgy and knew he needed to relieve some of his tension. He shouted loud enough so that he could be heard throughout the house. "Where's Tommy? It's time to play tackle! Tommy, where are you?"

And then, off in the distance from the other side of the house, he heard Tommy's faint voice yell back, "I'm busy right now. I'm watching a movie with Michelle."

Fine, Justin thought to himself, *be that way!* He then looked over at Sandy, their dog of thirteen years who was sprawled out on the recliner. *I'm guessing you don't want to play with me either?* Sandy yawned and went back to sleep. *I'll take that as a no?*

Halftime always drove Justin crazy. He never wanted to veer too far from the television in case he might miss something important, like a comment from a player or the first-half highlights. As a result, he carefully calculated his moves in between halves. Today, however, even contemplating whether or not to get up off the couch proved to be a difficult decision. *That's pretty sad,* he mused to himself as he belched and sat upright. Just then his eyes caught a glimpse of the floor, and the business section from the morning paper. It was lying right where it had landed when Megan had thrown it at him.

What was it she wanted me to read? he asked himself, dazedly. Unable to remember, he quickly glimpsed at the front page and spotted an advice column called "Ask Dr. Mac." *Could this be what she was referring to?* he pondered. Justin held the paper back just far enough so that he could read it without having to get up and retrieve his glasses.

It started out:

> Dear Dr. Mac,
>
> I have a coworker who continuously makes personal calls throughout the day. It would be one thing if this were just an occasional thing, but she....

and then Justin impatiently tossed the paper down on the floor.

Please! he cried inwardly, *I don't have time to read that crap!*

For the brief time that his mind had switched from the joy of football to the agony of work, Justin could feel a tinge of anger. He had read just enough of the article to stir up some bad feelings about Lee Ann, one of his coworkers, who apparently would rather spend her time at work making personal calls instead of taking customer orders.

Oh well, he thought, shaking his head, *it's not my problem. What do I care anyway? I'm not her boss.*

Just then the Bears came back on the field and Justin happily resumed his horizontal position on the couch. Tommy and Michelle finished their movie and quickly ran into the room and joined him on the couch for the second half.

I just love my Sundays! Justin mused. *Life is good.*

Savoring the weekend

I‍F SUNDAY AFTERNOONS WERE the best of times for Justin, then Sunday evenings were clearly the worst of times. When dinner came around, Justin could feel his weekend slowly slipping away. It was that unwanted transition from a nice, relaxing weekend full of fun, family, and football to thoughts about Monday, the workweek, and having to face a job that was quickly becoming mundane and unmotivating.

Justin glanced around the table and smiled, feeling an overwhelming sense of appreciation for his family. It was a moment in which he could have very easily lingered, but which ended abruptly when he heard Megan cry, "Tommy, Tommy, what are you doing?" from across the table.

But Tommy was in his own world, smashing green peas with his fork while softly singing to himself. Megan put her arm around him and whispered, "Honey, you can't eat your peas if you continue to smash them."

Just then Tommy broke out of his trance and looked up at Justin with a gleaming face. "Daddy, who won the football game?"

Megan could only shake her head.

Justin looked at her, trying not to laugh. "He gets that from me."

"I know he does," replied Megan, "and it's not one of your better traits," as she got up from the table, trying to conceal her smile.

Of course Tommy's words were music to Justin's ears. He loved the idea of having a son with whom he could share the game of football. "The Vikings won, son, but we'll get 'em next time. Right?"

"Yes, daddy, 'cause we're the Bears! Right?"

"Right, son, 'cause we're the Bears."

Justin got up to wash the dishes while Megan took the kids upstairs for their evening baths.

The weekend is ending too quickly, he thought. *I don't want to go to work tomorrow! They can't make me!* But he knew it was futile to whine. He had to work, and that meant adjusting his attitude between now and tomorrow morning. *I need to be upbeat and positive at all times,* he thought. Of course those weren't his words, but those of his supervisor, Christal. She was always throwing out catchphrases from whatever management book she was reading at the time. The problem was that she rarely backed the words up with any kind of consistent action, at least in his opinion.

Justin took a slow, deep breath in an attempt to shift his negative thinking away from Christal and back to salvaging what little time remained in the weekend.

Christal's really not that bad, he reflected, *and she did go out of her way to get me one of the highest raises in the department.*

Feeling slightly better, Justin poured himself a cup of hot tea and headed for the den to catch the remaining half-hour of *SportsCenter* on ESPN. This nightly ritual was his time to relax and put closure on the day. Of course getting one more dose of sports scores and highlights before bed didn't hurt either.

As Justin put his legs up on the coffee table, he spotted the Dr. Mac column on the floor. Although Megan hadn't brought the subject up yet this evening, he knew she was likely to quiz him on it before they went to bed.

All right, I guess I'll read the whole thing, he shrugged, and he took another deep breath before reading:

Dear Dr. Mac,

I have a coworker who continuously makes personal calls throughout the day. It would be one thing if this was just an occasional occurrence, but she is constantly on the phone, all day long, day after day. What's worse is that because we have cubicles, everyone can hear her talking out loud, laughing and having a good time.

I've tried talking to the supervisor but he tells me to mind my own business. It has gotten to the point that I can no longer concentrate and do the job I was hired to do. I'm about to give up!

Please help me.

Angry and Annoyed

Dear Angry and Annoyed:

Let me ask you this: If a coworker of yours had an issue with you, would you prefer that they talk to you directly about it or go to your supervisor first with their concerns? I'm guessing that you'd prefer they come talk to you directly first. With that in mind, you too have the responsibility to talk to the coworker directly about your concerns. Anything less would be disrespectful. And that includes talking "about her" to coworkers.

Next, you need to assess if her behavior is negatively impacting your ability to get your job done. I mention this because if her behavior is just annoying but doesn't really impact your work, then I'd have to agree with your supervisor and tell you to let it go. You are wasting a lot of valuable energy and time on something that is not really important. If, on the other hand, her behavior does indeed impede your ability to get your work done, then by all means, keep reading.

Confronting your coworker doesn't have to be a difficult experience. Sit down with her, one-to-one, and tell her what's going on with you, making sure you cover the following points:

1) *Begin by acknowledging the importance of having an effective working relationship with her.*
2) *Tell her that the purpose of your conversation is to share a concern that she may not be aware of.*
3) *Describe the particular behavior that is causing a problem for you.*
4) *Explain how the behavior is impacting your ability to get your work done.*
5) *Propose a solution.*
6) *Get agreement.*
7) *Thank her for her willingness to collaborate with you.*

It's important to remember when confronting a coworker that the key is not to make them wrong.

> *The key is to ask for what you need and to give them the same opportunity with you. Always remember to keep the focus on the working relationship. Personal attacks don't belong here. Finally, be respectful and polite and treat coworkers the same way you'd like to be treated.*
>
> *—Dr. Mac*

Hmm, interesting, Justin thought to himself. Megan was right; this situation *was* almost identical to what was going on in his office with Lee Ann. It was as if one of his coworkers had written the letter. And he really liked the fact that this Dr. Mac got right to the point, not to mention the fact that he had offered some really good advice.

A devious thought occurred to Justin. *Perhaps I should bring this article in and leave it lying on the table in the break room for others to read. Better yet, I could put it on Lee Ann's chair before she comes in!* Justin grinned as he imagined the look on his colleague's face as she read the article that mysteriously appeared on her chair.

Just then Megan called out from upstairs. "Honey, are you coming to bed?"

"Yes, babe!" was all Justin could muster as he reluctantly got up from the couch and shut off the television. The room became quiet for the first time that day. Unfortunately, the same could not be said for Justin's brain, which was buzzing with all kinds of thoughts—thoughts that weren't likely to go away anytime soon.

The 4 company

DATADUMP WAS ON THE CORNER of Maple and Oak Streets, just a short, twenty-minute drive from Justin's home in Winnetka, Illinois. The building itself was a very modern, three-story structure of dark brick with large tinted windows. On the back side of the building, next to the company parking lot, was a private recreational park just for DataDump employees, complete with picnic tables, a basketball and sand volleyball court, and a couple of outdoor grills.

The company itself was fairly new, specializing in computer software products. In the software industry, they were probably best known for their 100-, 250- and 750-MB zip disc series. Due in great part to the popularity of these products, DataDump had recently opened up a satellite office in Boulder, Colorado in order to create a regional presence out west.

Justin had joined DataDump five years ago when the company was just starting out. He was twenty-eight then and came over from another high tech company in nearby Evanston, where he worked in sales. The DataDump position was more of a lateral move for Justin but it provided a better salary and a much shorter drive, given that he and his family lived in the same town. When he first began at DataDump, he was in the Sales and Marketing Department and was primarily responsible for taking orders for their zip disc products. Although these products were still fairly new at that time, it took everything Justin and Charlie Pozzi had to keep on top of the daily orders.

Charlie, the other order-taker, was ten years older than Justin and had previously supervised an orders-fulfillment department with a large catalog company in Chicago. According to Charlie, he had purposely taken a step down in rank and in salary by coming to DataDump because he wanted be a little closer to home. Like Justin, Charlie placed great value in living and working in the same community.

Together, Justin and Charlie made a pretty good team. Even though they both experienced days of being overwhelmed with taking and fulfilling orders, both enjoyed working for such a small company with a family-like atmosphere. In the early years, DataDump had been a place where everyone knew each other, birthdays were celebrated together, and monthly barbecues out behind the building occurred on the fourth Friday of every month.

But times were different now.

In just five short years, the company had grown from twenty to eighty employees and there were no signs of things slowing down anytime soon. Future projections for their zip disc series were extremely favorable, not to mention that they were about to introduce an entire new line of complimentary products into the marketplace.

The Sales and Marketing functions were split into two separate areas, leaving Justin and Charlie as the first two employees of the newly developed Orders Fulfillment department, now under Sales. In the couple of years since then they had been joined in the home office by Will, John, Lee Ann, and Amy as additional order-takers. Christal Deeds, an experienced sales manager from New York City, had been brought in as the department manager responsible for overseeing both the Winnetka and Boulder offices.

For Justin and Charlie, going from a department of two to seven people in such a short span of time had been a challenge in itself. Nevertheless, the Orders Fulfillment *team,* as Christal liked to refer to them, still seemed to be coming together nicely, and without any major problems. Or so it appeared.

Part Two

The Promotion(s)

Christal's **5** promotion

CHRISTAL DEEDS WAS DESTINED to lead. Being manager of the Orders Fulfillment Department had clearly been a stepping-stone for her. It was now time to move up in the organization, and Christal had just been tapped to become the company's new Vice President of Sales.

The organization rejoiced.

An all-employee celebration party was held out back at the company park.

The Orders Fulfillment Department was in shock.

The other 6 promotion

AMIDST ALL THE EXCITEMENT and congratulations that surrounded Christal for the next few days was the rather difficult decision of choosing her successor. The person she chose as manager would not only oversee the staff in Winnetka but in Boulder as well. Not a simple task; nor was making this decision.

"Do you know who you're going to select?" asked J.W., the CEO of DataDump, as they sat at the conference table waiting for the senior management team to trickle in for their meeting.

"Yes and no," replied Christal. "I can easily narrow it down to two people, Charlie and Justin. Charlie is older and has management experience. Yet, I'm not convinced that he is the right person for the job."

"What do you mean?" asked J.W. "If he's got the experience—"

"That's just it," interrupted Christal. "He's already been a manager of an orders fulfillment department. Frankly, I can see Charlie helping us out in other areas within DataDump as we continue to expand. Wouldn't it make more sense to promote Justin now so that he could get some experience? That way, we can promote Charlie to manage some of our bigger projects once we expand and we won't have to disrupt the Orders Fulfillment Department for a second time."

J.W. smiled. "I like that. There's only one problem."

"What's that?" asked Christal.

"We won't be ready to make any official statements about our expansion plans for at least a couple months."

"So you are telling me I can't say anything to Charlie?"

"Correct. Would that change your decision?" queried J.W., as the other members of the senior management team walked into the conference room.

"Let me think about that," replied Christal.

The meeting began with a customary applause for Christal, their new Vice President.

"Thank you everyone," she said, feeling a little embarrassed, "I can't begin to tell you how excited I am to be a part of the senior management team."

As the applause died down and the meeting moved on to financial matters, Christal found herself more interested in the discussion going on in her head than the one going on in the meeting. She knew that promoting Justin would not only be a great opportunity for him but was strategically in the best interest of the company. Even J.W. agreed with her on that one. What's more, she knew she couldn't keep her old department waiting any longer. She needed to go ahead with her decision, even if it meant not being able to explain her rationale.

Abruptly, she stood up and announced, "I need to move on this. It will be Justin!" A look of relief came over her face as she walked toward the door.

J.W. looked surprised. "What? We're right in the middle of a meeting." He wasn't used to a member of his management team walking out on one of his meetings.

"Oh, I'm sorry," said Christal, as she addressed the whole group. "My department...I mean my old department, has been waiting for me to select my successor and I think I'm finally ready to do that. I mean, I am ready to do that, and I need to do it now."

At that moment the rest of the management team simultaneously smiled at Christal. Her overriding concern for her former department was refreshing and admirable. It had also broken up what was quickly becoming a somewhat less than dynamic meeting.

"Go ahead," called out J.W., trying to conceal his smile. "We need to take a break anyway."

And with that, Christal hurried out the door.

The calm before the storm

THE EMPLOYEES OF THE Orders Fulfillment Department were having a little difficulty accepting Christal's promotion. After all, this was a group who worked well under her strong leadership and direction but who also depended on it. Their sense of security was now being threatened by this unwanted change.

"It's not like we're losing her," Justin said to Will and Amy, speaking loud enough so the others could hear him from the break room. "She'll be around—just not our immediate supervisor anymore."

"Do you think they'll appoint Charlie to take her place?" Amy whispered. "I hope so," she added, her voice trickling off as Charlie walked into the room.

"Charlie would be the most obvious choice," Justin replied, smiling at Charlie. "What do *you* think, Charlie?"

Charlie smiled back. "If they hire from within," he said, "and they probably will, then I'd take it. Sure, why not!"

John popped his head inside the break room where the group was starting to gather. "What about you, Justin? Do you have any interest in becoming the manager?"

By now, Will, John, Amy, Charlie and Justin were all standing around in the break room having an impromptu meeting.

This was not an unusual occurrence in Christal's absence. The break room was where a lot of the informal conversations occurred. It was also the only place in the office to talk privately without everyone else hearing what was being said. Having six cubicles in the outer office made for very little privacy.

"Me?" replied Justin, a little embarrassed, "Oh no. Charlie has more experience than me. Besides, I wouldn't know how to manage. It would be Charlie for sure."

Just then a familiar, yet somewhat annoying laugh came from Lee Ann's cubicle. The group immediately exchanged knowing smiles.

"Personal call," mocked Amy. The rest of the group laughed as Amy shook her head in disbelief.

Lee Ann was twenty years old and had a habit of taking more personal calls during the day than customer calls. Although not an overwhelming problem in the scheme of things, it was difficult to ignore since she was so much louder and animated when talking to her friends. Nevertheless, it was one of many "little" problems that went unaddressed in the Orders Fulfillment Department, and one that had bothered Justin enough to mention it to Megan on more than one occasion.

"Charlie, looks like you got your work cut out for you," Will replied, pointing to Lee Ann. Everyone laughed as the informal gathering broke up.

Justin headed back to his cubical, still feeling a bit embarrassed. He had never aspired to becoming a manager, and really didn't know how to respond to John's question. Yet the more he thought about it the more he began to wonder if he shouldn't start considering the possibility of taking a management position some day. *Maybe in a year or two,* he mused.

Justin's surprise

CHRISTAL LITERALLY RAN from the conference room, which was on the third floor, all the way down the stairs to the first floor, where the Orders Fulfillment Department was located. Despite being out of breath, her excitement over arriving at a long-awaited decision energized her. She couldn't wait to see how the staff would respond to her announcement, and trusted that they would be both relieved and equally as enthusiastic about her choice of Justin as her replacement. She was sure of it.

"Department meeting in five minutes in the break room," shouted Christal, as she made her way through the maze of cubicles toward her old office. When she got to Justin, she smiled and said, "Can you come see me...now!"

"Sure thing," replied Justin, jumping up to grab his clip-board while simultaneously scanning the room for Charlie. But he was nowhere to be seen. *It must not be about the manager position,* he figured, as he followed Christal into her office.

"Please close the door," requested Christal.

As he shut the door, he once again noticed what a great view she had of Oak Street out her window. "How do you get any work done with that view?" joked Justin.

Christal smiled broadly. "I'm glad you like the view, Justin," and then she paused. "Because I've decided that it is going to be yours. I'm naming you as manager of this department and I know you will do a great job!"

Justin's jaw dropped. It was the same look he'd had on his face three weeks ago when a Giants defender picked up a Bear's fumble and ran it back ninety-five yards for the game-winning touchdown. He was in a state of shock then and was in a state of shock now. He couldn't believe what was happening.

"But, but what about Charlie? We all assumed he would become the manager."

Christal looked taken aback. "Justin, I've given this a lot of thought and feel that you are more of what this department needs right now. I think the world of Charlie, but I am asking you to step up and take on this position."

"Does Charlie know?" asked Justin.

"No, not yet, but he will in about thirty seconds. Are you on board?" Christal put out her hand in anticipation of a confirmation handshake.

"Yes, of course," replied Justin, still numb. "I'm just worried about how Charlie will take this, that's all. And please don't get me wrong, I'm honored to be asked and will do my best to make this work. It just surprised me." He then got up and shook Christal's waiting hand, noticing how much stronger her grip was than his.

"Don't worry, Justin, I'll be here to help you," smiled Christal, as they both walked out the door into the deserted outer office. Laughter could be heard coming from the break room where the rest of the department had gathered.

I sure hope they are still laughing in about ten minutes, Justin thought to himself.

The shocking announcement

THE GROUP WAS EAGER to hear the news. They couldn't wait to officially celebrate Charlie's promotion. Of course, with this group any reason to celebrate was a good thing, but today would be different.

Charlie's heart was pounding. He knew this was going to be a special day for him and he wanted to appear surprised when Christal named him as the new manager. He had even prepared a little speech.

Justin's heart was also pounding, only for a different reason. Appearing surprised when his name was to be announced wouldn't be a problem since he still was in a state of shock. This was a moment for which he was unprepared, and he wasn't quite ready to see it play out. He knew the rest of the department wouldn't be ready either for what they were about to hear.

As Christal and Justin walked into the break room together, it was obvious by Christal's smile that she had something important to say. This was a special moment for her. She not only was going to name Justin as the new manager, but she would officially turn over the reins of her department as well. As thrilled as she was to announce her decision, she experienced a wave of sadness with the realization that this moment also represented an ending for her. This would be her last meeting with this group as their manager. With all the hype about her promotion and concern over choosing a replacement, she had not given much thought to this moment and the impact that it would have on her.

With teary eyes, Christal invited everyone to sit down around the table and started the meeting. "Wow, I can't believe I'm getting so emotional. I came to tell you the news about your new manager and here I am feeling sad about having to leave you. Please forgive me."

The energy in the room suddenly shifted from a buzzing sensation to a very still and compassionate mood. Charlie spoke up, "No need to apologize, Christal, we're sad to see you go, too."

"She's not leaving," said Lee Ann, immediately correcting Charlie.

"I know, but she's leaving us as our manager...at least that is what I meant," replied Charlie, annoyed at being contradicted.

Justin bit his lip. Charlie was acting manager-like now, as if he needed to slowly transition himself into that role.

"I know, let's have two celebrations," urged Amy. "One to say goodbye to you as our outgoing manager, and one to celebrate Charlie as our incoming manager."

Christal immediately shook her head. "Wait a second, I've selected Justin as your new manager, not Charlie."

Christal looked around the room, searching for some kind of acknowledgement or endorsement for her decision. Instead, she was greeted with stunned silence.

Justin was frozen. He knew there would be a reaction, but he was not prepared for this awkward silence. He suddenly became self-conscious about everything. His hands—what should he do with his hands? The expression on his face—was there one? Should there be one? Was everybody looking at him? Should he look back? Where should he look? He suddenly didn't know what to do or how to act. He could only hope something would break up this uncomfortable moment.

"Why...why Justin?" stuttered Charlie, trying to sound neutral, while masking his deep disappointment.

Before Christal could answer, Amy exclaimed, "I'm sorry, I thought Charlie was going to be the manager because he has the most experience and because he was a supervisor already."

"Please," cried Christal. "With all due respect to Charlie, I felt that Justin would be the better fit at this point in time. You are just going to have to trust me on this."

Before anyone else could say anything, Christal got up and headed toward the door. "I'm so sorry that I can't stay and talk more but I have to get back to a meeting. Please know that I'm counting on all of you to make this work." She then looked right at Charlie. "Charlie, if you want to talk, let's set up an appointment. I know this was not what you wanted to hear."

Just as Christal disappeared, she popped her head back into the break room. "Justin, I'll talk to you tomorrow. Have a great day, everyone."

So much for the awkward moment going away anytime soon, Justin lamented.

Charlie got up, looked at Justin and angrily said, "Good luck. You're going to need it," and then stormed out of the room.

Amy jumped up and called out, "Charlie, hold on," and ran after him.

Lee Ann shook her head and said to the others, "I don't know what the big deal is. It's not like it really matters who our manager is. We just do our jobs and go home. It's not rocket science." And with that she got up and walked out of the room.

John walked by Justin, patted him on the arm and said, "Don't worry about it; you'll do just fine."

Will waited for the others to leave before clearing his throat to speak. "You gotta admit, Justin, Charlie got ripped off. He should have gotten the job, and you should have said something to him when you decided to apply for it."

"I didn't apply for the job!" cried Justin. "This was as much of a surprise to me as it was to you. I only found out about it five minutes before the meeting. How do you think I feel?"

"Well, all I can say is that it's not right, and you are going to have to work your butt off in order to get this group back together. I'm glad I'm not you," and he walked out of the room, leaving Justin sitting by himself, at the table, in the room where his life seemed to be turning upside down right before his eyes.

And then it got worse

JUSTIN KNEW HE NEEDED to do something if he was to begin establishing himself as the new manager, only he didn't know what that something would be. What he did know was that his department was crumbling right before him. The worst part of all was knowing that even though he wasn't the one who'd created the problem, he would be the one held responsible for solving it.

He took a deep sigh and mumbled, *Welcome to management!*

For the next few hours Justin hid away in his cubicle, trying to make sense out of the day's events. He was having a rather difficult time accepting his new role and the responsibility that went with it. Truth be told, he wasn't quite sure he wanted it.

It was late in the afternoon when Lee Ann approached him.

"How come you aren't moving into Christal's office?" she asked, surprised to see him still in his cubicle.

"Oh, I will," replied Justin, "I just thought I'd wait until the end of the day."

"Well, suit yourself," she shot back while walking away, "but I don't think it's going to change anything."

"Wait, what do you mean?" asked Justin. "Change anything?"

Lee Ann stopped and turned around. "What I mean is that regardless of whether you feel supported or not as the manager, you *are* the manager, and that is the manager's office," pointing towards Christal's old office. "Hanging out in your cubicle is not doing anyone any good. That's all I have to say." And with that, she walked away.

Justin didn't know what to say or how to respond, but he did know enough to concede that she had a point. Shortly thereafter, he stood up, picked up his clipboard and headed to Christal's office. Although he wasn't ready to move in, he knew he needed to do something, even if just for show. Besides, he wasn't exactly getting much done in his cubicle, and perhaps a change of scenery would provide him with the direction he so needed.

And then it happened.

Justin hadn't gotten halfway to Christal's office when he was struck with the solution of all solutions.

I've got it! he exclaimed to himself as he walked into the deserted office and sat in Christal's chair. *I know how to bring the staff together and make all this discomfort go away. I will simply turn down the promotion and hand it over to Charlie! That's right. I'm going to turn it down!*

Justin was beaming. A forgotten smile took over his face again. He could begin to feel the day's uninvited tension and pressure release from his body. He was becoming tingly all over, and knew it was a sign that he was making the right decision.

He continued talking to himself. *I'm clearly not ready, let alone prepared to be manager of this department. Plus the whole staff, including myself, wants Charlie to be the manager. Why, it's the best decision for everyone! I can't wait to tell Charlie.*

The phone rang. It was Helen, Christal's new secretary, calling from upstairs to set up a meeting between Justin and Christal for tomorrow morning.

"Sure, 8:00 a.m.—no problem," replied Justin. "And one more thing," he added, "could you put me through to Christal's voice mail? I want to leave her a short message."

Justin wanted to plant the seed of his decision with Christal before they met in the morning. He knew she didn't like surprises, especially ones that might reflect poorly on her. He needed for this to go smoothly.

Then he heard Christal's familiar voice on the phone. "Hello, this is Christal. I'm out of the office right now, but please leave a message and I'll get back to you as soon as possible. Beeeep."

Justin cleared his throat. "Hello, Christal, this is Justin. I'm looking forward to our meeting tomorrow morning at eight. I have an idea that I'd like you to consider. I'll see you tomorrow. Bye."

He smiled. He still had one more thing to do before day's end. He had to find Charlie and tell him about his plan. He jumped out of the chair and headed into the outer office.

"Where's Charlie?" Justin asked Amy as he peered into Charlie's empty cubicle.

With a disapproving glance, Amy replied, "He left for the day. He's pretty upset. To tell you the truth, I don't know if he is coming back," and then she picked up the phone as if to call someone.

"Well, I need to talk to him," retorted Justin as he maneuvered his way past Amy and walked into Charlie's cubical. Although slightly perturbed over her attitude, he knew it was more evidence that turning down the promotion would be the right thing. *The sooner I take care of this the better,* he thought, as he grabbed a pad of paper from Charlie's desk and wrote:

> Charlie, I need to talk to you. I have a plan to fix everything. I think you'll like it.
> —Justin

Finally feeling as if he were making some progress, Justin headed back to Christal's office. As he passed by Amy's cubicle again, he noticed that she had left for the day. It was only 4:40 p.m. Technically no one was supposed to leave before five, yet both Charlie and Amy were already gone.

Shaking his head, Justin thought to himself, *I'm glad I'm not going to have to deal with this,* and stepped into Christal's office, where he plopped himself down in her black leather chair for what he assumed would be the last time. He sat back and put his feet up on the desk, almost defiantly. He then looked out into the outer office from the big window in front of the desk and spotted Will and John whispering to each other over the cubicle wall, occasionally glancing in his direction. A tinge of paranoia came over him. He could not help wondering what he had done to deserve all of this sudden attention. It was supposed to have been a typical day.

Just then the phone rang. His first impulse was to let it go to voice mail, but then he thought it might be Charlie calling to talk. "Hello."

The familiar voice on the other end politely asked for Christal. Justin recognized that it was Claire from their Boulder office.

"Hi, Claire, it's Justin."

"Justin, hi! Hey, what's going on over there?"

"What do you mean?" inquired Justin.

"We heard about Christal's promotion, but no one has told us anything else. I was hoping someone would have called us to tell us who will be our new boss. You know, professional courtesy," she said sarcastically. "Is Charlie taking over? He sounded like he was expecting to be promoted. Has it happened yet? Don't keep us in the dark. We need help here. What's going on?"

The thought of calling the Boulder office had never crossed Justin's mind. Given the recent developments and his latest intentions, he thought it would be best to say nothing.

"Claire, we expect to have everything in place by tomorrow morning, and then someone will call to fill you in on all the details. There are still a lot of loose ends that need to be straightened out here. We haven't meant to neglect you; we just wanted to have everything in place first. Really!"

"Sweet. Can you at least tell me if Charlie is the manager or if they brought someone in from the outside?"

Justin wanted so badly to confide in Claire about the day's events and his decision to turn down the promotion, but instead stayed the course. "There's still some negotiating going on, so I can't give you an official answer. But I promise, you will be the first to know."

"Okay, be that way," replied Claire. "Whomever it ends up being, they are going to have their work cut out for them. We are having problems with Katie and Colleen again. Apparently the two of them had a misunderstanding over something Katie wrote to Colleen in an e-mail. Of course Katie says she was just kidding, but Colleen didn't take it that way and now they are both upset with each other. We need some help now! Any ideas?"

Justin politely declined. "Claire, it's probably best we wait on this until tomorrow when we have an *official* manager. But again..."

Claire jumped in and completed his sentence. "I know Justin, I'll be the first to know."

As Justin hung up the phone, he couldn't help but wonder why anyone would want to become a manager. *It is just one problem after another! The sooner I'm out of this dilemma, the better.*

It was after five o'clock. The office was empty and quiet. Justin sat back and reflected on all that had happened in this space over the past eight hours. The innocence with which he had begun the day was now gone.

Another perspective

THE SHORT DRIVE FROM DataDump to Justin's house barely provided enough time for him to think through the day's events and to decide which parts of it he would share with Megan. He knew she'd be just as surprised as he was to hear about the promotion. What he wasn't as sure about was how she would react to his plan of turning it down.

He began to rehearse. *The promotion caused more problems than it was worth, and my decision to turn it down is the only way to salvage the situation. In many ways, I'm doing the noble thing by turning it down. I'm essentially putting the needs of the department ahead of my own.* His eyes lit up.

Yes! That's exactly what I'm doing and Megan, of all people, should be able to understand such unselfish motives.

Justin smiled. He felt good about his strategy to resolve what he had perceived as an insurmountable problem. Now if only he could convince Megan.

Tommy ran to the window the minute he heard the familiar car door slam shut. With a big smile on his face he yelled out in excitement, "Mommy, mommy, its daddy!"

Justin managed another smile as he walked in the door and gave Tommy his traditional bear hug. "There's my boy! Where's mommy?"

Tommy pointed toward the kitchen. "Daddy, can we watch football tonight?"

In all the day's commotion, Justin had forgotten that it was Monday night. The Broncos and Dolphins were playing and he had promised Tommy that they'd watch the game together.

"Sure son. After dinner."

Megan was on the phone when Justin entered the kitchen. She smiled and, without speaking, mouthed the word, T-A-N-Y-A, so he knew who was on the other end of the line. Justin nodded back. He already knew it had to be Tanya, Megan's best friend of eight years. No one else could bring out as much animation and laughter from Megan as she could.

Justin looked back at Megan, pointed to the den and mockingly mouthed the word, D-E-N. He figured Megan and Tanya had more to discuss, and he wanted to relax for awhile anyway.

Megan covered the phone and said with a sarcastic look, "Shut up. I'll be off in a few minutes."

Justin laughed. He liked kidding with Megan and it helped lighten the moment. He never wanted to lose his sense of humor—something that hadn't been very visible lately.

Tommy was already in the den watching cartoons.

"Hey sport, do you want to watch the pregame?" asked Justin.

Tommy's eyes lit up. "Okay."

As the two of them snuggled together in front of the TV, Justin briefly closed his eyes, only to be awakened forty-five minutes later with Michelle shaking his arm. "Daddy, it's time for dinner!"

Feeling disoriented from his unplanned nap, Justin wearily stood up and mumbled, "Oh, okay, honey."

The whole family was already seated at the dinner table, patiently waiting for him. It was 6:30 p.m. and he had slept through his opportunity to talk with Megan before dinner. Now it would be much more challenging to find the right moment. This wasn't playing out like he had hoped.

"Rough day, honey?" inquired Megan, passing him the plate of chicken.

"Mommy, daddy was snoring," exclaimed Tommy.

Megan laughed.

Hoping to divert the focus away from him, Justin replied, "Oh, let's just say it was a rather interesting day. How was yours?"

"My day was great. I finished designing the logo for my hardware store client and met with a guy from Jay's Potato Chips to talk about some freelance work for one of their divisions."

"Wow, that's fantastic," cheered Justin.

"Thanks, but what did you mean by 'interesting?'" replied Megan, not letting his previous comment fall by the wayside.

"Actually, there is something I need to discuss with you," hesitated Justin, figuring now was as good a time as any. "But only if it's a good time."

Megan looked at him curiously. "Well, it depends if it's good or bad news. Which is it?"

Justin carefully chose his next words, "A little of both, I suppose."

"Then tell me the good news," replied Megan enthusiastically.

In looking around the table, Justin noticed the kids seemed as eager to hear what he was about to say as Megan was. "Okay, I will tell you guys, but then you two need to let mommy and daddy talk alone. Will you do that for me?"

"Yes, daddy," replied Michelle. Tommy, already bored, was on to his next project of trying to pour salt into the top of the pepper shaker.

Justin began very slowly. "Christal surprised us all this morning by selecting me to be the manager instead of Charlie."

"No way!" exclaimed Megan. "You've got to be kidding me!"

"I'm serious," insisted Justin, feeling a little impressed with himself for the first time that day.

"Justin, that's incredible news! I knew you could do it. I'm so proud of you! Kids, daddy is now the boss at work!"

"Yea, daddy!" screamed Michelle.

"Yea, daddy," added Tommy, trying to mimic Michelle.

Megan beamed. "Oh, this is such great news. I can't wait to hear all about it. How is Charlie taking it?"

Justin quickly turned to Michelle, "Honey, will you take Tommy to the playroom for a while?"

"But daddy, I want to hear more. Can't I stay?"

"I'm sorry honey," replied Justin, shaking his head.

"Okay." Michelle then grabbed Tommy by the hand and reluctantly headed off to the playroom.

Justin, frowning, returned to Megan's question. "Charlie's not taking it too well, to tell you the truth. In fact, it was a very unpopular decision," as his voice trickled off.

"So, what are you going to do?"

"I've been giving this a lot of thought...and...I'm going to turn it down."

Megan looked stunned. "You're what? Tell me I didn't hear you say you were going to turn it down! An incredible opportunity comes your way and you want to turn it down all because Charlie is having a hard time with it? Give me a break!"

"Honey, let me explain why I think turning down the promotion is in everyone's best interest, including mine."

"This must be the bad news," snapped Megan.

Justin nodded.

Megan stood up, noticeably upset. "You know what, Justin? I'm not ready to continue this conversation right now. I just don't understand you sometimes!"

Angered now, Justin retorted, "You don't understand me sometimes because you won't hear me out!"

"Oh, I see. Now it's my fault." Megan shook her head and walked out of the kitchen in a huff.

Justin threw up his arms in frustration. The irony was amazing. Disarray at work, in his decision, and now in his relationship. What else could go wrong!

12

Macology

Justin and Megan hardly said another word to each other that night. As they went to sleep, Justin put his arm around her as a kind of peace offering, but she turned away. She was not ready to talk to him, even if it meant going to bed mad—something they both had agreed never to do.

The following morning didn't improve his state. In addition to the tension with Megan, Justin was now starting to worry about his eight o'clock meeting with Christal. The decision that he had felt so confident about yesterday had turned into a contentious point in his marital relationship. He was torn. If it were up to him, he would turn down the promotion. But now he couldn't help wondering if that was the easy way out. Was it really the best decision for him and his family? Had he really given himself enough time to think through this decision? Despite all the sudden confusion, he did know that he needed Megan on his side in this dilemma—now more than ever. He approached her as she walked into the kitchen.

"Megan, I'm sorry about upsetting you last night. I am not thinking clearly right now and I just need to know that I'll have your support, regardless of which way things end up."

Megan's disposition softened as she smiled and looked into Justin's eyes. "Honey," she said quietly. "You can't just make independent decisions regarding your career without consulting me first. Maybe turning your promotion down might end up being the right thing to do, but I'd appreciate some input. After all, your career impacts my life just as my career impacts yours."

"I know, dear," replied Justin, happy to be talking again. "It was wrong of me to phrase it in such a way that you thought I wasn't open to feedback. I was and still am ready to hear what you have to say. Only, I can't stay and talk any more right now because I have to get to the office for my meeting with Christal."

"Can we talk about it later?" asked Megan, as Justin headed to the door.

"Yes, but I may not have the luxury to delay this decision. She is going to want to know this morning. I'll call you later." And out the door he went.

Megan watched Justin through the kitchen window as he got into his car. She really was very proud of him for being offered the promotion, even though she had barely shown it. It was upsetting that he never thought to consult her, but she was even more upset over the way she had responded to him. He was clearly struggling with his decision, and all she could do was react to it instead of helping him through it.

Meanwhile, as he drove to work, Justin found himself agonizing over his pending meeting and his sudden ambivalence about turning down the promotion. He was already halfway down Maple Street before realizing that he had no idea how he had gotten there. It was the words coming from the radio that finally caught his attention. "We're back with Dr. Mac, our special guest this morning. Call us at 555-WKBT if you'd like some Macology with your coffee. He's here 'til nine!"

Dr. Mac? Dr. Mac? Where have I heard that name before, he wondered.

"Hello, caller, you're on *Breakfast with Bobbie and Jay.* Do you have a question for Dr. Mac?"

"Yes, I do. Good morning Dr. Mac. My name is Linda."

"Good morning to you Linda," said the friendly and confident voice on the radio. "Ask away."

"Well, I'm the volunteer coordinator at my organization, and my job is to oversee the volunteers and to coordinate their assignments. A couple of days ago one of our younger volunteers, maybe eighteen or so, came in with a very noticeable nose ring plus a huge tattoo on the back of her neck. Now, don't get me wrong, I don't mind…"

Dr. Mac gently interrupted her and asked a few questions. As their conversation shifted from what was wrong to how to address the problem, it occurred to Justin where he had heard Dr. Mac's name before. He was the guy who wrote that advice column Megan had shown him on Sunday.

"This is *that* guy," he said out loud.

As Justin continued to listen, he couldn't help but wonder what Dr. Mac would do with *his* dilemma. Although initially just kidding, the more he thought about it, the more he realized that getting a second opinion from a management guru might not be such a bad idea. *Hmm?*

Just before the show went into commercial, the radio announcer repeated the station's phone number. Justin impulsively inserted the number into his cell phone and hit the send button just as he pulled into DataDump's employee parking lot.

"WKBT Chicago, do you have a question for Dr. Mac?" the voice on the other end asked.

Surprised by the immediacy of the response, Justin began stumbling with his words, now fearful that other DataDump employees might be listening.

"Sir, you are not on the radio. I am the station manager and I am selecting the callers to pass on to Dr. Mac. Please, just tell me the specific question that you'd like to ask Dr. Mac."

Feeling relieved, Justin said, "I was going to ask him if I should take a promotion I've just been offered, that's all. It is not that important...I really don't need to talk to him."

"Oh, that's a great question. We are getting too many complainers this morning, if you know what I mean. Your question will add a nice mix. Hold on, sir."

Justin's heart was pounding. "Oh, but..." and the next thing he knew he was on hold. His meeting with Christal was less than ten minutes away and here he was about to go on live radio from his car in the parking lot.

This can't happen, he thought to himself. And then suddenly he heard Jay, one of the co-hosts, come on the air. "Dr. Mac, we've got a caller who wants your advice on whether or not he should take a promotion. Personally, I don't know why you'd ever turn one down..."

"That's because you've never been promoted," joked Bobbie, the other host of the show. "Go ahead, sir!"

Justin tried to disguise his voice. "Ah...well...yes, I just wanted to know your thoughts on when it is a good idea to take a promotion."

"And your name is?" asked Dr. Mac.

"Just...um, just Paul," stumbled Justin.

"Okay, *just Paul,*" laughed Dr. Mac, "tell me a little more about your situation."

Justin carefully chose his words, trying hard not to reveal too much. "Well, I was unexpectedly offered a promotion the other day, and I'm not sure it is in my best interest to take it, that's all."

"Paul, do you know why you were selected for the promotion?"

"No."

"Do you value the opinion of the person who promoted you?"

"Yes."

"Paul, are you worried that someone you know might hear this conversation on the radio?" inquired Dr. Mac, perceptively.

"Yes."

"Okay, then let me do most of the talking and you just answer as best you can. Paul, does this promotion involve a position that you are capable of taking?"

"I think so."

"Then, what's the problem?"

"It's not going over too well with my coworkers."

"So let me see if I got this. You are worried about taking the promotion because your coworkers are not being very supportive of the idea. Is that what you are saying?"

"Yep."

"Paul, let me ask you something. If you turn down this promotion, what do you think the odds are that your organization will come back to you with another promotional opportunity in the near future?"

"Probably not great."

"Paul, listen to me. Do you want the promotion or not?"

"Yes, but—"

"Because to be real honest with you, it sounds like you are more concerned with what other people think of you than what you think of yourself. Your coworkers won't be deciding for you whether you take the promotion. You will. And, I might add, we are talking about a promotion that you ultimately want, that your boss thinks you should have, and that you are capable of taking. Please don't take this wrong, but this decision isn't about your coworkers, it's about you! Moving into a management position involves making a lot of decisions that will not always be popular, but that are in the best interest of the organization. Get used to it, son. This is not about looking for acceptance. This is about stepping up to the plate and taking on a challenge. If you want to move into management, then take the promotion and give it everything you've got. Your opportunity is right here and now."

Justin was moved by Dr. Mac's response and knew he was right. This was his moment to step up to the plate and he didn't need anyone else's approval to do so. He was going to take the position!

"Thank you so much Dr. Mac," said Justin, now feeling enlightened and energized. "You are absolutely correct. This is an opportunity that I'm not going to pass up. But can I ask one more question?"

"Go ahead."

"Do you have any advice for me? I've never been a manager before."

Dr. Mac paused before replying. "Paul, this may not be what you were expecting, but it is the best advice I could give you. Start keeping a journal. Write down your thoughts, feelings, and, most importantly, any and all insights you gain about yourself and about becoming a manager. Believe me, there will be a bunch of them."

Dr. Mac's advice, or "Macology," as the radio hosts preferred to call it, was exactly what Justin needed. Instead of dreading his meeting with Christal, he was now looking forward to it. Justin thanked Dr. Mac one final time and hung up. He didn't want to keep Christal waiting.

Part Three

The Learning Curve

A nonmeeting

JUSTIN HATED TO BE LATE for meetings, especially this one. Nevertheless, he knew that the cost of being a couple of minutes late was well worth it for what he had gotten in return from Dr. Mac. He was a different person now than he had been just a short fifteen minutes ago, and this sudden metamorphosis should greatly benefit both him and Christal.

Walking as fast as possible, Justin got to the Orders Fulfillment Department in record time, only to remember that Christal's office was no longer there. She was now with all the other vice presidents up on the second floor—often referred to as "executive row."

As Justin turned around toward the stairs, he glanced over at his new office through the glass doors. There, he saw a sight that he wasn't prepared to see. Charlie was sitting in his office, apparently waiting to discuss the note that Justin had left for him the previous day.

Oh, crap, winced Justin, *I forgot about the note!*

He looked at his watch. It was 8:10 a.m. There was no time to talk to Charlie; he was already late for his meeting with Christal. He turned and quickly headed up the stairs to the second floor, where Helen, Christal's secretary, was waiting for him.

"Christal called, and she's running late. She said to go ahead and have a seat in her office."

Justin was relieved. This meant he wasn't *technically* late, and would now have some time to collect his thoughts. Seeing Charlie had thrown him off stride. He had totally forgotten about writing that note—a note that clearly implied his intention to turn down the promotion so that Charlie could assume the role. And a note written in sheer desperation without any consideration for what a promotion would mean for Megan and the kids.

Moments later there was some commotion in the hallway as Christal stormed into the office, clearly out of breath from running up the stairs. "Justin, hi. I'm sorry to be late. I ran all the way from my car." She sat down and took a big breath. "I had a breakfast meeting that ran late and the traffic on Maple these days—what's going on with that?" she exclaimed.

Before he could respond, Helen popped her head in the doorway. "Christal, excuse me, you've got a nine o'clock with J.W. and your flight to New York leaves at 2:00 p.m. You need to be at the airport by noon."

"Thanks, Helen," smiled Christal, and she frantically looked at Justin. "Want to switch jobs?"

"I'm thinking no," replied Justin, trying to be funny.

"Look, about yesterday, the staff will come around; you just have to be patient. Okay?"

Amazed at how quickly she got down to the issue, Justin replied, "Well, what do I do if they don't?"

Helen popped her head in again. "Christal, it's J.W. on line two. He said it was urgent."

Christal excused herself and headed over to her desk. Looking up at Justin she said, "This may take a few minutes; do you mind waiting outside?"

"Oh, sure, no problem," replied Justin, and he walked out into the outer office, where he planted himself down on a couch. This was now the second time that morning that he found himself waiting on Christal. He took a big breath and let it out slowly.

Helen smiled at him from her desk. "Congratulations!"

"Oh, thank you," replied Justin.

"You'll do a fine job, I'm sure," she said, before turning her attention to another ringing phone.

The giddiness that Justin was feeling after his talk with Dr. Mac was now dissipating into an unsettling anxiety. All the problems that instantly evolved from yesterday were still looming large over his department and, once again, his problems to solve. The biggest one was Charlie, who was now waiting in his office, no doubt expecting to hear all about a plan that no longer existed. And then there was Amy and Will, who were mad at him, simply for being selected as the manager. Oh, and there was the Boulder office whose employees were fighting amongst themselves again. If ever Justin needed Christal, it was now.

He shook his head in frustration. *Whatever happened to a honeymoon period?*

Helen looked up from the phone at Justin, "Excuse me, Justin?"

"Yes," replied Justin, fearing her next words.

"I'm sorry, we are going to have to reschedule your meeting with Christal. How's next Tuesday at 9:00 a.m.?"

"Next Tuesday? Today's Tuesday! That's a week from now," Justin protested.

"Unfortunately that is the best we can do."

Knowing that he didn't really have a choice, Justin reluctantly agreed and walked out into the hallway, feeling more alone now than he'd ever felt. *How am I supposed to become a manager without any help? I have no training, and now I have abso-*

lutely no guidance from Christal. I feel as if I'm being set up to fail, and I haven't even started yet.

A familiar voice called out from the vicinity of the stairwell. "Justin, Justin!" It was David from Accounting. "Hey, was that you by chance on the radio this morning?"

"Me? What are you talking about?" asked Justin, feeling totally exposed.

"There was some guy on the radio talking with that psychologist dude who gives advice, and it sounded like you. Didn't you just get a promotion?"

"Who, me? Yes, sort of. But no, I didn't call a radio station. Why would I do that?"

Not waiting for a response, Justin headed down the stairs. It was barely nine o'clock in the morning and his first full day as manager was not off to a good start. This was going to be a day that couldn't end soon enough.

The note **14** gone bad

JUSTIN ENTERED THE DEPARTMENT feeling frazzled. He had spent so much time within the last twenty-four hours trying to get out of being the manager that he had never given any thought to actually being the manager. He wasn't sure what to do or where to begin.

John approached, looking somewhat frustrated. "Justin, are we going to have a meeting? No one knows what's going on!"

Feeling grateful just to have someone talking to him, Justin reassured him. "Oh, sure, that's a good idea. How about at ten o'clock in the break room?"

As he watched John walk away, he couldn't help but wonder what he would say in the staff meeting. Everybody would be looking to him for some kind of direction and he had none. *I need time to think...alone,* he thought to himself. And with that he headed into his new office, well aware that he was under the microscopic lenses of his coworkers. He shut the door, pulled out the big leather chair behind the desk, and planted himself. He looked out into the office through his big picture window. He then swiveled the chair around in the opposite direction where the view looked out on Oak Street. He swiveled back again, only this time noticing the top of his desk and a little note right by the blinking phone. Upon a closer look, he realized it was the note he had put on Charlie's desk the previous night. *Oops,* he cried out, *so much for preparing for the meeting. I need to talk to Charlie.* He quickly pushed two and then four on his phone, Charlie's extension, feeling uneasy about the conversation he was about to have.

"This is Charlie."

"Charlie, Justin. Can you come to Christal's office for a minute? Thanks."

Justin felt a little funny claiming Christal's office as his own—at least until he had the opportunity to establish himself as the new manager with Charlie.

Seconds later Charlie walked in, looking very businesslike. He immediately closed the door behind him, as if he were the one who had called the meeting.

"Can you explain that to me," he asked rather forcefully, pointing to the note on Justin's desk.

"That's what I wanted to talk to you about," replied Justin, forcing a smile. As he cleared his throat, wondering what it was he was going to say, he noticed that Will, John, Lee Ann, and Amy were all standing around John's cubicle in the outer office, pretending to have a meeting of their own. Had they all not been repeatedly looking through the window into Justin's office, he might have thought that their meeting had some legitimacy, but he knew better. If he'd been in their shoes, he'd be right there beside them.

"Charlie, I met with Christal this morning and...we didn't really get a chance to map out the next step."

"You don't have a plan, do you?" inquired Charlie, tight-jawed.

"Um, no, not yet," apologized Justin.

Charlie could only shake his head as he headed toward the door. "Justin, I need to take a couple of days off to think about all of this."

Justin stood up and protested, "Wait! I need you here!" But Charlie ignored the plea. He quickly swung by his cubicle to grab a large backpack and headed out the door. It was rather obvious that he was already packed up and ready for a quick and dramatic exit.

Justin's startled gaze was met by four other pairs of eyes from the outer office, all equally surprised. Amy and Will were shaking their heads in frustration.

It was now ten, and time for the staff meeting.

The slow descent

RUBBING HIS EYES IN FRUSTRATION, Justin slowly walked into the outer office and nodded his head in the direction of the break room. "Let's go! We've got a meeting." Without looking back to see if anyone noticed, he walked into the break room and sat down at the table, right smack in the middle. He looked around the empty room and had an instantaneous flashback of the previous day's meeting, where the slow descent of the staff had begun. He wondered if his new determination to accept the position had been the right decision after all.

Lee Ann was the first to walk in. She appeared very tentative as she looked around wondering where to sit. With Christal and Charlie now gone, even the break room had a different feel to it.

Will and Amy walked in and immediately sat down together on the opposite side of the table from Lee Ann. John then followed and sat by Lee Ann at the other end. With Justin in the middle, the dynamics looked more like a divorce hearing than a staff meeting.

Justin started things off. "I don't have a plan. I am not prepared for this meeting. I'm feeling overwhelmed."

"Well, that's just great. Justin," said Amy, intensely. "So what are we supposed to do?"

Will looked at Justin. "Did you just let Charlie walk out? You know, Charlie, the one guy who we need the most—more than you—to lead this group."

Startled by how quickly the confrontation escalated, Justin raised his voice. "Okay, hold on! I don't know why Christal chose me to manage this department over Charlie. Believe me, there was no one as surprised as I was to hear the news. Do you think this has been fun for me the last twenty-four hours? I wouldn't wish this experience on anyone!"

A brief moment of silence passed before Amy retorted. "Then why did Charlie storm out of the office, Justin. Why?"

"Because he thought I had a plan." Justin shook his head in disappointment. "Yesterday I thought the best thing was to turn down the position, but today I decided to take it. That's why he stormed out, if you want the absolute truth."

Amy responded in an almost maternal fashion, "Well, you need to go get him back, Justin. We need him here!"

"Don't worry, I'll get him back," replied Justin. "I just want to give him some time to cool off first."

Lee Ann jumped in. "But Justin, we're short two people. Who's going to do their work?"

Feeling attacked, Justin retaliated. "I guess it wouldn't be you, would it, Lee Ann!"

The room fell silent.

"What are you talking about?" demanded Lee Ann, her face turning bright red.

"I'm saying that if you spent more of your time process-ing orders, like you are supposed to, instead of talking to your friends all day—"

Lee Ann jumped up out of her seat. "You don't know what you're talking about. You have no idea what I do during the day, and it's none of your business anyway!" Then she picked up her notepad and stormed out of the break room.

Surprised himself over what had just happened, Justin turned to John and said, sarcastically, "So, how am I doing so far?"

John just shook his head and looked down at the floor.

The meeting abruptly broke up. It was a new low in the Orders Fulfillment Department and Justin could only blame himself. Lee Ann had headed upstairs to the second floor. That, of course, could only mean one of two things: either she went to find Christal, or she went to Human Resources to complain. Either way he knew he was in big trouble.

Justin's phone rang just as he walked in his office. Reluctantly, he picked it up. "Hello...I mean, this is Justin."

Megan was on the other end. "Hi, honey. I'm sorry for getting mad at you last night. I should have been more supportive."

Justin didn't respond. He didn't know what to say or where to begin. Last night seemed so long ago. He had been so consumed with knocking off his staff one by one that he had completely lost sight of the other part of his life, his family.

"Honey, are you there? Is everything okay?"

Justin sighed. "I've been better. I'll fill you in tonight on what's transpired, that is if I'm still here!"

"What do you mean? Are you alright?"

"Not really. My staff is rebelling and quitting on me. Christal has left me completely on my own to clean up her mess. Let's just say I've had better days. Basically, everything's falling apart. And your day?"

"Wow, slow down," cried out Megan. "You took the job?"

"Sort of. I'm in the process of trying to lose it right now. News at ten." Justin's sarcasm was even getting to him.

"Honey, I can see this is a bad time, why don't we talk tonight. Okay? You'll do just fine. I'm so proud of you," and she hung up.

Justin wasn't kidding, however. He now had alienated himself from his staff and was more than likely in trouble with

HR. He hadn't been the manager for more than a few hours, and the turmoil that surrounded him was unbearable. He had actually made things worse. He was on a crash course, and he was unable to stop it.

Suddenly some noise stirred from the outer office. As he looked out, he could see Lee Ann returning from the second floor. She stopped by John's cubicle and had a brief conversation with him before heading over to her cubicle. Justin was relieved to see that she didn't immediately start packing up her stuff. He couldn't bear to watch that scene play out again today.

The phone rang. Justin took a deep breath and picked up the receiver.

"Justin, this is Cynthia from Human Resources. I want to talk to you about one of your employees, Lee Ann."

Here it comes, he thought. "Yes, go ahead."

"She said you made some disparaging remarks to her in front of the other employees in your department. Can you tell me what happened and what you said?"

Justin had thought he had hit rock bottom when he inappropriately confronted Lee Ann but now knew that this was even worse. He sensed he was on the verge of being fired. This was bad!

He paused. With nowhere to go at this point, he decided to say what he really was feeling. "Cynthia, she's right! I lost my temper and made an inappropriate comment. I've never been a manager before, and Christal was unable to help me transition into this new role. My coworkers are mad at me because they wanted Charlie to be the manager, and...."

"Justin, Justin," interrupted Cynthia, "hold on a second. Lee Ann's very upset. You made a mistake. You need to apologize to her and make amends. It's not the end of the world; just go talk to her, now! Okay?"

Surprised by Cynthia's response, Justin felt the noose around his neck loosen a bit for the first time since being named the manager. He hadn't completely sabotaged himself after all; instead he'd been given an opportunity to correct a mistake. He felt very fortunate.

"Thank you for being so understanding. I will go talk to her right away. I'll fix this, you'll see."

Cynthia voice softened. "Hey, my first time as a manager wasn't very easy either. Get back to me and let me know how it goes."

As he hung up the phone, Justin felt a surge of renewed energy. This conversation with Lee Ann was going to be a defining moment for him as a manager, and he wanted to make it a positive experience for both of them. He knew the most important thing he needed to do was apologize for saying what he said to her in front of the staff. He also knew that he owed her an explanation as to why he said what he said. That was going to be the hard part.

And then a light bulb went off. *Wait a minute! That column by Dr. Mac on Sunday was all about dealing with a coworker who socializes on the phone!* And, Justin recalled, he also had offered the letter writer some pretty sound advice. He quickly turned on his computer and did an Internet search for Dr. Mac. To his surprise, up came hundreds of links, including the one he was searching for, from *The Daily Tribune*. Two clicks later and he had Sunday's *Ask Dr. Mac* column right in front of him. He read Dr. Mac's advice again.

Dear Angry and Annoyed:

Let me ask you this: If a coworker of yours had an issue with you, would you prefer that they talk to you directly about it or go to your supervisor first with their concerns? I'm guessing that you'd prefer they come talk to you directly first. With that in mind, you too have the responsibility to talk to the coworker directly about your concerns. Anything less would be disrespectful. And that includes talking "about her" to coworkers.

Next, you need to assess if her behavior is negatively impacting your ability to get your job done. I mention this because if her behavior is just annoying but doesn't really impact your work, then I'd have to agree with your supervisor and tell you to let it go. You are wasting a lot of valuable energy and time on something that is not really important. If, on the other hand, her behavior does indeed impede your ability to get your work done, then by all means, keep reading.

Confronting your coworker doesn't have to be a difficult experience. Sit down with her, one-to-one, and tell her what's going on with you, making sure you cover the following points:

1) Acknowledge the importance of having an effective working relationship with her.
2) Tell her that the purpose of your conversation is to share a concern that she may not be aware of.
3) Describe the particular behavior that is causing a problem for you.
4) Explain how this behavior is impacting your ability to get your work done.
5) Propose a solution.
6) Get agreement.
7) Thank her for her willingness to collaborate with you.

It's important to remember when confronting a coworker that the key is not to make them *wrong*. The key is to ask for what you need and to give them the same opportunity with you. Always remember to keep the focus on the working relationship. Personal attacks don't belong here. Finally, be respectful and polite and treat coworkers the same way you'd like to be treated.

—Dr. Mac

Justin smiled. This was exactly the kind of advice he needed right now. He then pulled an unused notebook off the shelf and decided that this was as good a time as any to start his management journal. The "Lee Ann incident" was already providing him with some insights that he needed to get down on paper right away.

Journal Entry # 1

a) If I can't say something nice, or at least in a supportive and constructive way, then I'm better off not saying it at all.
b) I need to take my concerns to the person I'm having the concerns with directly. Anything else would be disrespectful.
c) It's always a good idea to think through both the process and what outcomes I'm looking for before confronting another employee. And that includes trying to view the concern from their perspective as well.

Justin closed the journal and sat back in his chair. *That was helpful! That was very helpful.*

The first of many

JOHN POPPED HIS HEAD into Justin's office. "Are you aware that they are having problems down in Boulder?"

Not wanting to lose his momentum regarding his conversation with Lee Ann, Justin pleaded, "I need to talk to Lee Ann right now. Can we touch base about Boulder later?"

John nodded. He knew Justin and Lee Ann's conversation would set the stage for how the remainder of the day would play out. Boulder needed to wait. Besides, with the way things had been going, Justin might not even make it through his first day as their manager.

All remaining eyes were on Justin as he walked over to Lee Ann's cubicle.

"Can we talk?"

Lee Ann glared at Justin. "I have nothing to say to you. Your comment was hurtful, unfair, and *way* out of line."

"Lee Ann, you're absolutely right. I was wrong to say what I said, and I'm sorry. Can we go get a cup of coffee and talk? Please? You can still hate me afterwards if you like."

Lee Ann took a big breath and let the air out very slowly. "Okay, Justin, I'll give you ten minutes and ten minutes only.

Because of you I'm behind on my client orders...you know, the work that you claim I neglect!"

"Thank you!" replied Justin, purposely ignoring her last comment. "Just ten minutes, I promise."

They then walked out of the building and down the street to Stella's Coffee, the quaint little coffee house nearby. Stella's had become a regular meeting place for DataDump employees who needed a more private place to talk.

Once inside, Justin broke the uncomfortable silence by asking Lee Ann if it was okay to sit at the table farthest away from the front counter so they could have more privacy.

"Whatever, Justin. It doesn't really matter to me."

With two cups of coffee in hand, Justin joined Lee Ann at the table. He had the look of a puppy that knew he did something wrong as he began his apology. "I don't want to lose you because of something stupid that I said. This has been the hardest couple of days in my life, and I need help—I need *your* help."

Lee Ann paused for a few seconds and then replied, "Justin, this job isn't my life. It's just a job to me. So yes, I do talk to some of my friends from time to time during the day. But so does everyone else, including you! And singling me out for something that everyone does was just wrong!"

Thankful that Lee Ann was willing to get right to the heart of the issue, Justin clarified himself. "Lee Ann, as I said earlier, it was wrong, inappropriate, and unprofessional of me to do what I did. I should have taken my issue to you directly instead of letting it play out in front of others. I'm sorry. What can I do to wipe the slate clean with you?"

"It's not just me, Justin. You did that in front of Amy, John, and Will. I'm not the only one who was upset by your comment."

"So help me out here," pressed Justin. "What can I do?"

"You need to apologize to the whole group. And even then I don't know..."

Justin realized Lee Ann was right. He had not even considered the impact that his comment might have had on the others. At the same time, the thought of bringing this issue up to the whole group made him very uncomfortable. It would be like reliving a nightmare. Yet what choice did he have?

"And that will make it go away?"

"I'm not going to forget it, Justin, but I will forgive you."

He nodded. "Okay, I'll do it. But can we talk about the comment itself?"

"We just did! What else is there to say?"

"I meant what was *behind* the comment." Justin quickly reviewed Dr. Mac's advice to himself, and then began. "When you talk to your friends at work, you tend to talk louder and you become more animated."

"So what's wrong with that?" shot back Lee Ann.

Justin pleaded, "Hold on, let me finish. There is nothing wrong with that. But because of that, it is pretty easy to tell the difference between when you are talking to your friends and when you are talking to clients. And, from my perspective, you seem to get a lot of personal calls during the day. So this might be unfair, but it gives me the impression that you are not putting out the same effort with our clients that everyone else is in the office."

Lee Ann started to object, but Justin continued.

"Plus, because of the way our cubicles are designed and located, I can hear everything you say, and I'm having a hard time concentrating, particularly when you are talking to your friends."

"Can I talk now?" asked Lee Ann.

"Just one more thing," replied Justin. "Please know that I'm not saying I'm right. It's just my perception. But that's what has been bugging me for a while, and I didn't know how to bring it up to you, and I'm sorry for that."

Lee Ann's face softened a bit. "Wow, Justin. How long have you been upset over this?"

"Just for a couple of months maybe."

Lee Ann looked perplexed. "First off, how are you going to be a manager if you can't talk to me?"

"I can," pleaded Justin, "that's what *this* is!"

Accepting his response, she continued. "I admit that I probably do get a few more personal calls during the day than most people, but I take orders and make my client calls as well. You cannot make the assumption that just because I talk to my friends during the day I don't get my work done. I do. And really, shouldn't you and everyone else be minding your own business?"

Justin suddenly realized that he had no idea whether or not Lee Ann was meeting her orders quota. It was another assumption he had made.

"Lee Ann, you're right. I have no idea who is or isn't meeting their quotas. That clearly is something I need to be on top of from this moment on. Thank you for helping me realize that." Justin then lowered his voice to a whisper. "Could I ask you, however, to at least lower your voice when talking to your friends? I know I'm not in the cubicles anymore, but your voice can carry across the entire office."

Lee Ann consented. "Okay, I'll watch that. But will you promise to apologize to the rest of the staff?"

"I will," acknowledged Justin, "right when we get back... oh, and one more thing,"

"What's that?" asked Lee Ann.

Justin was smiling now as he spoke, "Thank you."

Lee Ann smiled back, "No problem. Just talk to me in the future, okay?"

"I will. I promise"

As they headed out the door, Lee Ann asked, "Justin, what are you going to do about Charlie?"

"I'll get him back. That is, if he's willing to come back."

Keeping his promise

JUSTIN FELT LIKE HE JUST EARNED his first stripe as a manager. He had worked through two issues with Lee Ann and was pleased that their working relationship was now better than it had ever been. He was proud of himself—so proud that he wanted to tell someone. He wanted to brag. He wanted some acknowledgement that he had actually done something right as a manager. But there was no time. He had too many other fires burning that required his immediate attention. He had to talk to his staff, he had to get Charlie back, and he had to somehow help the Boulder office resolve their problems. If it wasn't one thing, it was another. There didn't seem to be an end in sight.

What he did know was that his apology to the staff was now the most important task at hand and clearly the most difficult. Apologies in general weren't easy for Justin, and now he had to deliver his second one within an hour. He wasn't looking forward to this at all, but he also knew that it would only get worse if he didn't handle it right away. With that in mind, he popped his head into the outer office and politely asked everyone to step inside his office. Although staff meetings usually occur in the break room, Justin wanted the intimacy of his office as the backdrop. For whatever reason, it gave him more confidence, which was exactly what he needed most right now.

As the staff walked in, Justin directed them to sit around his mini-conference table, which could fit five comfortably. Will and Amy pulled their chairs back away from the table, forcing Justin to ask them to pull back in. They shrugged.

Amy spoke up. "Why are we all crammed up in *this* office," still unwilling to acknowledge that it now belonged to Justin.

Aiming to lighten the mood, Justin replied, "Because I'm batting 0-for-2 in the other room and needed to try something different."

No one laughed.

John came to the rescue. "So does this mean you strike out if you screw this one up as well?"

Now they laughed. Justin appreciated the humor. He hadn't laughed with the group for a few days and it really felt good, even if it was directed at him.

He began. "I met with Lee Ann earlier and now I wanted to meet with all of you." He took a big breath. *Here goes,* he thought. "It was inappropriate for me to say what I said to Lee Ann in the break room earlier today. It was equally inappropriate to say it in front of all of you. I've apologized to Lee Ann and now I want to apologize to the rest of you. It won't happen again."

Amy grunted, "Are we done? I've got stuff to do."

Justin bit his tongue. "Yes, that's all I had."

Before anyone could get up, Will jumped in, looking right at Justin. "Wait, someone said you were on the radio this morning with some shrink?

"Not true," lied Justin, "next question?"

Will reloaded. "Okay, then what about Charlie? What are you doing to get him back?"

Disappointed by Amy and Will's lack of empathy for his apology, Justin assured Will that he would try to contact Charlie to convince him to stay.

As the group got up to leave, John patted Justin on the back and whispered, "Good job."

Lee Ann waited for everyone to leave before approaching. "Thanks, Justin. I'm willing to start over again with you."

Justin smiled. "Thanks for giving me another chance."

Feeling like he could now put his morning mishap behind him, Justin closed the door and sat back in his chair. He had mixed feelings about what had just transpired. Although the staff was more divided now than they had ever been, he could feel he was making progress, albeit slowly. All in all, he was just thankful for still having a job. And then he remembered his conversation with Dr. Mac, which brought a smile to his face. *Whoever this guy is, he sure had an impact on me today.*

The ringing phone startled him.

He picked up. "Hello, this is Justin."

It was Claire from the Boulder office. "Justin, you're still there! Sweet."

"What's that suppose to mean," he asked.

"I always say 'sweet,' you know that."

"No, I mean you seemed surprised I am still the manager?"

Claire backed down, "It's just that we've been hearing different rumors about who was going to end up as the manager."

Justin shrugged, "Well it's me. Disappointed?"

"Oh no, personally, I'm glad," replied Claire. "You've always been nice to me."

After a brief pause, she continued. "We've still got a problem between Katie and Colleen. Now that I know it's you, I mean, since you are our new manager, I'm forwarding you the e-mail that started this latest episode."

Justin was having a hard time shifting his focus to the Boulder group. Here he was, barely surviving in his own department, and now Claire was expecting him to solve a problem in hers—a department that was in another part of the country and with a staff that Justin hardly knew.

"So, Claire, what is it you'd like me to do?" asked Justin, feeling overwhelmed.

Claire pleaded, "You need to handle it. I don't know what you should do or how; that's your job now, Justin. I'm just telling you about it. They're not talking to each other and Colleen was in tears the last time I saw her."

Trying to get some perspective, Justin probed. "Is this the first time this has happened?"

"No, are you kidding? Christal has known about the dynamics in our office. She even sent us all to a class together with one of those *kumbaya* dudes."

"Did it help?"

"For a while. But they're at it again! Maybe you should talk to Christal."

"Okay, let me try to talk to some people here and I'll get back to you, okay?"

"Okay Justin, but hurry. I don't know how long Colleen will wait around. I know she's looking for another job. Oops, I wasn't supposed to tell you that! Please don't tell anyone. She'll kill me if she finds out I told you."

Justin reassured her. "Don't worry. I won't tell anyone," and hung up the phone.

Before even thinking about anything else, he quickly pulled out his newly created journal. He wanted to record some insights from his reconciliation meeting with Lee Ann, not to mention the staff meeting afterward, while they were still fresh in his mind.

Journal Entry # 2
    a) Managing by way of assumptions only gets me into trouble. I need to have my facts straight before drawing any conclusions.

    b) Never, ever confront a staff member in front of his or her peers. It only makes things worse and requires twice as much repair work.

c) Apologies are difficult but necessary to do when I make mistakes.
d) It's important to role model the behavior I wish to see in others.

It was now after five o'clock and everyone in the department had left for the day. Although Justin still had a lot to think about and a lot more to do, he couldn't wait to get home and be with his family. After such a trying day at work, his family meant more to him now than ever. Everything else would just have to wait.

The **18** homecoming

MEGAN MET JUSTIN AT THE DOOR and immediately embraced him as if she hadn't seen him for days. Tommy and Michelle were impatiently awaiting their turn to greet him as well. Neither of the kids understood why this particular homecoming was such a special occasion, but they were eager to participate just the same.

Megan whispered to Justin so that only he could hear. "I am so proud of you, honey. I even made your favorite meal for dinner." Before she could finish what she wanted to say, the kids were jumping up and grabbing at his arms, demanding to be part of the celebration.

Justin smiled at Megan and shifted his attention to the kids. In one swift swoop he had Tommy in one arm and Michelle in the other. As he and the kids embraced, he couldn't help but notice the difference between how he was feeling now and how he had felt for most of the day. It really highlighted how much it meant to him to feel appreciated, and he wished the feeling would stay with him forever.

"Okay kids, let daddy change and relax a little," Megan said, shooing her husband away for a break before dinner. "And Tommy, can you set the table for mommy?"

Tommy, excited to have such an important role, ran over to the drawer where the placemats were and started pulling them all out onto the floor. Meanwhile, Michelle ran off to get her math quiz from Mrs. Henkel's class. She couldn't wait to show her *A* to her daddy.

With the welcoming party now breaking up, Justin headed upstairs for a hot shower. He was thankful for the opportunity to be alone for a few minutes and to reflect upon his day; a day that had clearly been among the most difficult ones he had ever experienced.

After toweling off and putting on his sweats, Justin plopped himself down on the bed. Although his body was physically exhausted, his mind was still racing. He couldn't stop processing the day's events. He still felt tension throughout his body.

He took a long, deep breath and let it out slowly. It dawned on him that in the past he had no problem leaving his work at the office. There really was no reason to take it home. Now, if this day was to be any indication, he might need his time at home just to debrief his workday. *That's not right,* he said to himself, and then continued to talk out loud, as if he were still talking to Megan.

Overall, it was a pretty good day. I stepped up to the plate— more than once, actually— and asserted myself as the new manager. He paused. *Yet in some respect I created as many problems as I solved. In reality, I'm still very much in the eye of the storm without any clear end in sight.* He paused again, now feeling the day's anxiety kicking back in. *Truth be told, it wasn't such a great day after all.*

Then, just as the aroma of spaghetti and meatballs permeated the air, Megan called Justin from the bottom of the stairs. "Honey, time for dinner."

He took another big breath and let it out slowly. He needed to get back into a positive frame of mind—and in a hurry.

Michelle was waiting at the bottom of the stairs. "Daddy, look, I got an *A* on my quiz."

Justin took the piece of paper and examined it with a big smile. He looked over at Megan. "Wow, honey did you see what our daughter did in school today? She got an *A*!"

Michelle was grinning from ear to ear.

Tommy ran up and pointed at the table. "Daddy, look, I set the table!"

Justin grabbed Tommy and started tickling him.

Megan intervened. "Okay you two, no roughhousing in the kitchen. Please everyone, sit down at the table."

Once everyone was settled in and grace was said, Megan began her interrogation. "Well, tell me everything! I want to know what made you change your mind this morning and what happened today. You sounded stressed when I called."

Justin was actually excited to tell the part about his phone call to the radio station. It was so uncharacteristic of him to do what he did that it made for a great story.

Megan glowed as she listened; she was pleased to know that she'd been the one who'd called Justin's attention to Dr. Mac's column.

"And so he told you to take the job?"

"Not exactly. It was when he said, 'this opportunity may not come around again' that it really hit home. The more I thought about it, the more I realized he was right. This was about me, not Charlie."

"Isn't that what I told you?" asked Megan, looking for some acknowledgment that she'd brought that point up the night before.

Justin nodded and then proceeded to methodically go through his day, telling her about his meeting with Christal, the Charlie incident, the first staff meeting, his *faux pas* and recovery with Lee Ann, the second staff meeting, and of course, the Boulder dilemma.

As their conversation started to wind down, Megan noticed that they had just enjoyed one of the liveliest dinner conversations that they'd had in quite a while. Justin, she observed, was more animated than ever before, and for the first time seemed to really care about his job. It was a passion that she had previously witnessed in him only when he watched football. She liked what she was seeing.

Justin got up to clear the dishes and gently kissed Megan on the cheek as he passed by. It was his way of thanking her for putting up with him the last couple of days. Her unyielding belief in him meant a great deal, especially considering all the problems that suddenly presented themselves to him at work.

Minutes later Justin took his tea and retreated to the den to watch *SportsCenter*. With Megan upstairs giving Tommy a bath and Michelle off doing her homework, this was Justin's time, which he cherished so much. Tonight, however, he had much more on his mind than relaxing and watching sports highlights—he had the additional burden of trying to figure out what to do about Charlie and the persistent problem in Boulder.

If only someone could just tell me what to do, he moaned to himself. *No, if only Christal could tell me what to do.* And then it came to him. *Why of course! I'll call Christal on her cell phone.* Justin felt energized. Although calling Christal after hours was supposed to be for emergencies only, this *was* an emergency! Surely she would understand, and more importantly, tell him what to do. He phoned her. After a couple of rings, her voice mail clicked in. "Hello, this is Christal. I'm unable to take your call right now, but please leave a message at the beep and I'll call you back. Beeeep."

Disappointed to get her voice mail, Justin focused on his message, trying not to sound too desperate. "Christal, Justin here. Sorry to call your cell, but we have a couple of problems that need some immediate attention, and I need your advice right away. Can you call me on my cell or at the office first thing tomorrow? Thanks. Oh, and I hope your trip is going well."

Just then Megan walked into the room and sat down with him. "Is everything okay?"

Justin put the phone down. "Not quite. I tried to reach Christal for some advice, but only got her voice mail. I'm not sure what to do."

Megan tried to reassure him. "Honey, isn't there someone else at DataDump you can talk with? Or what about my father? He used to be a CEO, you know. Maybe he could help. Or what about Dr. Mac?"

Justin's eyes lit up. He liked the Dr. Mac suggestion much better than the thought of talking to his father-in-law. "Hmm, Dr. Mac might be a good idea. I wonder if I can write a letter to his advice column using the newspaper's website and get a quicker response? What do I have to lose, right?"

Megan smiled at her husband's obvious preoccupation with his dilemma. "Just don't stay up too late. You need a good night's sleep." She stroked his face, kissed the top of his head, and left the room.

Justin smiled. "I'll be up in a few minutes, I promise!"

Desperate Dave

JUSTIN KNEW THE ODDS of getting Dr. Mac to respond right away to his letter, let alone respond at all, were pretty low. Nevertheless, he didn't know where else to turn. Christal was quickly becoming more unreliable than reliable, and, quite frankly, he didn't know if he could count on her or not at this point.

He pondered about what to write. Although he really wanted to ask Dr. Mac about the Charlie situation, he worried that someone at DataDump would figure out that the letter came from him. That could ruin him, especially since he'd already almost blown his identity by talking to Dr. Mac on the radio. The Boulder issue was clearly the safer one. No one, including most of his own staff, was very familiar with that situation.

With that decided, he began to type.

> Dear Dr. Mac,
>
> I'm a new manager in charge of a small department. Our company also has a satellite office in another

state, where I oversee the employees at that location. They essentially provide the same job functions as my employees here at the home office.

It has come to my attention that a couple of my employees at the satellite office are having a conflict. Considering that I just took over the managerial role, it doesn't make sense to me to go out there when I am still trying to establish myself with my employees here. As a result, I was thinking about hiring a consultant out in that area to assist them in resolving their problems.

Am I on the right path?

Justin read and reread his letter. Although he liked what he wrote, there was something missing...and then it came to him: he needed an alias! He then considered a variety of names before settling on "Desperate Dave." The "desperate" part was how he was feeling about being a manager and the "Dave" part was his brother-in-law's name. More importantly, it was a name that no one at DataDump could possibly trace back to him.

Now he just had one more thing to do before sending off the letter. He went up to the subject line of his e-mail and typed in the word "URGENT" in capital letters. *Why not?* he mused to himself. *Maybe it will get someone's attention.*

Justin's first full day as manager was finally coming to an end. It was now after ten in the evening and he could only hope that this was not an indication of what he could expect in the days to come.

More bad news

20

THE NEXT MORNING CAME all too soon. Neither Justin nor Megan had slept very well, but for very different reasons. For Justin, it was that his brain had refused to shut down for most of the night. For Megan, it was the fear that Justin's job was going to absorb whatever time he had left for her. Both were fairly quiet that morning until Justin finally spoke up.

"So, what do you have going on today?"

Megan, who was zipping up Tommy's coat, replied, "I've got to meet with a couple vendors in town for one of my clients and then I'm helping Michelle's teacher during fourth period. Why?"

"Just wondering," replied Justin, sensing some tension.

"What are *you* doing today?" asked Megan.

"I'm going to try to get through another day without getting fired," replied Justin, attempting to lighten things up.

Megan snapped back, "Don't be so pessimistic. Maybe you'll have a great day. You always think the glass is half empty."

Justin could see that his sarcasm wasn't helping the situation. He needed to find a way to connect with Megan, not push her away.

"Honey, I'll try to come home a little early today so that we can spend some time together and get caught up. I feel like we haven't had enough time to talk since all this started going on. Hopefully things will slow down today."

"I'd like that," replied Megan, as she put on her coat and yelled for the kids to get into the car. It was her day to drive them to school.

After hugging his kids goodbye, Justin pulled Megan over and gave her a big kiss. Sometimes something as simple as a good kiss did wonders when he and Megan were at odds. He then followed his family out the door and both cars departed the O'Brien household at the same time.

The drive to DataDump was pretty calm compared to the commotion going on in the lobby as he walked in the front entrance. Mary Lou, the receptionist, called out the moment she spotted him. "Justin, you need to go see Melvin immediately."

Melvin was the senior vice president and second in charge behind J.W. He was often referred to around the office as "Number 2," a nickname that J.W. had coined and that had stuck with him ever since. At DataDump, all the VPs reported to Melvin, including Christal.

Justin could feel his heart pounding. *Why Melvin? Why now?* He knew something must be terribly wrong. There could only be one reason Melvin wanted to see him. He was going to be fired! What else could it be?

Perspiring now as he walked past the Orders Fulfillment Department, Justin noticed that his staff was huddled together at one of the nearby cubicles. Again, another bad sign. He wondered if they were talking about him or if he would ever see them again.

At the top of the stairs, he saw Ginger, Melvin's executive secretary, waving him over.

"Justin, Vice President Coleman will be right back. Please have a seat in his office."

Justin forced a smiled and walked past Ginger into Melvin's office. Ginger was the only one in the company who referred to Melvin using his title and last name. Many employees poked fun at her for her formality, including Justin, but today her words felt more chilling than funny.

As he sat in Melvin's office, a room three times the size of his own, Justin began to contemplate what he would do if he got fired. It was a scenario that he hoped he wouldn't have to face—yet why else would he be there?

Melvin walked into the room, looking very concerned.

Here it comes, he thought.

Expecting the worst, Justin was surprised by Melvin's uncharacteristically soft voice as he said, "Hi, Justin, come sit over here," pointing to a couple of comfortable chairs away from his desk.

Melvin cleared his throat. "Justin, Christal is in a hospital in New York; she got hit by a car last night."

21

Regrouping

Justin couldn't believe what had happened. As Melvin explained it, Christal had left her hotel shortly after 5:00 p.m. yesterday to go jogging, and was struck by a hit-and-run driver. She was rushed by ambulance to New York Presbyterian Hospital, where she currently resided in serious condition. Her injuries included a fractured pelvis, some broken ribs, and a punctured lung. Her family had been notified and J.W. was on his way out there to join them.

Melvin could not have been more compassionate as he walked Justin out of his office and down the hall. He was even missing an emergency management meeting in order to keep Justin informed.

"Let me know if you or your staff needs anything, Justin. I'll get word to you when we get more information."

Justin felt numb as he worked his way down the stairs toward his department. If he had gotten fired, at least his choices would have been obvious. But this was an entirely different situation. He couldn't control what was happening with Christal's life. He felt both helpless and at a loss for what he needed to do or say to his staff. What he did know was that he wanted to be with them now more than ever.

Lee Ann, John, Will, and Charlie all looked up from the break room as Justin entered.

John jumped up. "What have they told you?"

Seeing Charlie caused Justin to do a double take and quickly brought him back to reality. He walked over to the group, acknowledged Charlie, and told them everything Melvin had told him. Amy was not in the office.

"Where's Amy?" Justin inquired.

"She called in sick," said Lee Ann. "She won't be in today. Oh, and you are supposed to call your wife."

Justin looked at the group, "Let's touch base after lunch, and I'll see if I can get more information about Christal. Charlie, do you want to talk in my office?"

Before Charlie could respond, Lee Ann suggested sending some flowers to Christal.

Justin nodded. "Yes, certainly. Would you mind handling that?"

Lee Ann smiled, "Sure, no problem."

Justin was thankful to see that Lee Ann was truly trying to be helpful. Yesterday's talk had evidently been a success. He was equally thankful to see that Charlie apparently had come back.

Charlie put on his coat and headed to Justin's office.

"Charlie, why do you have your coat on?" asked Justin, confused.

"Because I'm going home. I just came in because I heard about Christal and was concerned. We were supposed to meet this coming Friday when she got back from New York." Charlie was shaking his head now in disappointment. "But obviously that's not going to happen either!"

"Hold on a minute," inquired Justin. "Just because Christal's not here, do you think you can just come and go as you please?"

"For your information Justin, I had this already pre-approved. You see, in anticipation of being named the new manager, I had planned to take a few days off to celebrate with my family. Of course there's not a lot of celebration going on in my household right now. How about yours?"

"What's that supposed to mean, Charlie?"

"Justin, I find your innocence awfully hard to swallow. I'm sorry, but I don't believe that all of this was a surprise to you," as he pointed around Justin's new office.

Justin was getting angry now. He really wanted to tell Charlie what he could do with his perspective, but knew better. He carefully chose his next words. "We need you here. I need you here."

Charlie shook his head, got up, and started toward the door. "Justin, to be honest with you, I just don't know if I can work for you, and I don't think I'm the only one." He opened the door, looked back at Justin once more and said, "Sorry, but you asked!"

Justin sat down, feeling like he had just been punched in the stomach. The phone rang. This time it was a welcome diversion.

"This is Justin."

It was Megan. "Honey, I called earlier. Didn't you get my message?"

Debating whether or not to tell her what was going on, he decided the easiest thing right now was to apologize. "Sorry, I was just about to call you."

"Justin, you got an e-mail from the newspaper asking you to call them. The message said it was urgent."

Justin was confused. "The newspaper? I can't imagine why they are contacting me. Are you sure they weren't trying to sell us a subscription or something? I bet it's a telemarketer."

Feeling a little insulted, Megan retorted, "You need to give me a little more credit than that, honey. It looks like a personal note."

Justin backed down. "I'm sorry, I'll call. What's the number?" He then thanked her and told her he loved her before hanging up.

By now his blinking phone already had four messages and the day had only just begun. He knew at least one had to be from Claire in Boulder—a call he wasn't ready to return just yet. He pondered. Then he decided to call the phone number Megan had given him. He knew he'd never call the newspaper unless he did it right now and got it over with. *I feel sorry for the sales person who tries to sell me a subscription,* he mused.

The phone call

An ENTHUSIASTIC VOICE picked up. "Dr. Mac."

Justin was thrown off. He had expected to be talking with a telemarketer, not Dr. Mac. And then he remembered that he had e-mailed the columnist the previous night. He instantly became nervous as he mumbled, "Hello?"

"Yes, this is Dr. Mac, how can I help you?"

Justin lowered his voice so no one could hear his conversation from the outer office. "Um, my wife told me to call this number at the paper."

Dr. Mac had a very caring voice. "Is this Desperate Dave by chance?"

Now it was all coming back to Justin, including the way he had signed his letter. "Okay, yes," he said, chagrined. "This is Desperate Dave. Is this really Dr. Mac?"

"Desperate Dave! Yes, this is Dr. Mac. Listen, I don't normally e-mail or consult over the phone with people who have written to my column." He paused. "Guess how many letters I get a day?" Not waiting for a response, he answered himself. "I get over three hundred letters a day!"

"Wow, you sure are a popular guy," Justin said, not knowing what else to say.

"I e-mailed you back because it sounded like you needed a response right away. It takes quite a while before a letter makes it into my column. I didn't want to make you wait for an answer."

Justin was feeling a little foolish for taking up Dr. Mac's valuable time. "I can't believe you contacted me. You're amazing!"

"Desperate Dave, I'm just an old man trying to be helpful, that's all. Now let's talk. I've got about ten minutes before I have to go to a meeting. I have your letter right here. Let's see, you were wondering if you should hire a consultant to handle the conflict that is going on at your satellite office. Is that right?"

Justin was feeling grateful to have the man's interest. He also liked being called Desperate Dave. It felt like an endearment that only a good friend would use.

"Yes, that's right. I'm fairly new here as the manager and I didn't think it would be a good idea to go to Boulder right now. That's where the satellite office is located."

"Well, if I had the time, I'd love to talk about this more in-depth. However, let me just give you my two cents worth right now. In my opinion, you need to get out there and establish yourself as their manager right away. These people are also your direct reports, and they need your supervision. A consultant will only muddy the water. Please understand: I'm not against using consultants, especially since I'm one myself. It's just that your first three months as a manager are critical in establishing yourself with the people you manage."

"But Dr. Mac, I can't be in all places at once!"

"It's not an ideal situation, is it? It never is. Let's look at it from a different angle. What message will it send to your Boulder people if you bring in an outside consultant?"

Justin stopped to think about that one before responding. "In one sense, they'll probably be happy that I'm addressing it right away. But in another sense, they might be disappointed that I didn't handle it myself."

"Very true. Both urgency and leadership are needed right now. More importantly, you don't want the Boulder group to feel as if they don't matter to you as much as the home office group does. That could create an unwanted *us* versus *them* situation. And think about what message it could send to your employees in the home office. They may think that you don't trust them enough to go out to Boulder. Also, it is important to role model effective leadership to both groups consistently. Every one of your actions says something about who you are as a leader. Your people in the home office need to understand that you manage both groups and that they need to be able to perform their job functions to the best of their ability whether or not you are there. How else can you establish that independence if you don't allow them to flourish and perform on their own? A lot is at stake here, Desperate Dave—look, I've got to go. Did that help a little?"

Actually, it had helped a lot. Justin was floored at how direct and concise Dr. Mac's advice had been. He himself had been struggling for twenty-four hours over what to do about Boulder, and here Dr. Mac had rattled off a solution within a couple of minutes. "Of course that helped. All I can say is thank you! How do you know all of that stuff?"

Dr. Mac chuckled, "I'm not an expert, Desperate Dave. I just gave you my two cents, that's all."

Justin thanked Dr. Mac again and hung up. Having a clear direction gave him an incredible sense of relief. Granted, he still had his hands full with Christal's hospitalization, Charlie's near insubordination and now a necessary trip out to Colorado, but none of it seemed as overwhelming as it had just ten minutes ago. At least now he felt like he had a fighting chance to succeed. Dr. Mac was quickly becoming his hero. He whipped out his journal.

Journal Entry # 3

a) I need to manage both the Winnetka and Boulder departments equally and respond to either when needed. And if they continue to see themselves as separate entities from each other, then I have not done my job.

b) Don't opt to use a consultant to do the work that I should be doing.

And then his thoughts shifted for a second as he wrote,

c) Charlie's a jerk!

Justin shook his head. He knew full well that he was now reacting emotionally. His eyes glanced up to his previous journal entries, especially 1a and 2a.

1a) If I can't say something nice, or at least say it in a supportive and constructive way, then I'm better off not saying it at all.

2a) Managing by way of assumptions only gets me into trouble. I need to have my facts straight before drawing any conclusions.

He took a deep breath and took in his own advice. He crossed it out.

c) ~~Charlie's a jerk!~~

With that, he put his journal away and picked up the phone. He needed to get a flight to Colorado.

23
Feeling supported

LEE ANN POPPED HER HEAD in the doorway. "Justin, I've ordered the flowers. Is there anything else you think we should do?"

Justin was happily impressed with Lee Ann's initiative. "Wow, that's great. Thanks for taking the lead on that."

Lee Ann smiled. "No problem, I just wasn't sure if it's enough. Do you think we can call her?"

"I don't think so. It will probably be awhile before she's well enough to receive calls. But let me talk with Melvin this afternoon and see if her condition has improved. I'm guessing she's in a lot of pain right now. Perhaps we could follow up the flowers with a get well card that we all sign or something. What do you think?"

"Sure, why not. I'll pick a card up at lunch today."

"Hey, Lee Ann," Justin said softly. "Thank you! I really mean it. Thanks for everything."

Lee Ann's eyes met Justin's. "I'm just doing my job. But thanks for noticing."

As Lee Ann walked away, Justin sat back in his leather chair, feeling a tremendous sense of appreciation for her and for their transformed relationship. It was such a powerful sensation that he pulled out his journal one more time and wrote:

Journal Entry # 4

a) It takes a lot of work to turn a "strained" relationship into a "supportive" relationship, but it certainly is worth the effort.

Justin reread his entry before closing the journal. The insights that were beginning to fill the pages were already becoming very empowering for him, and he had only just begun. He especially liked the idea of having all his thoughts and insights together in one place. Perhaps this journal might become the management skills manual that he had never received. He could only hope.

Meeting with Melvin

I T WAS LATE IN THE DAY when Melvin stopped by the office. Although he had sent an all-employee e-mail updating everyone on Christal's condition, he wanted to personally talk with the Orders Fulfillment Department.

"Melvin," cried out Justin loud enough so everyone in the outer office could hear him. "Welcome."

All eyes immediately shifted to Melvin as he walked through the office toward Justin.

"Justin, I'm sorry it's taken all day to get back to you. Can I have a moment?"

"Of course," replied Justin, as he signaled to his staff to join them. "Why don't we all gather in the break room?"

Will, John, and Lee Ann shot up out of their seats like a bolt of lightning had struck them. After all, it wasn't every day that Executive Vice President Coleman stopped by.

Melvin waited for everyone to be seated before beginning. His disposition was clearly more relaxed than it had been earlier in the day. "Welcome, everyone. I wanted to—" and then he stopped for a second and looked at Justin. "Where is the rest of your staff?"

Justin jumped in before anyone else could respond. "Oh, um, Amy is out sick and Charlie is...well, he's taking a couple of vacation days."

Amy would have been the most likely one to challenge his words at that moment, but fortunately for Justin, she wasn't there today.

Melvin, satisfied with Justin's response, continued. "Okay, well, I stopped by because I wanted to see how you were all doing and to answer any further questions you might have about Christal's condition. I'm sure you've seen the e-mail I sent out earlier to the whole company. That was mainly to keep everybody informed about her condition."

Will was the first to speak. "What exactly happened? All we know is that it was a hit-and-run accident."

Melvin leaned in as he responded. "Here is what I know. Christal had just left her hotel to go jogging yesterday when she was hit by a car while crossing the street. According to eyewitnesses, the car that hit her was turning left and sped up as it made the turn in order to beat the oncoming traffic. Unfortunately, that was right at the time that Christal was crossing the same street. The driver apparently saw her at the last second and tried to swerve out of the way but to no avail." Melvin was now using his hands to demonstrate the collision. "The car hit her pretty much head on and knocked her over onto the curb. We're told that the driver slowed down after hitting her and then immediately sped away. There were a couple of witnesses, as I mentioned, and they were able to describe the make and color of the car. Nobody has been arrested yet, at least as far as I know.

As for Christal, she fractured her pelvis, broke a couple of ribs, and punctured one of her lungs. They took her to New York Presbyterian Hospital, where she's listed in serious condition."

"Will she fully recover?" asked John.

"Although there is always a chance of complications, the doctor seemed pretty optimistic about a full recovery. Fortunately, she won't require any surgery to repair her pelvis. However, it's going to be a long, slow recovery process that will entail extensive bed rest and physical therapy."

"Is she awake and able to talk at all?" asked Lee Ann.

"Yes, she has been able to talk but is in an incredible amount of pain. We ask that you don't try to contact her until we know that her condition has stabilized."

Melvin then looked around at each staff member. "I apologize for being so lengthy, but I wanted to make sure you knew everything that I know. Is there anything else you need right now?"

A few glances were exchanged before Justin spoke up. "Well, we know where you are in case a question does come up," hoping that his comment would wrap things up. He was afraid that the conversation might shift from Christal to how things were going in the department, and he didn't want to go there with Melvin in the room.

"I have another question," replied Will.

Justin held his breath.

"Whom will Justin be reporting to during Christal's absence?"

Melvin was a bit taken aback by the odd question and responded rather sternly. "He'll still be reporting to Christal. Why'd you ask?"

Will backed off, noticing Melvin's tone of voice. "Oh, I was just wondering."

"Will, we fully expect for Christal to recover and be perfectly capable of providing Justin with whatever advice or support he needs, even if it has to be from her hospital bed. Besides, I would hope that you'd take any concerns that you have directly to Justin. After all, he is your manager. "

Justin bit hard into his lip, hoping the pain would subdue his grin. Watching Will get "schooled" by Melvin was well worth the temporary pain. It was the same sensation he used to get when his older brother got caught taunting him when they were kids. It was enjoyable then and it was enjoyable now—a kind of sweet justice.

But despite the immediate satisfaction that Justin was feeling, it didn't explain what happened next. In a complete about-face, Justin spoke up on Will's behalf. "Melvin, Will was merely asking that in a supportive way. He knew I was concerned about it, that's all."

"Well then, no problem," replied Melvin, smiling at Justin and getting up from the table. "Be sure to let me know if you need anything."

A mass exodus erupted the moment Melvin left the room. It was after five and everyone, including Justin, was ready to call it a day.

John, in what was now becoming a predictable gesture, passed by Justin and mentioned to him that it was a good meeting.

When Will walked past Justin, he said nothing but managed to give an acknowledging nod. Although minor in some respects, Justin knew it represented a shift in their relationship.

The surprise meeting

THE WEEK ENDED WITH SOME good news about Christal. Her condition had stabilized and she had been moved into a wing with her own room. It was the weekend now and Justin was reflecting about his upcoming trip on Tuesday to the Boulder office. He hated to even think about work on the weekend but given the week he'd had, he couldn't seem to stop. Work was slowly taking up what little energy he had left for his family.

Megan came up from behind the couch and put her arms around him. "Hello, my name is Megan and I'm your wife, just in case you may have forgotten."

"Oh, sorry, babe. I was thinking about my trip out to Colorado."

"Honey, this is the weekend. Remember, a time for family, fun, and anything but work!"

Justin shook his head. "I'm just getting so tired of not knowing what to do. I feel so ill equipped to handle this promotion."

"But I thought you were starting to turn things around. Are you expecting too much of yourself?"

"That would be an understatement," said Justin. "I wish I had asked Dr. Mac what I should be *doing* with the staff in Boulder instead of just asking him if I should go or not. I had the man on the phone, for Pete's sake, and dropped the ball!"

Justin knew that there was nothing Megan could do, and that complaining about it wouldn't make his frustration go away. What he did know was that his weekend was about to pass him by and he needed to try to enjoy it.

He stood up and put his arm around Megan. "Honey, thanks for listening. Don't worry, I'll figure something out. I have until Tuesday to come up with a plan." He paused long enough to feel his energy kick back in. "Now, let's talk about today. What would you like to do?"

Megan appreciated this sudden change in attitude. "Well, what I'd like *you* to do is to take Sandy out for a walk and take Tommy with you. Go to the park or something. The fresh air will be good for you."

Justin looked out the window with a renewed sense of adventure. He went to the front door and popped his head out where he was suddenly overtaken by a sensory explosion. He could feel the warm sun shining on his face. The sounds engulfed him as well: kids playing, birds chirping, lawnmowers blazing away. He spotted neighbors talking to each other across lawns, and the beautiful autumn leaves just beginning to turn into their vibrant seasonal colors. It was a symphony of fall sensations just waiting for him to experience.

And then, just as fast as it had started, Justin's love-fest with the great outdoors was interrupted by a barking dog and a screaming son.

"Daddy, we've been looking for you! Can we go to the park, please, please?" Both Tommy and Sandy looked up at Justin with great anticipation. Tommy, with his coat on and his favorite red tennis shoes already tied, had his hand firmly around Sandy's leash.

"Daddy, can I hold her?"

"Okay, but remember to hang on to the leash when we get to the park. I don't want to have to go running after Sandy again like I had to the last time. Remember?"

"I promise, daddy," said his son.

The park, also known as the Village Green, was only a few blocks away. It was just the right amount of distance for a Saturday afternoon walk. Short enough to get to and from the park in a reasonable amount of time and yet long enough for Justin to feel like he was getting some exercise.

Justin grabbed his coat and off they went, waving to various neighbors as they strolled by. Once at the park, Tommy immediately spotted his best friend Brian, over at the swings. "Daddy, can I go on the swings? Brian is over there."

Justin smiled, "Sure, just stay there so I can keep an eye on you," as he took over Sandy's leash. Sandy was an aging mutt with shaggy hair who used to love to run around the park and chase squirrels. However, at thirteen, she was perfectly content just finding a suitable spot to nap.

As Justin walked over toward the swing set area, he could see that all the park benches were already occupied—that is until an elderly woman got up from one of the benches to leave, revealing an available seat right in front of the swings. Justin walked over and approached the elderly man who appeared to be the woman's companion.

"Excuse me sir, is she coming back?"

The older man looked up and smiled. "Oh, yes, but please, have a seat. We'll be leaving in a minute," as he patted the spot right next to him.

At this, Sandy immediately jumped up on the bench, thinking the older man was inviting her to sit next to him.

"Sandy, down!" cried Justin, embarrassed. "I'm so sorry."

"Oh don't be," replied the older man as he started petting Sandy. "I love dogs."

A reluctant Sandy slowly got down, clearly preferring the bench to the grass.

Justin took over the unoccupied seat. "Sure is a nice day."

"Isn't it, though?"

The man's voice sounded very familiar, causing Justin to wonder if they had met before. "So what brings the two of you to the park today?"

"We just had to be out on this beautiful day. Can you believe how rainy it's been?"

Justin nodded in agreement.

"How about you?" asked the man.

Justin pointed towards the swing set. "That's my boy over there. You've already met Sandy. We just needed to get out. The wife tells me I'm thinking about work too much."

The man seemed to understand. "Yes, I know what you mean. I'm not sure I've mastered that one myself."

"What do you do?" asked Justin, still trying to figure out where or how he might have met this man.

"I'm retired for the most part. Do a little writing and consulting. Drives Daisy, my wife, crazy. Says I need to relax more and quit working."

Justin now was certain he knew this man, and finally asked, "Have we met before? Your voice sound very familiar."

"I'm Ken McDiffett. Your voice sounds familiar as well. You are?"

"I'm sorry, I'm Justin O'Brien."

"Nice to meet you, O'Brien. If we haven't met, let me say that it's nice to meet you."

Justin smiled. "McDiffett, McDiffett. Can't say your name rings a bell. What kind of consulting do you do?"

"I dabble in management consulting. Helping people work better together."

Suddenly a light bulb went off in Justin's head. "Do you have a nickname, by chance?"

The man smiled modestly and leaned in close, as if he only wanted Justin to hear. "They call me Dr. Mac."

"You're Dr. Mac!" burst out Justin, stunned. Just then a couple of people looked over curiously. "Oops, sorry. I'm guessing you don't want that broadcast throughout the whole park."

"I do try to keep a low profile. If Daisy sees me talking shop she'll ground me," jokingly replied Dr. Mac.

Justin couldn't believe his luck. He was sitting next to *the* Dr. Mac on a park bench, of all places. Go figure!

Off in the distance Justin spotted Dr. Mac's wife walking toward them. Although Dr. Mac just said he wasn't supposed to "talk shop," Justin knew he might never get this opportunity again. He had to make his move and quickly.

"We actually talked on the phone last week. I'm Desperate Dave!" Justin put his hand out.

"I kind of thought you were," said Dr. Mac, shaking Justin's hand. "Aren't you going out to Colorado?"

"Thanks to you I am. I mean that in a good way. Only I was hoping to pick your brain sometime about *how* to actually handle that situation. You've been so helpful. Oh, and, I've even taken your advice about the journal."

As Daisy reached the bench, Justin instantly realized that Dr. Mac's journal advice had not come from his Desperate Dave letter. It had come from their conversation on the radio show! *Yikes, I hope he doesn't pick up on that*, he thought to himself. *Otherwise, he'll think I'm a total loser.*

"Hi, dear, how was your walk?" Dr. Mac said to his wife warmly. "This is Justin O'Brien."

"Hi, Justin," said Daisy McDiffett. "Glad to meet you." She then looked directly at Dr. Mac. "Honey, we need to get going."

Dr. Mac nodded.

Daisy smiled at Justin. "It was nice to meet you, Mr. O'Brien."

Dr. Mac got up and locked hands with his wife. As they started to walk away he turned toward Justin. "O'Brien, can you meet me here on Monday at 3:00 p.m.?"

Justin's face lit up. "I'll be here. Thank you, sir!"

Reliving the moment

THE WEIGHT JUSTIN HAD BEEN CARRYING around all morning had simply dissipated. He couldn't wait to tell Megan what had just happened. His weekend had shifted for the better and he had her to thank.

"Mommy, daddy talked to a man at the park," cried Tommy upon seeing his mother.

Megan looked inquisitively at Justin. "You talked to a man at the park?"

"Honey, you are not going to believe this. Guess who I accidentally ran into!"

Megan hated these guessing games. "I don't know. Charlie? Just tell me, okay!"

In order to keep the suspense, Justin decided to tell the story. "Tommy goes off with Brian to play on the swings—"

Megan interrupted. "Not by himself, I hope."

"Honey, let me finish the story. And no, of course I wouldn't leave him alone. Anyway, all the benches by the swings were taken. The park was packed. Then, this elderly woman gets up and heads down the walkway, leaving one seat available next to her husband."

"You took an old woman's park bench seat?"

"No, of course not. I did, however, go up to the man and ask if they were going to be leaving anytime soon. He said they were, and invited me to join him in the meantime."

Tommy was laughing now as he interjected about Sandy jumping up on the bench.

"Oh honey, you let Sandy—" Justin interrupted. "No, no, Sandy thought the guy was inviting her up on the bench."

"What? I'm confused."

Justin continued. "The point is that I ended up sitting there and talking with the guy for a while. And then that's when it hit me. I knew I had met him before, but couldn't quite figure out where or when. That is, until I asked him what he did for a living."

"And what did he say?" asked Megan curiously.

"He said he was retired, but did a little management consultant and writing."

"And that told you what?"

"Nothing at that point, but it was when he said that he helped people work better together that I figured it out. Honey, I was talking with *the* Dr. Mac!"

"No!"

"Yes! And get this. After he introduced himself— he said his name was McDiffett—I asked him if he had a nickname."

"Why did you ask that?"

"Because there is no way that Dr. Mac could be his real name. And sure enough, this Mr. McDiffett grabs my arm, leans in and whispers, 'They call me Dr. Mac."

"You're kidding me!"

"Nope. And then we formally introduced ourselves. Oh, and you'll love this. Now he calls me *O'Brien*!"

"Not Justin or Mr. O'Brien but O'Brien?"

"Yep. Isn't that cool?"

Megan agreed. "That *is* cool. So, did you ask him about Boulder?"

"Even better, my dear. We are meeting on Monday at that same park bench to discuss Boulder. I'm going to be Macologized."

"Justin, that's not a word."

"Well I don't think Macology is either but everyone uses it in the same sentence with Dr. Mac."

Megan looked up at the ceiling. "Whatever!"

A Sunday gone sour

JUST KNOWING THAT HE WAS going to be meeting with Dr. Mac on Monday allowed Justin to relax and enjoy the remainder of the weekend. On Sunday the O'Brien family and neighborhood friends played a friendly game of touch football out on their front lawn. Since the Bears had a bye, touch football was the next best thing to help curb Justin's football craving. And even Megan joined in on the festivities. It truly was an O'Brien family event.

Sunday night dinner was yet another O'Brien family event. For Megan, there was no better tradition than preparing a special meal and gathering the whole family together to enjoy it. It was her favorite night of the week. Tonight she had made her special lasagna along with salad and French bread.

"Sure was a nice weekend, wasn't it?" commented Megan, passing Justin the bread.

Justin agreed. "Had I not accidentally run into Dr. Mac, I might not be saying that."

"Daddy, who's Dr. Mac?" asked a curious Michelle.

Justin's response was interrupted by the ringing phone.

"I'll tell you in a second," said Justin, as he got up to answer the phone. Usually the only calls they got during dinner were from telemarketers. But it was Sunday, and Justin figured that even telemarketers got that night off. It must be someone they knew.

"Hello."

"Hi Justin, it's Christal."

Justin's jaw dropped. "Christal, how are you? How are you feeling?" He glanced over at Megan.

Megan nodded. That was her way of giving him permission to take the call.

"Justin, I hope I'm not interrupting anything. Is this a good time to talk?"

"Oh, sure, no problem," replied Justin, as he headed into the den for some privacy.

"I'm going to be going through more testing the next few days and may not be able to talk to you for a while so I thought I'd check in with you now as opposed to later."

"I'm glad you called. We've all been so worried about you. How are you feeling?"

"I'm surviving, thanks in part to the pain medication. To tell you the truth, I feel pretty lucky to be alive. It could have been much worse."

"I can only imagine," replied Justin, noticing a slight slur in her voice.

"Please say thank you to the staff for the beautiful flowers. It really meant a lot to me."

"No problem. Lee Ann was the one who pulled that together for us. You would have been proud."

Christal sounded a bit surprised. "Lee Ann? You're kidding!"

"No, she's really come around."

"Wow, that's great to hear, Justin. So how are you doing?"

Justin paused, not knowing where to start or how much to say. "I guess you are aware that Charlie is pretty upset that you selected me over him."

"Why would I know that?" she asked surprisingly.

Justin was confused by her reaction. "I got the impression you two had talked and that you were planning on meeting with him this past Friday to talk more about all of this."

"All of what, Justin?"

"The reason why you selected me and not him as the manager."

"Justin, I never talked with Charlie, let alone scheduled any sort of meeting. And even if I had, I certainly would have let you know what was going on. Just because I'm laid up in a hospital doesn't mean I have forgotten how to manage."

"I'm sorry, maybe I misunderstood him," replied Justin, wondering if Charlie had lied to him. He decided to change the topic.

"I'm going out to Boulder on Tuesday."

"You're what?"

This was not the supportive response he was hoping for. "They are having some problems out in Boulder and I've decided to go out there to help them work it out."

Christal sounded frustrated. "Justin, you have no experience as a manager and have no idea what's going on in Boulder...or what has gone on for that matter. You need to cancel your trip."

"But Christal, it wasn't my idea, it was Dr. Mac's."

"What? Who?"

"Dr. Mac. He's a management coach who writes a column in the *Daily Tribune* called 'Ask Dr. Mac.' You haven't heard of him?"

"No, can't say I have. So what do you mean it was his idea for you to go out to Boulder?"

"Claire asked for help and I didn't know what to do so I wrote a letter to Dr. Mac's column."

Barely able to mask her anger, Christal laid into Justin. "Let me see if I got this right. You contacted some guy who writes a 'Dear Abby' column in the newspaper in order to help you make that decision! My God, Justin, who will you contact next, the 'Psychic Hotline'?"

"Hold on…"

"No, you hold on," insisted Christal. "I have a consultant I've used who has helped me with the Boulder staff before and who has gotten results every time. You've got to understand, it is not cost-effective for you to go out there every time a situation happens."

"Christal, I need to establish myself as their manager and am going to use this trip to do that as well as help them work through the problem."

"Is that right? And tell me, Justin, what is it you plan on doing?"

Justin knew better than to say what he was about to say but he said it anyway. "I don't know, but Dr. Mac has agreed to meet with me tomorrow and he is going to help me come up with a plan."

Christal's voice softened a bit as she regained her composure. "Justin, Justin, listen to me. Is this Dr. Mac guy your supervisor? Does he know anything about DataDump? Has he been with the Boulder staff before? Is he even qualified to be giving you advice?"

The conversation was heading south quicker than his food was getting cold. Justin just wanted to get out alive. He backtracked.

"I would have consulted you, but we were told not to contact you until your conditioned stabilized. Please, Christal, I'm not trying to circumvent you as my supervisor. I was just trying to solve a problem. Besides…the tickets are non-refundable. I can't cancel the trip."

Christal paused. "Why don't I call Claire in Boulder and see what I can do."

She's just not getting it, Justin thought to himself. "Christal, I'm sorry for not discussing this with you beforehand, but it is important to me that I handle this myself. I promise you that you will be consulted throughout this whole thing."

Christal reluctantly gave in. "Alright, but I want a full report, and I especially want to know what your *plan* is upon going out there. I'm not thrilled about your seeking advice from a newspaper writer. Do you know what could happen if this gets out. You'll be the laughingstock of the company."

"This guy is an established management consultant in the community and he is even on the radio. He's not just a newspaper reporter."

"Fine, Justin, just confer with me in the future on these types of matters, okay?"

"Okay, I will. I'll talk to you in a couple of days."

As they hung up, Justin could feel the tension throughout his body. *I've never seen that side of Christal before,* he thought to himself. *Perhaps the painkillers had something to do with it.* He could only hope.

"Justin, are you in here?" Megan popped her head into the den. "Honey, do you think you can join us for dessert at least?"

Justin forced a smile. "I'm not hungry anymore. Do you mind if I just sit here for a while longer?"

Megan could tell his conversation hadn't gone well. "Sure, honey. Do whatever you need to do. Just don't put your game face on yet. We aren't ready to give you up for the weekend."

Megan used the term "game face" in reference to the serious look Justin would have on his face whenever he started thinking about work. He was notorious for wearing his game face on Sunday nights, usually right after dinner.

"I'll try honey," replied Justin, knowing full well that it was too late.

In preparation

JUSTIN'S GAME FACE LASTED through the evening and into Monday morning. He was still having trouble understanding why Christal was so upset with his decision to go out to Boulder. Clearly he had touched a nerve.

Once he'd arrived in the office, John waved Justin over to his cubicle. "Hey. I saw Charlie out front. Do you want me to go get him?"

Justin's stomach tightened. In one sense he was glad Charlie was on the premises, but in another sense he was bothered that he wasn't already at his desk working. Something seemed fishy. He looked around the office. At least everyone else was in and accounted for, including Amy.

"Don't worry about it, John."

Justin wasn't quite sure if John was trying to stir things up or if he was actually trying to be helpful. Although supportive of Justin in private, he would rarely demonstrate any allegiance to him in front of the whole staff. He seemed to be playing both sides of the fence, depending on whomever he was with at the time. It made Justin a little suspicious.

"Can everyone come into my office?" yelled Justin across the outer office. "I talked to Christal yesterday and wanted to give you an update."

Just then Charlie walked into the outer office, wearing a silly grin on his face. "What's up?"

Justin ignored Charlie's grandstanding entrance and stood by his door. Lee Ann was the first to walk in, followed by Will and then John. Charlie stopped in to see Amy in her cubicle and the two of began to talk and laugh, paying little attention to Justin's request. It was becoming more and more apparent to him that Charlie's defiance over his promotion was far from over.

With a lot on his mind and a very busy few days ahead, Justin was determined not to get caught in a power play with Charlie (or Amy for that matter). It was a battle that would have to wait for another day.

"Where's Amy and Charlie?" asked Lee Ann as she looked at Justin.

"Oh, they're talking over in Amy's cubicle. This isn't a mandatory meeting, so it's no big deal." He then cleared his throat. "Christal called me at home last night. She's doing a little better and wanted to make sure you all knew how much she appreciated the flowers." Justin then looked right at Lee Ann. "I told her that you were primarily responsible for handling all of that and she was very impressed."

"Justin, they were from all of us."

"I know. I just wanted to make sure you got the credit you deserved, that's all."

Lee Ann blushed.

"What else did she say?" asked John.

"Basically that was about it. She's not going to be available for phone calls for a while but she wanted to make sure we knew she was alright." After a short pause, Justin decided to go ahead with the other piece of information that he wanted to talk about. "But I do have one more thing."

Before Justin could get his next words out, Amy and Charlie walked into the room. Amy sat in the remaining empty chair at the table while Charlie went behind Justin's desk and pulled out his big leather chair and rolled it over near the group. Nobody knew whether to laugh or be dismayed.

Charlie was still wearing the silly grin as he commented to the group. "What? There weren't any other chairs!"

All eyes moved to Justin in anticipation of a reply or at least a reaction.

Justin looked at Charlie. "Just don't put your feet up on the desk!"

Laughter broke out in the room. Even Charlie smiled.

Justin was relieved. He had forgotten the value of humor in times like this. He continued with his second item. "As you may or may not know, they've been having some relationship problems in the Boulder office and I've decided to go out there tomorrow to help them resolve things."

The response from the group was very similar to their response to Christal's announcement that Justin would be her replacement—shock.

"You're going out there?" asked Charlie, implying that Justin was making a big mistake.

"Yes, I am their manager, too."

Amy smirked. "Justin, you don't know the first thing about what to do for them. You could actually make things worse."

Lee Ann spoke up, trying her best to be supportive. "We don't exactly have it together ourselves right now. Do you think this is the best time for you to go out there?"

Justin didn't like having his decision challenged for a second time within the last twenty-four hours. And he wasn't about to make the same mistake of bringing up Dr. Mac.

"Look, I—"

"Don't worry about it," interrupted Will as he spoke to the group. "We'll handle things here. They need you out there."

Amy's jaw dropped. Charlie's silly grin evaporated. The room was silent.

It was now Justin's turn to be in shock. Will had just made a supportive statement.

John, now sensing the shift, commented. "I agree with Will. We'll handle things here."

Charlie apparently wasn't inclined to let this moment go without an argument. "Of course we can handle things here; my concern is whether you have the ability to handle things there!"

Justin looked right into Charlie's eyes. "It is a situation that can't wait any longer. I've conferred with Christal already and will be getting some more advice later this afternoon. I'm just going to do the best I can, Charlie."

Charlie blatantly shook his head in frustration. "Yeah, whatever!"

Lee Ann broke the tension with a question. "Who'll be in charge while you're gone?"

Justin smiled. He knew Lee Ann meant it rather innocently, but he also knew it was a loaded question. Certainly the obvious choice would be Charlie, but that would only stir the fire of his discontent. And naming someone else would have its own ramifications. The truth was he had no one at this point whom he trusted. Hence, his response was short and diplomatic.

"No one. You've all worked here long enough to know what you need to do. If something comes up, call me on my cell. You also have Cynthia from HR or Melvin in case she's not around."

"You forgot about Christal," replied Amy.

"As I already mentioned, Christal said she would not be available by phone for a while," retorted Justin.

When the meeting finally broke up, Justin made eye contact with Will as he was walking out of the room. "Will, hold on a second. For what's its worth, thanks for your comment."

For a moment Will seemed at a loss for words. Then he said, "Well...I...I guess I owed you one!"

They exchanged nods and moved past each other.

Justin stepped back into his office and sat down. He had a few loose ends to tie up before leaving for his meeting with Dr. Mac. But before he could do any of that, he pulled out his journal. He had a couple of insights he wanted to get down from the past few days.

Journal Entry # 5

   a) Always support my employees in front of senior management, even when they are being difficult.
   b) Don't be afraid to use humor to lighten up an uncomfortable situation.

Justin still had an unsettling feeling as he put away his journal. He was happy about the sudden change in Will but unhappy about Charlie's growing negativity. *Why is it that with every positive there has to be a negative,* he lamented to himself. *I can't seem to sustain any forward momentum.* Justin knew that eventually the tide would have to turn if he wanted to keep his job. *Batting 500 might work in baseball, but it's not good enough in business,* he reminded himself.

Macology in the park

I⊤ WAS 2:45 P.M. and Justin was on his way to the park. He was very careful to duck out of the office without any fanfare, successfully avoiding any questions as to where he was headed. As much as he hated to admit it, Christal was probably right when she said that he could be the laughingstock of the company if people found out about Dr. Mac. He was better off just keeping it to himself.

The afternoon temperature was slowly dropping as a cold front worked its way through the North Shore town of Winnetka. Actually, it wasn't that unusual to see the clouds rolling in each afternoon, nor was the sudden influx of wind off Lake Michigan, for that matter. But cold air in September was something no one expected or wanted. Illinois winters were bad enough without having to have subtle reminders early in the fall.

Justin arrived at the Village Green with notepad in hand. His primary goal for the meeting with Dr. Mac was to come out with some sort of plan for the Boulder group. He also hoped to slip in some conversation about Charlie.

Dr. Mac was already at the bench. Despite the cooler temperature and occasional blast of wind from the east, he seemed to be enjoying himself as he tossed breadcrumbs to the assembling pigeons.

"Hi there, Dr. Mac!" said Justin as he approached the bench.

"Ah, O'Brien, I'm glad to see the cold didn't keep you away."

"Are you kidding, I wouldn't miss this for anything."

"How are you?" asked Dr. Mac as they shook hands.

Justin joined Dr. Mac on the bench, while tightening his coat for extra warmth. "Beginning to feel like winter out here!"

"Yeah, Daisy made me wear a scarf today, can you believe it?" smiled Dr. Mac, pointing to a very colorful scarf.

Justin smiled back. He was amazed at how unpretentious and *real* Dr. Mac was.

Dr. Mac leaned toward Justin and spoke softly. "O'Brien, how can I help you?"

"Dr. Mac, first off, I'd like to thank you for meeting with me today. I'm sure there are hundreds of people who would love to be sitting in my shoes right now, and I feel pretty fortunate."

"I like you, O'Brien. I don't know what it is, but I enjoy talking to you. Even your letter stood out for me. It's weird, I know."

"Well, whatever it is, I'm certainly glad it's there." replied Justin. "But I do want to pick your brain on what to do with my other staff in Boulder, where you so elegantly convinced me to go tomorrow. I'm a little anxious, to say the least."

Dr. Mac nodded in agreement. "That's because you are carrying too much of the load, O'Brien. It's not your problem to solve; it's theirs."

"But Dr. Mac, then why am I going out there?"

"I don't know why. You tell me!"

Justin was confused now. "Because you told me to go out there. Don't you remember?"

Dr. Mac remained calm as he asked again. "Why are you going out there?"

Justin realized that *because you told me to* was obviously not an acceptable answer. He thought about it and then answered again. "I'm going out there for two reasons: First to connect with my new staff and to establish myself as their manager."

Dr. Mac's eyes lit up as he nodded in agreement.

"And secondly, I am going out there to help them work through whatever issues they need to work through so that they can function better together."

"Ah, that was a much different answer than your original one," replied Dr. Mac.

"Okay, okay, I get it. I had the answer all along."

"O'Brien, your first task is to believe in yourself. You'd be surprised at how much you do know," said a convincing Dr. Mac.

Justin was starting to feel better. It meant a lot to have someone believe in him like Dr. Mac apparently did.

"Dr. Mac, let me try a different question on you. I do understand the *why* part of why I'm going out there but it is the *how* part that I'm worried about right now. Can you help me with that?"

"Be more specific. What's going on?"

"Here's what I know. There is some kind of conflict going on between two of the employees, Katie and Colleen, that started from a comment that one of them made to the other in an e-mail. Apparently, it has blown up from there and now neither of them is speaking to one another. I'm guessing there's more to it, but that is what I know at this point in time. I just need to know how to address and/or resolve this."

"Do you have a full understanding of who is involved and what the issues are?" asked Dr. Mac.

"I have a general idea."

"Did you talk to both parties?"

"No."

"Do you think that might be helpful?"

"Yes."

"Then tell me what your first step will be once you are out there."

"I will meet individually with both parties first."

"Then what?"

"Well, I'll then consult with Claire, who is the team lead, and we'll decide what to do. It will either be disciplining one person or possibly mediating between two."

Dr. Mac nodded. "That's good. But what if there is more to it, as you had mentioned. How will you determine that?"

"Okay, I see where you are going with this. I need to also get an idea of what Claire has done in the past to address this and other problems. Perhaps she's reinforcing the problem by not addressing it. And now that I think about it, I need to also talk to Taylor, the other employee, to get her perspective and to see if the problem between Colleen and Katie impacts her as well."

"And what if it does?"

"Then I'll know that the solution needs to go beyond Katie and Colleen. They all need to be a part of it."

"I'm impressed O'Brien," replied Dr. Mac. "But I got one more question for you."

"Shoot."

"Should an incident occur between these two employees in the future, how do you want it handled?"

"Truthfully?"

"Is there any other way?"

Justin expected that. "Although I'd like Claire to consult with me, I would prefer that she attempt to handle it first. I don't want to have to play this 'parent-child' game where they expect me to solve their problems. They need to do that themselves."

Dr. Mac was smiling now. "Did you just hear yourself?"
"What?"

"Ah, never mind," said Dr. Mac, giving him a nudge.

Justin was all excited now. "So I also need to empower Claire so that she is clear on her role in the future. It's probably why we both need to be involved in this together, so that the rest of the employees know we are on the same page."

"You didn't need me here; you already knew all the answers!" beamed Dr. Mac. "Let me just add a couple of things. Empower Claire privately first, and then in front of the whole staff while you are out there. When I say empower, I mean spell out your expectations for her as a team lead and make sure everyone else understands those expectations. Secondly, make sure Claire and the staff understands your role. I'm not a big proponent of managers managing satellite locations. However, if you have to, then you better have very clear expectations on all fronts from roles and responsibilities to a problem-resolution process."

"Got it. I can do that," responded Justin. "Is it okay to take the staff out to dinner?"

"Why wouldn't it be? They need to know you as a person as well. Just always be respectful and aware that you are still on the job."

Dr. Mac looked at his watch.

Seeing this, Justin quickly asked if he could ask one more question?

"Make it quick," replied Dr. Mac as he got up from the bench, "I do need to get home. Have some letters I need to respond to."

Justin got up along with him. "Real quick. Thanks to your help, more and more good things are happening for me as manager. However, it seems that for every good thing that occurs, one or two bad things always seem to follow. In other words, I'm not sure I've been making forward progress since becoming a manager. I know it is not a specific question, but are there any thoughts you could share on this for me? I don't think DataDump believes that *barely surviving* is good enough to keep me in my job."

"O'Brien, I want you to make a list for me of all the good things and all the bad things that you are referring to. Let's meet here again in a week and we'll go over your list. In the meantime, should you ever have a pressing question in between our meetings, just send me a Desperate Dave letter and I'll do my best to respond immediately. But keep that just between us, okay? I really do need to go now."

Before Dr. Mac could turn away, Justin did something he rarely did with another adult, even with Megan. He gave Dr. Mac a hug. Needless to say, it surprised Dr. Mac as well.

"Thank you, thank you, thank you, Dr. Mac. You have made my day!"

Dr. Mac, still a little taken aback from the surprise hug, humbly replied. "I'm just an old man trying to be helpful, that's all."

"You are much more than that," said Justin.

The **30** good and bad

THE DRIVE TO THE AIRPORT turned into a family affair. Justin's flight was early enough to allow Megan plenty of time to drop him off first, get the kids to school, and still make her nine-thirty meeting with one of her clients. Megan prided herself on her planning and organizational skills, and this morning would be no different.

"Justin, you've been kind of quiet since last night," commented Megan as they approached Chicago's O'Hare International Airport. "Are you doing okay?"

Justin put his hand on the back of Megan's neck and began rubbing. "I'm fine. Got the old game face on, that's all."

Responding in kind, she put her hand on his knee. "You'll do fine, honey. Just be yourself. Those women will be awed by your warmth and sincerity. I know I was."

Justin's raised his eyebrows as he focused on the word *was.*"

"And still am...of course," added Megan. "That is what I meant to say."

They both laughed as the car pulled up to the drop-off curb.

This was Justin's first-ever business trip. And although he was only going out to Colorado for one night, trying to get out of the car amidst all the kissing, hugging, and goodbyes felt more like he was leaving for a month. Yet he really didn't mind. It was at times like this when he appreciated his family the most.

The flight out to Denver would take about two hours—providing Justin with enough time to begin working on his homework for Dr. Mac. As he pulled out his journal on the plane, he smiled at the thought of having homework again. Opening to a new page, he wrote the following title:

Homework for Dr. Mac

He then added two subheads:

Good Things that have happened since being manager

Bad Things that have happened since being manager

Too wordy, he thought to himself. He simplified.

<u>Good Things</u>   **<u>Bad Things</u>**

And suddenly his pen had a life of its own. Within one minute he had the following list:

<u>Good Things</u>	<u>Bad Things</u>
Charlie came back	Charlie's attitude
Will's recent support	Amy's lack of support
Dr. Mac	Argument with Christal
Lee Ann's turnaround	John's wishy-washiness
Journal writing	Boulder dilemma
Cynthia & Melvin's support	My lack of confidence

Putting his pen down, Justin reflected on his list, looking for anything that stood out. And then he saw it. First, both lists were primarily people-related. Being a manager is as much, if not more, about relationships. Secondly, Will and Lee Ann made it to the *good list* because of something he did. He made a difference by actually doing something or saying something with both of them.

It wasn't until that moment that Justin realized how close he had come to alienating his whole staff. Yet it didn't happen. It didn't happen because of *actions* he took to improve or address his relationship with both of them.

Just then the intercom interrupted his train of thought. "In preparation for landing, please place your seats and trays in the full upright and locked position."

Justin quickly flipped to his "Insights" page and wrote two new insights as the plane descended toward Denver International Airport.

Journal Entry # 6

a) Supervision is about action. I cannot manage people by doing nothing.

b) It's a lot easier to manage tasks than people, but my ultimate success depends on being able to do both effectively!

It was now time to shift gears. It was a matter of minutes before he'd see Claire and he needed to clear his head a bit. *Maybe I should have relaxed on the plane,* he thought as he closed his journal.

Part Four

Only in Boulder

Boulder, Colorado

"JUSTIN, JUSTIN, OVER HERE!" cried Claire, waving wildly in front of the escalator.

Turning toward the sound of his name, Justin spotted Claire, and, to his surprise, Colleen standing next to her. *Ah, for some reason I thought Claire would come alone,* he thought to himself, unable to think through if it mattered or not.

"Hi, Claire." He nodded. "Hello, Colleen."

"How was your flight?" asked Claire.

"Uneventful," replied Justin. "I mean nothing happened. But that's good these days, right?"

"That's for sure," agreed Colleen, as she gave him a welcoming hug. "It's so nice to see you!"

Justin smiled. He liked Colleen. She always made a point to connect with him the two times they had previously been together at a company function. That meant a lot to Justin. Unfortunately, it didn't seem to mean as much to Christal. For some reason, she treated both departments as separate entities and never made much of an effort to bring the groups together, even though they essentially performed the same job functions for the same company. It was something Justin never quite understood but never questioned either—that is, not until this very moment. As the trio started striding away through the concourse, Justin asked:

"Does it seem odd to either of you that our two groups haven't collaborated more together?"

Claire looked puzzled. "Why do you ask that, Justin? You were with Christal every day; didn't she ever say anything?"

"Nope. I just accepted it. How's that for a poor answer?"

Colleen jumped in. "Speaking of Christal, how is she doing?"

"Gosh, we have neglected you, haven't we?" apologized Justin. "I'm sorry. I should have called you with the latest."

Colleen and Claire exchanged a look and nodded.

"What?" asked Justin. "What was that *nod* for?"

Claire smiled at Colleen before responding. "Justin, we've been DataDump's redheaded stepchild since the Boulder office opened last year. No one tells us anything, and when we do find something out it is usually told to us instead of anyone taking the time to seek our input. It has always been that way. So, no, it doesn't surprise us that you forgot about us—again."

"I'm so sorry," apologized Justin for the second time. "Did you ever ask Christal about that? I'm sure she had her reasons." Not waiting for a response, he added, "but either way, I will do my best to make it different. I promise."

"Seeing is believing," replied Claire. "And no, I never did ask her about it. I guess that's partly my fault."

"Well, I can't speak for Christal, but you need to be able to talk to me about things like that. I'm serious."

"Okay Justin. I'll do my best."

Justin nodded in agreement. "But back to your question, Colleen. She is doing better. As you know from Melvin's e-mail, she broke her pelvis, a couple of ribs, and also punctured a lung. Yet despite all of that, her spirits are good and she won't need any surgery."

"That's good. When is she coming back?" asked Claire.

"My understanding is that once she gets out of the hospital she will be heading to her mother's house in Redlands, California for her recovery and rehab. It's going to be a long haul for her."

"Thanks for the update, Justin," said Colleen. "We really do care, even though we may seem frustrated."

As they walked out of the airport toward the parking lot, Justin couldn't help but notice how comfortable he was already feeling with Claire and Colleen in just ten minutes. It was a refreshing change to have a completely unobstructed conversation with coworkers for once.

"So how's your wife and kids?" asked Claire, as they got onto I-70 heading west.

"They're great. Megan is still freelancing with her graphics business from home and has started helping out at Michelle's school in her spare time."

"She's incredible, Justin. You're a lucky man," said Colleen.

"Believe me, I know. And Michelle just turned eight and Tommy is five and both are into sports."

"Sweet!" replied Claire.

"Last time I recall talking to you, Colleen, you were engaged to some real tall guy, weren't you?" ask Justin.

Claire started laughing.

"That was a year ago, Justin. And yes, that one went by the wayside," joked Colleen.

"But she's in love now!" laughed Claire, as she winked at Colleen.

The conversation stayed light with a reasonable amount of kidding until they passed the Broomfield exit off of U.S. 36. They were only fifteen minutes away from the office, when Claire decided it was time to talk shop.

"Justin, I assume you read Katie's e-mail that I forwarded to you yesterday afternoon?"

"Oops, I ended up leaving early yesterday and never actually saw it," he said apologetically.

"No problem," smiled Claire, "I have an extra."

Justin decided to ask the question that hit him the moment he saw Colleen at the airport. "Do you think that Katie will be upset that the two of you picked me up from the airport?"

"Why would she?" asked Colleen innocently.

"Well, it may look like preferential treatment. You know, me spending quality time with the two of you and not Katie."

The more Justin thought about it, the more he realized that he should have insisted on Claire coming alone to the airport. Although he enjoyed Colleen, and wished that he had more people like her to work with in Winnetka, he was feeling uncomfortable with how this might look.

Claire tried to downplay her decision to bring Colleen along. "Don't worry, Justin. Colleen and I do a lot together, both in the office and outside the office. So I don't think it will look as if we were contriving to gang up on Katie."

Justin acknowledged that he might be unnecessarily concerned, but added, "I'm sure it's fine; I just don't want to give Katie or anyone else at your office any reason to believe that I might be biased. I truly am coming out here to make this a win-win for everyone. Assuming that's possible."

As they pulled into the parking lot behind their building, Claire asked Justin what he'd like to do first. Since Christal never came out to Boulder, Claire wasn't sure what to do with a manager.

Justin looked at his watch, remembering to subtract one hour to account for the time change. "Why don't you and I meet before lunch, Claire, and then I can meet with Katie, Taylor, and Colleen right after lunch. I'd also like to take everyone out to an early dinner tonight."

"Sweet," said Claire as she looked at Colleen, "I like this guy!"

Getting acquainted

T<small>HE</small> O<small>RDERS</small> F<small>ULFILLMENT</small> D<small>EPARTMENT</small> at DataDump was the only department that had a satellite location in Boulder, at least for the time being. There was talk about expanding the Boulder office to include other departments from the home office in Winnetka, but so far all it had been was talk. In the meantime, *the Boulder group,* as they were often referred to back in Winnetka, consisted of Claire, Colleen, Katie, and Taylor. Their office was actually a large room that was subdivided into cubicles and which sat above a bank on the Pearl Street Mall. Fortunately for Justin, Claire had reserved the conference room downstairs in the bank for his meetings with the staff. It was the only place in the building where you could have a private conversation without everyone else hearing it.

"I'm the team lead of this group in title only," complained Claire, during her one-on-one meeting with Justin. "Please don't get me wrong; I think the world of Christal. It's just that she pretty much gave us directives. I haven't really had any authority other than to make sure her directives were carried out."

"Claire, I can only speculate as to why that was. But as I said earlier, I'm going to do it a little differently. You will be involved in decisions, especially the ones that impact you out here."

"And what about Christal?" asked Claire.

"What about Christal?" replied Justin.

"Justin, please don't take this wrong, but you're pretty new as a manager. Do you really think she'll just let you change things around here?"

"Claire, you worry about Claire and the Boulder group and let me worry about Christal. Besides, she's already mad at me, so what do I have to lose anyway?"

"Why is she mad at you?"

"Oh, it's nothing," said Justin, now trying to downplay it. "Go ahead and tell me about what's going on here."

"Okay, but do you want the long version or the short version?"

Justin knew Claire had a tendency to be long-winded so he quickly chose the short version.

"Alright then," said Claire, not sure whether to take that as an insult. "Let me start by sharing a little bit about their personalities. First there is Katie. She is blunt, direct, and often insensitive. She's been known to say inappropriate things on occasion and can sometimes be considered outright rude, especially in some of her intra-office e-mails."

Claire pulled out a copy of Katie's latest e-mail—the one that had upset Colleen so much—and showed it to Justin. She continued. "Yet despite all of that," as she pointed to the e-mail, "she is probably the hardest worker I have."

Justin looked up from reading. "This isn't as bad as I imagined. Granted, telling Colleen to 'grow up' is not an appropriate comment to make, but there must be something else going on here."

"I agree, Justin, and that brings me to Colleen. She is very sensitive, caring, and doesn't like conflict. She's also probably my *best* employee, and I'm not just saying that because we are friends. Her problem is that she wears her feelings on her sleeve, if you know what I mean. And I think this latest e-mail from Katie just put her over the edge."

"I'm beginning to see the picture," replied Justin. "But what about Taylor? I haven't heard her name mentioned in all of this."

"That's because she pretty much keeps to herself. She's quiet—very quiet. And she's careful not to side with either of them when these kinds of incidents happen."

"So the conflict is pretty much between Colleen and Katie?"

"For the most part. The bigger problem is our work space."

"How so?"

"Come on Justin, think about it: four women, four cubicles plus a bathroom and water cooler. Welcome to our world! There is no privacy here! We can hear everything everyone says, whether it's to each other or on the phone. And frankly, that's why we tend to e-mail each other fairly frequently."

"Because it's the only way to have a private conversation without leaving the office?" guessed Justin.

Claire nodded. "Exactly."

"So you're saying that the size of the office itself is contributing to the problem? Or to put it another way, the confined space amplifies the personality differences and the lack of privacy within the group."

"Justin, I'm impressed. Have you been taking management classes?"

"I wish. I just got lucky."

"Well I think you hit the nail on the head. If we were more spread out, the personality issues would be minimal. We wouldn't be in each other's space and we'd be able to have an occasional private conversation."

"So what about you?" asked Justin.

"So what about me?" retorted Claire.

"What do you do when an incident happens between Colleen and Katie?"

"Usually nothing. Most of the time these *tiffs,* as I call them, go away in a day or two. Sometimes Katie apologizes. Sometimes Colleen apologizes. But most of the time they both just drop it after a while."

Justin started rubbing his neck as he leaned back in his chair.

"Are you okay, Justin?" asked Claire.

"I'm fine. I was hoping there would be a clearer answer. Based on what you've told me, I haven't the faintest idea what to do. And I don't think getting you a bigger office is a recommendation that I can make."

"Welcome to management, Justin!"

"Well, let me ask you this. Have you as a group ever done anything *formally* in the past to address these 'tiffs,' as you call them?"

"Christal has talked to Colleen and Katie before and asked them to apologize to each other. That works fine for a couple of weeks or until our workloads became overbearing again. Justin, we're fine when we can manage the workload. Things tend to flare up when we get swamped, like we've been the last few weeks. Again, four women in tight quarters—not a pretty sight."

Justin found it interesting that Claire was blaming the small office quarters as the main culprit for the occasional conflict between Colleen and Katie. Although his time with her was almost up, he decided to probe some more.

"Didn't you guys also use a local consultant named Walt before?"

"Why does everyone in Winnetka think we brought in a consultant? We went to a half-day workshop, a public workshop no less, together as a staff. Walt was the guy who led the program. There were over fifty people from all different companies there. It certainly wasn't any kind of intervention or teambuilding for just us."

"Well then, what was it? Christal seemed pretty impressed with this guy."

"Justin, Walt's program was one of those motivational workshops where we did values clarification stuff. And get this—we broke boards!"

"You broke boards?"

"Yep. It was pretty funny to watch Colleen and Taylor. Taylor finally had to be brought to a private room because she couldn't break her board. But then she did and when she came back to the room, everyone cheered. She actually had tears in her eyes. It was pretty cool."

"Okay, you've got my curiosity up now. What did breaking boards have to do with goals and motivation?"

"I don't know. I think it was some kind of metaphor to demonstrate that people are capable of overcoming things that might initially seem impossible. Anyway, that was as close as we've come to teambuilding. Christal thought that sending us all to a workshop would solve things. Probably to her it did but I can tell you that we never talked about it afterwards as a group. In fact, Katie still makes fun of it to this day."

As the clock struck noon, Justin ended the interview and thanked Claire for her candidness. She had given him lots to think about and he needed some time alone to process everything. Fortunately it was a beautiful Colorado fall day and Justin was able to snag a hotdog and secure a bench out on the mall, albeit right in front of a street juggler. Nevertheless, it was Boulder, and he was willing to take in the culture as well—that is until he heard off in the distance, "Justin, Justin!"

There, about fifty yards away were Katie and Taylor, smiling at him as they approached, with sandwiches and drinks in their hands. "Hey, guy," said Katie, "have we gotten so dysfunctional that we need reinforcements from the home office?"

Feeling a little disappointed that his quest for solitude had ended so soon, Justin smiled and invited both to share his bench.

Katie and Taylor smiled at each other and immediately sat down next to him.

"Hi. My name is Justin, and I'll be your new manager," joked Justin.

"Great, now everything's gone to hell," replied Katie.

Justin appreciated her humor, even though it was a bit abrupt. He didn't know Katie well at all, but he was already getting a taste of her personality.

"So, what's up?" asked Justin.

"Not much," replied Taylor, so quietly that Justin could barely hear her over the yelling juggler.

"Justin, what are you really out here for?" asked Katie in a rather business-like manner.

Justin threw the question back at her. "What did Claire say?"

"Just that you were going to meet with all of us."

"And take us out to dinner tonight," added Taylor, enthusiastically.

"All true. All true. I want to touch base with each of you and then see if there is anything that I might be able to help you out with. At the very least, I think it's important to get to know each of you a little better, given that I'm your manager."

"That's cool," said Katie. "We never saw much of Christal."

Although having only been in Boulder for a couple hours, two things were becoming increasing clear to Justin. First, there was not an *issue* per se to solve or fix. It seemed to be exactly as Claire said it had been, personality differences. Secondly, the Boulder group had really felt neglected by Christal.

"Will you ladies excuse me?" asked Justin as he got up from the bench. "I want to get some things together before we meet this afternoon. It was nice talking to you, and I'll see you, Katie, at one o'clock and you, Taylor, at three o'clock, right?"

Both Katie and Taylor simultaneously waved without saying a word, almost as if they had expected Justin to excuse himself.

The crowd in front of the juggler had grown to about twenty-five. Justin would have loved to stay for the show, but knew he needed some time to map out his strategy. His confidence was waning a bit since the problem seemed so intangible. *What on earth can I do to address personality differences?*

Back in Winnetka

"**I**S IT JUST ME or is anyone else finding it a little odd that Justin went to Boulder?" inquired Amy as she sat down for lunch in the break room.

Charlie welcomed the speculation. "Personally, I find it odder that Christal would support him going out there. She never did, and things ran fine."

Lee Ann was about to step out of the break room, but couldn't resist responding. She stepped back into the room. "She never did what, Charlie?"

Charlie looked surprised by the question. "She never went out to Boulder. I agree with Amy, it's a bit odd. That's all I'm saying."

John walked in with his lunch in hand. "What's going on?"

Lee Ann stayed focused on Charlie. "Well, we don't know what's actually going on in Boulder, so all we can do is take Justin's word for it. Why do you care, anyway?" asked Lee Ann.

"I don't," snapped Charlie. "Why do you?"

"What?"

"Why are you suddenly Justin's best friend?"

Lee Ann glared at Charlie. "I don't know what you are talking about."

"Yes you do," continued Charlie. "You've been his biggest fan since he became manager."

"It has more to do with Christal for me than it does with Justin—if you want the absolute truth. I like Christal and am willing to trust her decision. Sure Justin is pretty green, but at least he's trying—and I give him credit for that."

An awkward silence took over the room. The battle lines had been drawn, and both sides could see the conversation was at a stalemate. And then John spoke up.

"I talked with Claire in Boulder."

Immediately everyone looked at John as if he had something to say that might push the conversation one way or another.

"So, what about it?" asked Charlie, waiting for him to speak.

"Well, she did say something about an offensive e-mail that Katie sent Colleen."

"And?" cried out Amy impatiently.

"That's pretty much it," said John, now realizing by the look on everyone's face that they were expecting more.

Amy and Charlie shook their heads disdainfully and got up from the table. Lee Ann saw the impasse as an opportunity to head back to her cubicle as well.

Will had been watching the dynamics from just outside the break room. Now he approached John. "Boy, you sure know how to clear out a room. What was all of that about?"

"Ah, they were getting on Justin and I shared what I knew about the stuff going on in Boulder."

Will's interest heightened. "Do tell, my man."

"Apparently it's not worth repeating," shrugged John, regretting that he had spoken up at all.

"Alright then. So did I miss anything else?"

Unsure as to which side of the Justin likeability scale Will was now on, John thought it best to yield. "Not really. You know, just the same old stuff."

Information gathering 34

THE REMAINING INTERVIEWS with Colleen, Katie, and Taylor went pretty much as expected. Colleen primarily blamed herself for the problem with Katie, citing her oversensitivity as the reason. Taylor didn't think there was a problem, but enjoyed the workshop where they broke the boards. Katie admitted being undiplomatic and blunt at times, but also blamed Colleen for being overly thin-skinned. And both Colleen and Katie were back to talking to each other again, even though neither one ever apologized to the other.

By the end of the workday, Justin was no closer to a solution than he was when they first began. He scratched his head. *I guess the good news is that this is not a volatile situation. Yet, in many respects, it might have been easier if it had been. At least then I could get my hands around the problem and tell them to stop doing whatever it was they were doing. But dealing with different personalities is something that everyone has to deal with from time to time. I don't think there is a solution. And I know there is nothing I can do about their cramped quarters.*

Justin didn't like where his thoughts were headed. He reluctantly began to entertain the idea that maybe Christal had been right all along. Perhaps he really didn't need to be in Boulder.

Moments later, the four women joined Justin in the downstairs lobby.

"So where we going for dinner?" Taylor asked.

"I was hoping you would suggest some place. Is there anything good out on Pearl Street?"

The ladies all looked at each other and began laughing. Boulder was a pricy place, and that could have been a rather dangerous question. Fortunately for Justin, they were just playing with him. Claire had actually made reservations at the popular Jax Fish House for six o'clock.

Jax was a casual place on the mall where many locals congregated after work. Although it was only a Tuesday night, the place was buzzing with lively conversations and laughter. Even the DataDump table was doing their part to contribute to the energy in the room as the group told stories and teased each other. Justin hadn't laughed like this for quite a while and equally participated in the jousting that went back and forth. Amidst it all, he couldn't help but notice how comfortable the ladies were with each other. *You'd never know there was ever a hint of tension between any of these women,* he thought to himself.

The mood was soon broken as Katie shifted the conversation back to work. "So Justin," what's on the docket for tomorrow?"

"I wish I knew," replied Justin, causing the group to laugh. Unfortunately he was telling the truth.

Claire jumped in. "Actually, we've got the conference room downstairs from nine to ten-thirty. We'll all be together with Justin." She then looked at him for confirmation. "Isn't that right?"

"Yeah. My flight leaves at 1 p.m. so I thought we could use that time to tie up any loose ends and perhaps define ways that I could best support you. You know, that kind of stuff."

"Sweeeet!" said Katie, mocking Claire. The group roared with laughter. Then Taylor copied Katie, "Sweeeet," and then Colleen did her rendition, followed by, of all people, Justin, "Sweeeet." Claire could only shake her head.

Needless to say, it was one of those impromptu moments that took on a life of its own and quickly spread throughout the restaurant. First the table to the left picked up on it, followed by the table to the right, "Sweeeet!" Now versions could be heard from all over the room. Quickly the room sounded like a giant birdcage, filled with laughter and assorted versions of, "Sweeeet!" Even Claire joined in, now enjoying her sudden celebrity status. People from the bar were popping their heads into the dining section to see what all the commotion was about. It was one of those moments in time that could never be explained adequately or re-created.

Katie looked at Justin and cried out over the chaos, "Welcome to Boulder!"

This trip had already become a memorable one, and Justin still had another day to go. But it was that *day left to go* that began troubling him as the night went on. By the time he got back to his room at the historic Boulderado Hotel, it was late and he still needed to call Megan. He picked up the phone and called his house, hoping she was still up.

Megan answered on the first ring. "Hello."

Justin was relieved to hear her voice. "Hi, honey, how's everything?"

"Hi, babe. Everything is great here. I just put the kids down and am making some bread for our ladies' night out tomorrow evening. Don't forget that I'm not going to be home until late. You've got the kids."

"Yes, I remember. No problem."

"So, tell me," inquired Megan, "how bad is it?"

"Actually, not very bad at all. In fact, they are a much healthier group than my own staff."

"Really?"

"Yep. So pack up the kids, we're moving to Boulder."

"Funny, Justin. Now, what's really going on out there?"

"I'm serious. I met with everyone individually today and asked all the tough questions. The *conflict* per se that Claire was talking about is really nothing more than four very different personalities trying to work together in a very small office. For the most part, they all get along exceptionally well. They laugh together, joke with each other, and seem to work just fine together. When the occasional rub occurs, what happens is pretty predictable. Katie, the one who had sent the e-mail, is fairly blunt and direct when she communicates. And Colleen, the other woman involved, is very sensitive. Every once in a while Katie will say something that hits Colleen the wrong way. Colleen will then get upset and the problem starts to escalate. That is until someone apologizes to the other and then things are usually fine again."

"It all sounds pretty normal to me." said Megan.

"I know. I said the exact same thing myself. Now I just have to figure out what it is that I'm going to say or do tomorrow to help them out."

"Justin, why do you feel like you have to have some kind of solution?"

"Megan, I was asked to come out here to help them. How else do you suggest I help them?"

"Don't get defensive. I'm just trying to help."

"I'm sorry, it's been a long day. My concern is that if there is not something tangible that I can do to help them, then in actuality, I probably didn't need to come out here...and then Christal would have been right all along."

"Honey," and then Megan paused.

"What? Go ahead, say it."

"It's just that you seem to be making this more about Christal and proving her wrong than it is about these four women in Boulder. Maybe it's not about answers or solutions. Maybe it is just about connecting with them. I think you are over complicating this a bit."

Justin knew there was some validity to what Megan was saying. He was also exhausted and thought it would be best to sleep on all of this before deciding what his approach would be.

"You may be right, babe, I'll think this through some more in the morning. Sorry again for getting defensive. This job doesn't seem to ever get any easier."

"You'll do just fine tomorrow. You know I love you. Sleep tight."

"Love you, too." Justin hung up the phone and crawled into bed. It may have only been nine o'clock out in Colorado, but according to his body, it was much later. He could only hope some insight would come to him by way of the morning.

Morning coffee

INSTEAD OF WAKING WITH the anticipated insight, Justin woke with a rather large headache. He had forgotten Megan's advice to drink extra water yesterday, and as a result he ended up with what's called in Colorado an "altitude headache."

Yet, despite the pounding in his head, Justin wanted to take full advantage of the warm and beautiful fall morning in Boulder, and decided to have his breakfast outside at the little café at the base of the hotel. He was fortunate enough to have experienced a piece of Boulder the previous night at the restaurant and now he wanted to take in the awesome view of the flatirons as well.

Sitting at his table with his favorite hazelnut latte in hand, he leaned back, let out a big breath, and reflected on his conversation with Dr. Mac. Although only a mere two days ago, it already felt like a week had passed since the two had met on the park bench. He thought to himself. *Actually, Dr. Mac never told me what to do. Our conversation focused more on the process than any solutions. In fact, all he did was ask questions and I did the rest. Hmm.* Then Megan's words from last night popped into his head. *Maybe it is not about answers or solutions. Maybe it is just about connecting with them.*

"More coffee?" asked his waitress Janice, who was sporting a number of piercings all over her body, including in places that Justin found truly surprising.

"No thanks," he replied, now looking as if he had just figured out the answer to life's most important question. "I don't need coffee...and it's not my responsibility to have all the answers either!"

Janice looked confused. "What?"

Smiling now from ear to ear, Justin finished his thought. "Janice, sometime it's more about the question than it is about the answer. Know what I mean?"

Janice nodded as if she knew exactly what he was talking about. "I couldn't agree with you more, mister."

Justin jumped up from his chair, energized. He had just figured out his strategy. He was simply going to pose questions to the group so that *together* they could define how to create a work environment that worked for everyone. That way, they would feel some ownership over the results and feel more empowered over the process. It really wasn't his sole responsibility to provide them with solutions after all.

It's all about the question

THE CONFERENCE ROOM WAS fairly small, but very comfortable. It had a long table and eight recliner-type leather chairs. *It will do just nicely for today*, thought Justin.

Claire popped her head in. "Ready for us, Justin?"

"Always."

"Do you need me to do anything or say anything in the meeting?" asked Claire, wondering what Justin had planned.

"You know what, Claire, I am basically just going to pose some questions for discussion. I'd like you to sit back and fully participate. Nothing more."

"Sweet," replied Claire, as she took a seat at the table. Justin laughed, remembering last night.

Colleen and Taylor came in next, both looking a little wan.

"Morning," said Justin cheerfully. "You guys alright?"

Colleen smiled, rubbing her eyes. "Yep, just a bit tired, that's all."

Katie was now coming down the stairs, talking so loudly on her cell phone that the bank employees were all looking at her as she passed by on her way to the conference room. "Look, I'll call you back. I'm in a meeting. Okay? Bye."

Once everyone was seated, Justin began. "Welcome everyone. First, I want to thank you for taking the time to meet with me yesterday and for being so hospitable and entertaining last night."

He knew what was coming next from the group. "Sweeeet! Sweeeet!"

"Anyway, for today's meeting I would like to pose some questions for discussion."

Katie interrupted. "I swear Justin, I didn't do it this time."

The group roared. The laughter began filtering out into the bank before Justin got up to close the door. "Any other things I should know before we begin?"

More laughter.

"Seriously, I want to get this all in before I have to leave." Justin flipped a sheet over on the flip chart to reveal his three questions:

1) What are your strengths in working together?
2) Where do you need to improve?
3) How can I help?"

"Wow," exclaimed Claire, "I'm impressed, Justin!"

Taylor was the first to offer a response to question one. "I think we like and respect each other. That's important."

Justin went over to the grease board and starting writing down the comments. Within the next forty-five minutes the group had discussed and completed the first two questions.

What are our strengths?
- We like and respect each other.
- We try not to take things too seriously!
- We support and help each other out when needed.
- We laugh a lot!

Where do we need to improve?

- We need to address problems and conflicts right when they happen.
- We need to talk "to" each other instead of "about" each other, especially if there is a problem.
- We need to be respectful and diplomatic at all times with each other and in all forms of communication.
- If we cannot resolve a problem with a coworker directly, we will ask Claire to intervene. If that does not resolve things, then Justin is notified.

Before moving on to the third question, Justin went over to the grease board and crossed out the heading of the second question and replaced it with the words, **"Our commitments to each other."** He then asked if everyone was willing to abide by these commitments as well as hold each other accountable to them.

Everyone raised their hands in support, followed by a chorus of "Sweeeet!"

Justin was smiling. "You guys are great. Can I take you all back to Winnetka with me?" Before they could respond he continued. "Seriously, the third question is as important as the first two. I'd like to ask you to provide me with feedback on what I can do to better support you."

No sooner had Justin finished stating the question, all hands immediately shot up. He first pointed to Claire.

"Stop referring to us all the time as the *Boulder group.* Everyone in Winnetka calls us that. We do have names!"

Justin rapidly began writing down their comments. He then pointed to Taylor.

"Fill us in on what's going on over there. It's our company, too."

And then Katie added, "Yeah, and preferably when it happens instead of three weeks later."

Justin's wrist was getting tired now. He pointed to Katie.

"Justin, let us be a part of the decision-making process from time to time. We have opinions and would like the opportunity to give them."

Then to Colleen.

"Don't be a stranger. We are tired of being the redheaded stepchild that gets ignored."

"Oh, can I add one more?" asked Colleen.

"Of course," smiled Justin.

"When we come down for the company-wide retreat in January, can we be more integrated with your staff instead of separated from them? We really are one big department, aren't we?"

"You can count on that," assured Justin.

It was now about ten-thirty and time for the meeting to close. Justin asked the group to take a quick glance at the third list to see if anything else needed to be added.

How I can help:
- Stop referring to us as the Boulder group. We have names.
- Fill us in on what's going on at the home office. We do care.
- Let us be part of the decision-making process.
- Don't be a stranger.
- When we come out for the annual company-wide retreat, bring us into the fold with our counterparts.

Katie spoke up. "Looks sweeeet to me!"

Everyone laughed again as Justin ended the meeting.

After all the goodbyes were said, Claire made sure to walk Justin out to the car so that she could thank him for giving her more authority amongst the group. She then gave him a big hug and gave her car keys to Colleen, who would drive him to the airport.

"Be careful, Colleen. And no speeding!"

157

"Don't worry, he's in good hands," replied Colleen.

Once they were on the highway, Justin finally allowed himself to relax. He felt great about his trip to Boulder, every aspect of it. His decision to let go of trying to solve the problem and dictate a solution was what had made the difference in the meeting. He was proud of himself. But more importantly, he was proud of Claire, Taylor, Colleen, and Katie. He couldn't wait to tell Megan and Dr. Mac all about it.

Reflections

Justin REALLY ENJOYED talking to Colleen. The ride to the airport only reinforced that—especially when she confided that she was interested in applying for his old position at the Winnetka office.

"Send your resumé to Cynthia in Human Resources within the next week or so, okay?" said a rather pleased Justin.

"Are you sure it won't seem weird for me to transfer to your office?" asked Colleen.

"Not at all; in fact, you'd be a welcome addition."

Colleen had family out in the Chicago area and frankly was getting a little tired of Boulder. Justin, on the other hand, had fallen in love with Boulder and could see moving there someday with his family. But this wasn't the time or the place for that conversation. He wanted Colleen in Winnetka and wasn't concerned about her being "oversensitive." If anything, he felt the Winnetka office could use a little more sensitivity.

Shortly thereafter, Justin was en route to Chicago, anxious to continue with his journaling. He had more lessons and insights to jot down.

Journal Entry # 7

a) Sometimes asking the right question is a better intervention than trying to provide the right answer.

Three good questions to periodically ask the staffs I manage:
1) What are your strengths?
2) Where do you need to improve?
3) How can I (your manager) help?

b) It's important for a staff to think through how they want to handle conflicts <u>before</u> they have a conflict. That way they have a process already in place.

As Justin looked over his latest entry, he could tell he was improving as a manager. The insights in his journal were proof enough. Granted, his development as a manager was evolving mostly through trial and error, but he was still improving.

He then turned back to his Dr. Mac homework and took delight in moving the Boulder Office from the "Bad" to the "Good" column. Then he moved "my confidence" over to the middle. He wasn't where he wanted to be with his self-confidence yet, but it sure had improved over the last couple of days. His revised list was as follows:

<u>Good Things</u>
Charlie came back
Will's recent support
Dr. Mac
Lee Ann's turnaround
Journal writing
Mary Lou & Melvin's support
Boulder Office

<u>Bad Things</u>
Charlie's attitude
Amy's lack of support
Argument with Christal
John's wishy-washiness

My confidence

Human Resources

DESPITE HOW GREAT HIS Boulder experience ended up being, Justin knew he was returning to a much different staff—one that he hoped some day would have the same sense of mutual likeability and support that the Boulder employees had for each other. He could only hope.

The next morning Justin bypassed the Orders Fulfillment Department and kept walking upstairs to Human Resources. He wanted to talk with Cynthia about Charlie. His trip out west gave him some additional motivation to tackle what he saw as his biggest problem.

"It sounds as if Charlie's acting out and directing some of his anger toward you. Is that your take?" asked Cynthia.

Justin nodded in agreement. "Yeah. It sure seems that way. I just wish he and Christal had had a chance to talk before she announced her decision. But that didn't happen and now here I am the bad guy in his eyes."

"That's unfortunate. Is she planning on talking to him anytime soon?"

"According to Charlie," replied Justin, "they were supposed to have had a meeting last Friday. However, when I asked Christal about that, she said they never talked, let alone scheduled anything."

Cynthia had a puzzled look on her face. "So do you think he lied to you?"

"Either that or they had a misunderstanding. Regardless, it's tied into why I came in to see you this morning."

"Go ahead."

"Well, what do I do if he continues to be disruptive? What recourse do I have?"

"Justin, first and most importantly, I suggest you talk with Christal and get her thoughts. I know she is not going to be as available as you'd like right now, but she is an integral player in all of this. It is important for you two to be on the same page with whatever you end up doing. You will need her support and backing."

Justin nodded. "Right, I agree."

Cynthia was saying pretty much what Justin had expected—but he wanted more. He decided to press her a bit. "What would you do if you were in my situation?"

"Again, Justin, I see this as something that you and Christal need to address before I would ever get involved."

"I understand that, and of course I will talk to her. But off the record, what would you do?"

"You are not going to let this go, are you?"

"Nope."

She paused. "Alright. I would initiate a conversation with him privately and share my observations about what I see going on. I'd then ask him if he is going to be able to support me in this position. Assuming he says yes, I'd then ask for his support. Also, I'd make sure to ask him what I could do to better support him in return. In regard to your situation, both of you have needs that aren't being met right now. That's why the conversation has to go both ways."

"But what would you do if he said he couldn't support you?" asked Justin.

"Well hopefully that doesn't happen, because his options would be limited to either leaving the company or possibly getting transferred to another department. However, I can tell you that an employee who asks to be transferred because he or she can't work with their particular manager is not something that this company would view very positively."

"I see. Boy, Cynthia, that was helpful. Why couldn't you just tell me that outright?"

"Justin, of course I'll always be happy to share my thoughts with you at any time. With that said, I do believe that HR shouldn't take the place of a manager's manager, especially around topics that should initially be dealt with within a given department first. So, even though Christal is out right now, I don't want to cloud things by getting involved in something that I know she would want to address with you. Does that make sense?"

"Oh, of course. I just didn't know who to talk to about these kinds of things. I'm not sure what the proper protocol is. No one has told me anything, so how am I supposed to know?"

"I understand Justin. I'm not saying you were wrong to come to me. I'm just trying to give you some guidance."

"Sorry, Cynthia, it's just been difficult learning how to be a manager with so little help. I apologize if I came across as defensive. You have been great."

Cynthia warmly shook his hand and began walking him toward the door. "No problem. I hope you know that I have all the confidence in the world in you." Then she stopped. "Oh wait, I forgot to mention that we'll be posting your order-taker position today internally and tomorrow in the local newspaper."

Justin's eyes lit up. "I'm glad you mentioned that. Colleen from Boulder asked to apply for it. What do you think?"

"Wow, that's great. Of course we still have to go through the process, but she'd be terrific! How did that happen? I don't think you could get me to leave Colorado."

"Apparently she has family out here and wants a change."

"Well keep me posted, okay?"

Justin nodded as he headed out the door. He felt a little better about how he was going to handle Charlie and even about being back in the office again.

39

More support

"**I** SEE WE ARE ON executive hours now," commented Charlie upon seeing Justin walk in a little past nine.

Justin forced a smile, "Not exactly, Charlie. Had a meeting."

"How'd Boulder go?" asked John, looking up from his cubicle.

"It went very well. They're a good group."

John looked surprised. "Really?"

"Yep."

Justin surveyed the room and noticed that everyone was in and at their cubicles. *That's a nice change.* He then made sure he had everyone's attention before making his announcement. "Staff meeting in the break room at ten," and then promptly went into his office and shut the door. He had an important phone call to make.

"Hello."

"Christal?"

"Yes, Justin?"

"Hi. How are you feeling?"

"All things considered, I'm doing okay, I guess. I have a fever and am still pretty sore. I tried standing up yesterday, but couldn't even..." and then there was silence.

"Christal? Are you okay?"

Christal sounded uncharacteristically restrained. "I'm sorry Justin. It's just been hard."

Justin was caught off guard. He was expecting to be on the receiving end of Christal's wrath once again for not calling her while he was in Boulder. Instead he was picking up on a much different Christal on the phone and wasn't quite sure how to react.

"Are you sure you're alright?"

Sniffling now, as if she was on the brink of crying, Christal continued to apologize. "I feel so bad that I haven't been there for you Justin. It's not right. I've put you in a bad position and I'm sorry."

Immediately feeling a sense of compassion, Justin responded in kind. "Christal, you got hit by a car, for crying out loud; it's really okay."

Her emotions continued to spill out. "I haven't been able to do anything. J.W. and the whole executive team had such high hopes and expectations for me and here I am lying in bed in a hospital watching *Oprah*, of all things! I'm letting everyone down!"

Justin felt badly. Here he had been selfishly focused on what she wasn't doing for him instead of even considering that there might be something that he could be doing for her. He had been too self-absorbed. *That needed to end*, he thought to himself.

"Christal, tell me what I can do for you?"

"It's just that I hate to let people down," she lamented.

"Christal, you have not let me down. In fact, in many respects you have done me a tremendous favor."

Christal found Justin's comment amusing as she regained her composure. "Oh, do tell, Justin!"

"What I meant is that I've probably learned more about managing, albeit through trial and error, than I would have learned if all I had to do was ask you what to do. Do you know what I mean?"

"So you would prefer that I stay here in the hospital?" she said sarcastically.

"No, of course not, but I've been writing down all the things I've learned and it's quite a lot. And—are you ready for this—it's all in a journal I've been keeping."

"You're kidding! Wow, I think that's a great idea, Justin. I'd love to see what you've written...or is that too personal? Can you at least tell me what you've learned?"

"Definitely. And it was Dr. Mac who suggested the idea. I know you're not too crazy about him, but he's really helped a lot."

"Justin, I'm sorry about what I said about Dr. Mac. It's just that it was my fault that you even had to seek him out, that's all."

"But Christal, I see it slightly differently. To me it's a good thing that so many people, including Dr. Mac, have stepped up to fill the void while you are recovering. Melvin and Cynthia have helped me as well.

"Melvin? You never told me that he's helped you."

"Well, he has, and he told me to feel free to come to him for anything during your absence."

"That was sure nice of him."

"Christal, the bottom line is that I can't wait for you to return. I miss talking with you. But I also would rather have you back healthy and in one piece. So I'm willing to seek out whatever support I can get until you're back. I need you to be okay with that."

"Justin, thank you. I must say, I'm certainly impressed with you. You've really stepped up into the position. I guess I should be thanking your Dr. Mac, not to mention Melvin and Cynthia."

"Well..."

"Before you say anything Justin, I have something else. What in the world did you do in Boulder?"

"What do you mean?"

"Claire called me this morning, just raving about your trip out there and how helpful you were."

"Oh, that. It was nothing."

"Look, I was wrong in arguing with you about your trip out there. It's evident to me that it was the right thing to do. I was feeling out of the loop and probably got defensive. No, not probably, I did get defensive, and lashed out at you. You are proving to be every bit the manager I was, if not more. I am so proud of you. Do you hear me, mister? I am proud of you!"

Justin's day could have very easily ended right there. He was hearing the most important words he could ever have imagined hearing.

"Thank you, thank you, thank you. That means a lot to me. No kidding."

"Well, don't be applying for the vice presidency just yet. At least wait until I come back so that I can give you a fair fight."

"Christal, I wouldn't be here if it weren't for you. Don't think I don't appreciate you every day for giving me this opportunity."

Justin could see that it was approaching ten o'clock, and he hadn't even talked about Charlie yet.

"I've got a staff meeting in a couple of minutes, but I do need your input and advice on a matter. Can we talk later today?"

"Sure, I'm not going anywhere. Call me when you get a chance."

Justin smiled. "You got it."

As he hung up the phone and sat back in his chair, he couldn't help noticing how connected he suddenly felt to Christal. Initially he thought it was due to the incredible compliment that she had given him. But the more he thought about it, the more he realized that it was her authenticity—her raw courage to be vulnerable and to apologize to him—that impressed him so.

The line in the sand

It was a couple of minutes after ten and no one moved toward the break room. Justin wasn't surprised. He cleared his throat so everyone could hear him when he yelled across the outer office. "Let's go. Staff meeting."

Although he didn't want to get caught up comparing the Boulder office to the Winnetka office, it was difficult not to. Oddly, just a couple of days ago he had thought the Winnetka group was the better of the two. But that was before his trip. Now his position had reversed.

Lee Ann walked by with a plate of homemade cookies. "My roommate and I made cookies last night and had a few left over. I hope you don't mind."

"Of course not," replied Justin, as a slow procession ensued right behind her. First John, then Charlie, then Will, and finally Amy, bringing up the rear.

Amazing what a few home-baked cookies can do, Justin thought to himself, as he walked into the break room. "Okay, everyone have a seat. I have a couple of things to discuss."

Charlie didn't wait for the rest to be seated before beginning his arsenal attack. "So tell me, Justin, how is it you decided to go to Boulder?"

Will intervened in an attempt to be funny. "Why? Did you want to go?"

Charlie acknowledged Will with a smile. "I guess my real question is," as he looked at Amy and then back at Justin, "who's supervising you?"

Everyone was now seated at the table and curious to see what Justin would do.

"It sounds like you are, Charlie," responded Justin, trying to match his tone.

"No, if I was, your butt would have been here, not in Boulder with those misfits."

Charlie glanced around the table for support, but found none. He had been absent when Justin made his inappropriate comment to Lee Ann the previous week, and had no idea of the ramifications that had created.

John jumped in to ease the tension. "So Justin, can you fill us in on the Boulder group. What's going on out there, and what did you end up doing?"

Justin had had just about enough of Charlie and was trying to regain his composure before responding. He had no intention of going toe-to-toe with him in front of the other staff members.

"First, you need to know that the women in our Boulder office have asked that we use their names instead of always calling them "the Boulder group." I happen to agree with them and ask you do the same."

"Wait, I'm confused," interrupted Lee Ann. "We're supposed to say each of their names each time we refer to their office? That sounds kind of crazy."

Justin saw her point, but decided to ignore it for the time being. "Secondly," and then he looked right at Charlie, "Christal is my supervisor, and we have been talking quite regularly, thank you very much. But I'll be very happy to inform her that you had a problem with me going out to Boulder. No wait, I'm your manager and you need to take your concerns to me directly. Let's you and I discuss this further in my office imme-diately after this meeting. Perhaps I can shed some light on the situation for you."

The room was rife with tension, as everyone was waiting to see what Charlie would say next.

But instead it was Amy who entered the fray. "Justin, I'm really getting tired of all of this. You clearly do not have con-trol of this group. I think Christal needs to know what's really going on here."

"Go ahead and call her then, if you're so concerned," replied Justin.

"I will."

"Fine."

Justin was very aware that he and Amy were beginning to sound like two little kids, each threatening the other. He shifted gears and went back to John's original question.

"Regarding your question, John, everything is good in Boulder. The staff has asked to be more connected with the home office, especially to our department and to me, now that I'm their manager."

Charlie shrugged.

Justin continued to ignore him. "We talked through some issues that they were having and successfully resolved them. That was really it. I'd be happy to talk further if any of you want to know more than that."

Amy shot up out of her seat, thinking the meeting was over.

"Not so fast," said Justin, "I have one more thing. I need a complete list of each of your clients and your order sheets for last month on my desk by Tuesday of next week."

Instantly the group moaned.

Justin was still fuming over Charlie's attack and decided to abruptly end the meeting by saying, "Charlie, I'll see you in my office."

"Wow, Charlie," said Amy, sarcastically, "looks like you're going to have to stay after school."

The showdown

JUSTIN DIDN'T EVEN WAIT for Charlie to sit down in his office before addressing him. "What's going on, Charlie?"

"I don't know what you mean."

"Yes, you do. Ever since Christal asked me to be manager, you've been nothing but a pain-in-the-rear."

Charlie remained standing as his face reddened with anger. "You little scab. Who the hell do you think you are?"

"Me? Me?" replied Justin as he stood up.

"That's right Justin, you! Don't think your little 'I didn't expect to get promoted' song is fooling anyone out there."

"First off, Charlie, this isn't about *them*!" as he pointed in the direction of the outer office. "This is about you. That's right, you. And you are bordering on insubordination right now."

"Give me a break, Justin. You don't know the first thing about being a manager, so don't be threatening me with something you know nothing about."

Justin tried another tactic. "Charlie, let me ask you a question. Where do you see yourself in three years? Do you think you might be a manager by then? Better yet, do you think you can get there without me, or in spite of me? Because I got news for you, buddy, I ain't going nowhere. So it's your choice. You can work with me or you can work against me. But I will guarantee you this: you will not become a manager at this company without my support. And that isn't gonna happen if I can't count on your support right now."

Justin knew he was way out of line, but it didn't matter any more to him. "So here's what I'm going to do, Charlie. I'm giving you until Monday at 8:00 a.m. to decide if you still want to work here. At that time you are either *on board* and in alignment with me or you can forget about coming in, because you're going to be fired. So give it some thought, and go home. I don't want you here for the rest of the week."

"You have no right to say that, Justin, and you can bet I'll be calling Christal. You're the one who'll be out of here, not me."

"Well, Charlie, you're going to have to get in line behind Amy. The difference is: you'll be calling Christal from your home. You are out of here until Monday."

"We'll see."

"Yes, we will."

The aftermath

CHARLIE'S ABRUPT EXIT wasn't what startled the other staff members—it was Justin's yelling from his office that grabbed their attention.

Despite both the formal and off-the-record advice that Cynthia had given him, Justin had forgotten everything she had said, lost his composure, and proceeded to make an ultimatum that he was not authorized to make; but he didn't care. He never felt so powerful as he did in those moments going toe-to-toe with Charlie. It was invigorating to take a stand and to finally flex his muscle—that is until a disturbing thought entered his mind. *What if he comes back with no intention of cooperating? What if he calls my bluff?*

Justin began getting anxious again. If in fact Charlie came back with his bad attitude intact and he couldn't fire him, he could stand to lose the respect of his whole office. His word would be useless.

He then remembered what Dr. Mac had told him to do if he ever had a pressing question in between their meetings. He was to submit the question to his column using his Desperate Dave alias. Dr. Mac had promised him that he'd try to answer it immediately.

He flicked on his computer and went right to Ask Dr. Mac on the newspaper's website. He began writing, carefully altering the situation enough so that no one from DataDump would recognize it.

Dear Dr. Mac,

How do you know if you've gone too far? I may have overstepped my authority by sending two employees home with an attitude problem while threatening to fire them if their behavior doesn't change. What do I do if they come back with an even worse attitude? Have I backed myself into a corner?

Desperate Dave

Okay, he thought to himself, *that should do it*, and sent it off to the newspaper with the word "urgent" placed in the subject line.

Just then he heard someone knocking on his door.

Justin looked up only to see Cynthia standing outside his doorway. Needless to say, his *deer in the headlights* look revealed his surprise. "Well, hello."

"Are you okay?"

"Yeah, why?" replied Justin, trying to regain his composure.

"I don't know; you looked a little surprised to see me."

"Oh that, no, that was my 'too many things going on in my head' look."

Seeming to accept that, Cynthia lowered her voice. "Hey, I didn't see Charlie out there. Did you talk to him?"

"Um, well, no, not exactly. What I mean is, we're going to talk on Monday."

"Are you sure you're okay? You seem a little edgy."

"No, no, it's all good!"

"Well, okay. But on another note…"

"Yes?"

"I'll have some resumés for you early next week. When can you start the interview process? You need to fill that spot."

Justin stood up. "I'll put together an interview team and we'll be ready to go as soon as we get the resumés. Besides, with Colleen applying, I'm feeling pretty confident that we've got the best candidate already."

"Now Justin, you don't know for sure she's the best candidate. Let's just see how things go."

"Sorry, you're right. But she'll sure be a welcome addition, don't you think?"

"If she's the best candidate, then yes, she'll be a great addition." Cynthia smiled and shook her head as she walked out of Justin's office. She was really beginning to like him, but she could also tell that something was up.

Meanwhile, Justin headed out to Lee Ann's cubicle. "Lee Ann, would you help organize the interview process for my replacement...for my old job that is."

"I knew what you meant, Justin." smiled Lee Ann. "Do you want everyone involved?"

"What do you mean?"

"I mean are we all interviewing each candidate or just some of us?"

"I don't know. What do you think?"

"I would think everyone, but that's for you to decide. I don't want to get involved in choosing people. There's enough *stuff* going on around here."

"Okay, then let's have everyone involved."

Justin took two steps and then turned around and walked back to Lee Ann.

"What do you mean, 'there's enough stuff going on around here?'"

Lee Ann reluctantly leaned toward Justin and whispered, "You've got a big problem with Charlie and Amy. They're going to Melvin to complain, and they are trying to get Will and John to join them."

Justin could only shake his head. *Will it ever end!*

The getaway

THE MOMENT JUSTIN WALKED back into his office he noticed the blinking light on the phone. Afraid that word may have already gotten to Melvin about Charlie and the potential mutiny of his staff, he couldn't get up the nerve to pick up the message. Instead he decided to get out of the office and opted to go down the street to Stella's for a latte. He needed to collect his thoughts. He grabbed his journal and bolted out the door.

The coffee shop was busy as usual—including an assortment of DataDump employees spread throughout the shop. One department was even having its staff meeting there. Justin grabbed a table as far away from them as possible. *So much for getting away.*

Remembering the importance of asking the right question, he opened up his journal to a new page and wrote the following:

Questions on my mind
1. Do I come clean with Cynthia about Charlie, or wait to see what happens on Monday?
2. What do I do if the staff goes to Melvin? Should I try to head this off at the pass?

3. What do I tell Christal?
4. What about Colleen? Is this the kind of work environment she would really want? Isn't this partly what she is trying to get away from in Boulder?
5. What if Charlie comes back with a vengeance? Will he have won?

These questions pretty well captured the struggle that was going on in his mind. As he reflected on each one, he realized they were all pointing to a sixth question.

6. Am I really improving as a manager? Am I even management material?

Justin shut his journal. The questions were depressing him and he couldn't seem to muster up the energy to address them. Everything suddenly seemed dismal. He needed to get away and not think about work. He needed to go home.

He picked up his cell and called Lee Ann.

"Hello, this is Lee Ann. I'm either away from my desk or on the phone, please leave a message and I'll get back to you as soon as possible. Beeeep!"

"Lee Ann, Justin. Hey, I'm not feeling well and am going to go home for the rest of the day. Call me on my cell if something comes up that needs my immediate attention—otherwise I'll see you tomorrow. Thanks."

For Justin, the highs and lows of the job were becoming increasingly difficult to handle. So far, with every step he had taken forward there was always something that pulled him right back. *It shouldn't be this difficult,* he thought. *Perhaps it's me that is the problem.*

The remainder of the day consisted of lying on the couch, watching TV, napping, and occasionally throwing a ball out back for Sandy. The latter activity proved to be a lot more work, given that Sandy would chase the ball but would never return it. Nevertheless, the time away from the office did help provide Justin with the break that he so needed—that is until his cell phone rang.

"Hello."

"Justin, Christal. Are you okay?"

Springing immediately up from the couch, Justin remembered that he was supposed to be sick. "I'm doing a little better. I think it was a twenty-four-hour bug that I caught from Megan."

"I was concerned when you never called me back."

"Called you back?"

"Yes, you said you were going to call me back."

"Oops. Sorry. I went across the street for coffee, thinking that perhaps something warm would make me feel better but it actually made me feel worse. So, I just went home."

"Justin," and then she paused. "Oh, never mind. I have a more important bone to pick with you."

"You must be talking about Charlie."

"Charlie, Amy, what's going on over there?"

"Why, what did they tell you?"

"I haven't talked to either one yet. Amy left me a voice mail claiming that it's been nothing short of chaos ever since you took over. And is it true you sent Charlie home and threatened to fire him?"

"That's one perspective, certainly," replied Justin.

"Justin, you can't threaten employees! Why didn't you talk to Cynthia about this before you did what you did?"

"I did talk to Cynthia."

"And?"

"She gave me her advice."

"And?"

"And I got upset and forgot to follow it. There, was that what you wanted to hear?"

"Justin, listen to me. There is no place for emotions in confrontations. No one wins when that happens, and you usually say something you regret later. Trust me on this."

Justin knew he was in trouble. "I'm sorry. He triggered me and has not respected me ever since I became manager. I guess I had just had enough."

"Was Charlie what you wanted to talk to me about?"

"Yes."

"Well, I guess I'm partly to blame for this. I should have sat him down before I made the decision public."

"That would have helped, Christal. So, how much damage did I do?"

"You weren't really sick today, were you?"

"What? Where did that come from?"

"Justin, why did you really leave early?"

I'm so darned transparent; I can't even lie very well.

"Alright, you got me. Christal, I was so frustrated with Charlie and then Amy...and then Lee Ann tells me that all of them are planning on going to Melvin. I just couldn't handle it anymore. To be perfectly honest with you, maybe they are right. Maybe Charlie would have been your best choice all along."

"Oh I see, just quit on me. Things get a little tough and you want out. Well look here, Justin, I selected you because you have what it takes to lead this department into the future. Whatever gave you the idea that being a manager was going to be easy? Leadership is about staying strong during the tough times. How do you think character is built—by reading books? By taking a class? No, leadership is built by dealing with real-life situations. So if you're hoping that I called to give you the easy way out, you're wrong. You are their manager, you will be their manager, and I have no plans on changing that."

"Really?"

"Really."

Justin was beginning to feel some hope again. "So what should I do now?"

"You need to go talk with Cynthia. I need to talk with J.W."

"Why J.W.? How much trouble am I in?" asked Justin.

"We both could have handled some things differently. I'm going to have to call you back."

As they hung up, Justin realized that the situation with Charlie was far from over and would require his immediate attention. Amy would just have to wait. Hopefully, with Christal's help, he'd be able to manage for another day. Hopefully.

Working it out with Megan

MEGAN WALKED IN THE DOOR with a bag of trinkets from the field trip in one hand and a big bag from Kentucky Fried Chicken in the other. Tommy was crying as he entered and walked right past Justin on his way to his room.

"And don't come down until you can be nice to your sister!" yelled Megan.

"Rough day, honey?" asked Justin as Michelle ran up and gave him a hug.

"You have no idea. What are you doing home so early?"

"Took the afternoon off—well sort of."

"Must be nice, honey. Maybe next time you feel like taking some time off you can be the one to chaperone fifteen screaming kids at the zoo."

"Sorry. Can I do anything?"

"You can go talk to your son. He's been uncontrollable all day long and wouldn't leave Michelle alone while we were driving home. I can't handle two kids at once and run a business out of the home. I need more help around here!"

"Honey, don't get mad at me. I'm on your side, remember!"

Megan shrugged. "Then show it for once," and proceeded to walk out of the kitchen.

Michelle looked up at Justin from the kitchen table. "Daddy, is mommy mad at you?"

"Honey, no. I think she just had a tough day. Mommy and daddy love each other."

It was times like these that Justin particularly hated. Megan's *hit and run* tactics of dealing with conflict were both unfair and unproductive for him and for their relationship. Worse yet, they were indirectly teaching the kids not to deal with conflict, and that bothered him even more. Yet despite the pattern, Justin knew full well that he only contributed to it. He never tried to change things, particularly because Megan would usually come around an hour or so later.

Not sure exactly what to do, Justin decided to pull out his journal in hopes that perhaps one of his previous insights from work might also apply to what was going on right now between him and Megan.

For the next fifteen minutes or so he searched and searched for a solution or an answer but found none. And then he tried a different approach. *What would I do if Megan was an employee of mine and we had this dynamic going on,* he thought. Once again it took the right question to spark the answer. *Why, I'd acknowledge the problem and share my perspective. From there, I'd get her perspective and then together we would brainstorm a resolution that worked for both of us. In essence, I'd do the same thing with Megan that I did with Lee Ann.*

The sudden clarity was a mixed bag for Justin. On the one hand he had a solution, but on the other hand, it involved Megan instead of a work relationship. It was the same but it wasn't.

I guess it comes down to this, he thought. *Is the present situation with Megan acceptable or unacceptable?* Justin didn't need to give this one any more thought. *Of course it's unacceptable.* He headed upstairs to their bedroom.

"Knock, knock...can I come in?"

"Justin, not now. I'm not feeling well."

Justin walked in the bedroom anyway and sat down on the bed. "Honey, you and I have never been very effective in dealing with conflict between each other. The truth is, we rarely actually address what's wrong. I think it's time we change that."

"What are you talking about?" replied Megan, somewhat startled and unprepared to have this discussion.

"I'm talking about the pattern we seem to have when one of us is upset with the other."

"And your point is?"

"I think it's time we talked about *us*. I need to know from you what's working in our relationship and what's not working. I need to know what you need from me."

Megan had no response, so Justin continued. "To be completely honest with you, I love our relationship when everything is going well but I don't enjoy it as much when things are not going well. I'd like to change that."

Megan turned away from Justin and began crying into the pillow.

Justin put his arm around her while wondering if she was about to tell him something that he really didn't want to hear.

Megan turned over with tears in her eyes. "Justin, it's not you, it's me!"

"What?"

"Honey, I love you and always have. I hate being needy, but I can't help it. You have your work and now this promotion and you even have a special relationship with the kids that I don't have. I am not even sure if I make it into your top five!"

"Honey, you are number one and always will be!"

"Well, I don't feel like it. And then I start thinking negative thoughts and end up getting madder at myself."

"At yourself?"

"Yes. Sometimes I think that if I just learned to like football that you'd love me more."

"Oh honey, that's not true." Justin had absolutely no idea that Megan had these thoughts and feelings. He blamed himself for only now having this conversation. "You say it's not about me, but it is as much about me as it is about you. I haven't been meeting your needs."

"Yeah, but I never told you," replied Megan.

"Let's forget about who is or isn't at fault. We are both wrong for not communicating better. Please, let's make this right. What can I do on my part to improve our relationship? You are the most important thing to me. You need to know that."

For the next hour, Justin and Megan shared their feelings and recommitted themselves to their relationship. More importantly, they agreed to always talk out their conflicts in the future.

By the time the kids were in bed and Megan was upstairs, Justin once again pulled out his journal as he watched *SportsCenter*. Although he was feeling emotionally drained from his intense conversations with Charlie, Christal, and now Megan, he wanted to put some perspective on the day before going to bed.

His journal opened to the page he'd written earlier that day, which he titled, "Questions on my mind." Although it had only been about six hours since he'd written down the questions, he now felt ready to respond to each.

Questions on my mind

1. Do I come clean with Cynthia about Charlie or wait to see what happens on Monday?

Response: I need to come clean with Cynthia first thing tomorrow morning. Covering it up will only lead to further lies. She doesn't deserve that.

2. What do I do if the staff goes to Melvin? Should I try to head this off at the pass?

Response: I don't think this will happen, but if it does, I will be sure to let Melvin know that a) Christal and I are in alignment on what I'm doing, b) share with him the progress that has been made, including with the Boulder group, and c) let him know what my plans are for moving the department forward.

3. What do I tell Christal?

Response: Already done!

4. What about Colleen? Is this the kind of work environment she would really want? Isn't this partly what she is trying to get away from in Boulder?

Response: Assuming she gets the job, I need to have a heart-to-heart with her about the current situation and share with her what I've done and what I plan to do. I want the same kind of supportive environment that she does. I will also emphasize to her that her personality and skills will be a great addition to the group dynamics.

5. What if Charlie comes back with a vengeance? Will he have won?

Response: First off, the only "winning" will be if Charlie and I can reconstruct our relationship for the betterment of the department. Anything else will be a loss. Secondly, should he come back with an attitude, I will initiate a meeting between myself, Christal, and Cynthia to discuss our options. This is also why I need to come clean with Cynthia. If we are a united front, Charlie will have nowhere to go.

6. Am I really improving as a manager? Am I even management material?

Response: Hopefully I'll get better at not freaking out every time something doesn't go the way I want it to. Of course I'm improving, only sometimes it's small victories that aren't readily visible. The key is to always be up front with Christal and Cynthia so that I can fully access their advice, suggestions, and experience. How can I go wrong with support like that!

Justin's eyelids were getting heavier and heavier, yet he didn't want to go to bed without writing down his three insights from the day.

Journal Entry # 8
a) The easiest way to learn from a mistake is by owning up to it. Granted it may be difficult in the moment, but it certainly is better in the long run.
b) Standing up for myself and for what I believe in is invigorating!
c) The key to an effective relationship, whether at work or at home, is open and honest communication. Of course that's easier said than done, but critical just the same.

With a smile of content, Justin closed his journal and went upstairs to snuggle with Megan. It would be the perfect ending to an incredible day.

Telling the truth

I T WAS 7:30 A.M. and Justin was camped outside Cynthia's door. He wanted to come clean with her about Charlie before she found out on her own. It was important he got to her first.

"Hello, Justin."

Justin turned around with a rather surprised look on his face. It was Melvin.

"Hi, Melvin. How are you?"

"More importantly, how are you?"

Worried now that Melvin was aware of the problems occurring in his department, Justin quickly changed the direction of the conversation. "I'm doing okay. Talked to Christal."

Melvin's eyes lit up. "Me, too! She seems to be doing better."

"Yes, I got that impression as well," added Justin.

"Hey, come by later today if you would."

"Sure," replied Justin, still unsure if he was in trouble or not.

Cynthia came around the corner. "Alright, what are you two up to?"

"Melvin put his index finger up to his lips and looked at Justin, "Shhhh, she's here; let's keep this between you and me."

Cynthia gave Melvin a withering look. "Very funny."

As Melvin walked off, he glanced back and said to her, "See you at one o'clock?"

"If you're lucky!" quipped Cynthia.

Turning now to Justin, Cynthia looked excited. "Come in; I have something for you."

"That's funny cause I kind of have something for you as well," said Justin.

Right then Cynthia pulled out the morning newspaper from her bag and opened it up to page seven. "You've got to see this."

Justin looked closer and immediately recognized the "Ask Dr. Mac" column. He smiled as he realized that Dr. Mac was responding to his "Desperate Dave" letter!

"Did you already read this?" asked Cynthia, spotting his smile.

"Sort of. I saw the question but hadn't read the response, yet. But it's obvious that this Desperate Dave guy has a similar problem with his employees that I have with Charlie. Was Dr. Mac's advice helpful?"

Cynthia was nodding. "It's right on. This guy is good."

Justin knew this was the perfect opening to say what he needed to say to Cynthia. "Actually, I have more in common with Desperate Dave's letter than you probably want to know."

"What's that supposed to mean?" asked Cynthia, anticipating something bad.

"I didn't really tell you the whole truth about Charlie yesterday."

Cynthia had figured as much. "Is that why you were acting all weird? I knew something was up."

"Yeah, that's why. To tell you the truth, I kind of blew it."

"What do you mean you *blew it*?"

"I did talk to Charlie and out of frustration ended up sending him home."

"Alright, that's not that bad."

"There's more."

"Oh no."

"Yep, I told him that if he didn't come back with a different attitude by Monday that he would be out of a job."

"No! You didn't!"

"Yes. I did."

"Oh, Justin, we went over this."

"I know, I know."

"You know you can't threaten someone that way!"

"Threaten is such a strong word. Nevertheless, my brain wasn't in synch with my mouth at the time. I screwed up!"

Cynthia looked disappointed. "So much for my Friday starting off easy. Now I have to do damage control."

"I'm sorry about what I did, and especially for lying to you. I really screwed up...again!"

"Justin, this is twice now that you've said things to employees that you should not have said. Are you with me here?"

"Yes. But I have tried to do my own damage control on this one."

"What have you done?"

"I talked to Christal."

"And?"

"And I got the same reprimand from her as I'm getting from you."

"And?"

"And she said that she would support my decision."

"What!"

"I know what you are thinking—"

"Do you, Justin?"

"I know that two wrongs don't make a right," pleaded Justin.

"Oh, well, that helps," replied Cynthia sarcastically. "Thanks for being so understanding."

"What I mean is..."

Cynthia cut him off. "Okay, look, I've got to take this to Melvin. Hopefully everything will work itself out, but I know that he's going to want to know. He hates surprises."

Justin had hoped for a somewhat different reaction from Cynthia. He now wondered if it was a mistake to drag Christal's name into this. *What if I get her in trouble?*

"Justin, wait here," Cynthia said. "Let me see if Melvin is available."

As Justin watched her leave, he could feel his body tensing up. He knew he was in trouble, but this was beginning to look even worse than imagined. He shrugged. *Now what have I done?*

After about ten minutes of sitting and worrying, Justin realized that he hadn't even read Dr. Mac's response to his letter yet. *That might have some information I can use right now,* he said to himself, and he grabbed the paper off of Cynthia's desk.

Dear Dr. Mac,

How do you know if you've gone too far? I may have overstepped my authority by sending two employees home with an attitude problem while threatening to fire them if their behavior doesn't change. What do I do if they come back with an even worse attitude? Have I backed myself into a corner?

Desperate Dave

Desperate Dave,

Hopefully you've put the same question to your human resources manager as well. If you haven't done that, then that is what you need to do. It is not my place to circumvent a process that most likely is already in place within your company. Of course I'm speaking about the employee disciplinary process.

All supervisors need to be clear on what they can and cannot do with regard to disciplinary procedures. This is especially important to know before taking any action. But the responsibility doesn't stop there. Employees should not be left in the dark either on the consequences for inappropriate or disruptive behavior. And I'm talking about more than simply passing out employee handbooks to all employees. More needs to be done.

I'm a firm believer that no employee should ever be surprised by any kind of disciplinary action or performance review for that matter. Should that ever be the case, I can usually predict that there are some communication issues, or lack there of, between the supervisor and his or her employees that are contributing to whatever the problematic situation is. In those cases, the supervisor/manager needs to shoulder some of the blame. But I haven't answered your question yet, have I?

I think that you were okay to send your employees home, but probably overstepped your boundaries by limiting the consequences to being fired should their behavior persist. Had you said that there would be further disciplinary action taken, up to and including termination, *you would have been better off. In these types of disciplinary situations, try not to define a specific outcome, but instead a range of outcomes. When you are too specific, you essentially lock yourself into an action that may or may not be appropriate. Plus, since your comment may not have been sanctioned by your organization, the last thing you want to do is narrow down what the consequences will be.*

So here is my long-awaited answer to your question. I suggest you get together with your human resources manager and your immediate supervisor and discuss the situation, what you've done thus far and what you think needs to happen. Then come up with an agreed-upon plan that you know they will both support. This is a critical first step.

Then, meet with the two employees, either separately or together, and share the plan from your previous meeting. Help them understand the reasons behind the performance expectations and how you will support them in achieving those expectations. Once the expectations are completely understood, ask for a commitment from each of them to move forward. Help them understand that they have control over the consequences of their behavior and that you'd much prefer to shower them with praise than to pull them through this process again.

Hope this helped.

—Dr. Mac

Justin had just finished reading the last sentence as Cynthia walked in...followed by Melvin. Both looked concerned.

Cynthia picked up the Dr. Mac column and handed it to Melvin. "Here's that column I was telling you about."

Melvin didn't even look at it; he just slid it inside a folder he was carrying with him. "I'll look at it later."

"Can we fix this?" asked Justin.

The lighthearted jousting that had occurred between the three of them earlier that morning was clearly gone now. In its place was an uncomfortable brittleness that seemed to permeate the room.

"Tell me again exactly what you said to Charlie," asked Melvin, sounding rather lawyer-like.

Justin proceeded to go through the whole incident again, step by step and word for word. Although he knew he should not have threatened to fire Charlie, he didn't think it was the kind of mistake that should warrant this kind of scrutiny. Nevertheless, he was going to comply fully. Cynthia and Melvin were two of his biggest supporters and he didn't want to appear resistant to their help.

Finally Melvin had heard enough. "Justin, here is what we are going to do. We will call Charlie at home and ask him to come in for a ten o'clock meeting with the three of us, and hopefully Christal."

"Yes, but—"

Melvin held up his hand to indicate he wasn't finished. "At that meeting we will do all the talking. Do you understand that?"

"Yes, but—"

"Justin, listen to me. We are going to handle this. Charlie will be asked to come back to work immediately and we will apologize to him, on behalf of the company, for what you said. I don't want you to say anything in that meeting."

"I don't understand. Why can't you just let me handle this? I don't need a formal meeting to apologize."

Melvin clearly was not receptive to having a discussion. "You've said more than enough right now. I understand that things got out of hand and emotions were high. Nevertheless, we are going to move forward with the meeting."

"Alright," said Justin, feeling frustrated.

"One more question, Justin," added Melvin, "about Christal…"

Justin interrupted, "Christal had nothing to do with this. It was all my doing. I talked to her after the fact and she said she would support my decision, even though she didn't agree with it."

Melvin and Cynthia glanced at one other with curious looks.

Cynthia spoke up. "Justin, what are you saying?"

"I'm saying that she was upset as well with what I did and told me in no uncertain terms what I *should* have done. She then went on to say that she felt somewhat responsible for what happened since she was unable to talk to Charlie before she left for New York. She also said she felt bad for not being available to mentor me more in this role."

Melvin looked over to Cynthia with an approving glance. They both seemed to appreciate Christal's comments.

Justin decided to make one more plea. "Look, Christal did everything she could have done given that the situation had already occurred by the time she found out. If you need to fire anyone, it's me!"

Melvin shook his head. "Justin, we're not going to fire you—*yet*, that is! But I'm telling you, keep this up and this will be the last time that this company is going to come to your rescue. If you become a liability, I know for a fact that J.W. will not stand for it—not from anyone, especially one of his managers. Do we have an understanding?"

"Yes sir, we do. Thank you for giving me one more chance."

Melvin opened his folder and glanced at the Dr. Mac column. "Cynthia, do you suppose we can get this Dr. Mac to coach Justin?"

Justin was pleasantly taken aback. He thought about volunteering that he was already seeing Dr. Mac, but quickly thought otherwise. He didn't want Dr. Mac associated with this latest mishap, even if he had nothing to do with it.

"I'll call the newspaper and see if I can get ahold of him. It's worth a try."

Justin nodded in agreement. "That would be great. Again, thank you for taking another chance on me."

The meeting ended abruptly. Justin had had no idea that what he did was so wrong. Yet, if it led to formalized coaching with Dr. Mac, perhaps it was a blessing in disguise. He could only hope.

Girlfriend talk

MEGAN SMILED AFTER RECOGNIZING Tanya's knock at the front door.

"Hi, honey," said Megan, as she greeted her best friend, "come on in, the coffee's warming up and I've got some pie that's to die for."

Tanya gave Megan a big hug before the two headed toward the kitchen. "I can't wait; I'm starved. If there was ever a great indulgence for breakfast, it's pie!"

"You can say that again."

Megan and Tanya loved getting together for what they fondly called "girlfriend talk." It was their weekly ritual of intimate conversation sprinkled with a little neighborhood gossip.

"So, girl, come clean," exclaimed Tanya, "I know you've got something on your mind."

Megan blushed. "You're not going to believe this."

"Oh, I can't wait."

"Justin is becoming a communicator. He is actually beginning to use his feminine side."

Tanya's jaw dropped. "Honey, let me get this straight. Your husband, the couch potato chairman of the board, the 'get out of the way, I'm watching football' lug—is finding his inner self? Absolutely no way!"

"Way!"

"What did you do, slip him a pill?"

"It's this promotion he got. He's become a different man."

"You know dear, not to pour cold water on your parade, but Lamar went to some workshop way back when, and he came back a new man as well."

"See, it can happen."

"That lasted two weeks. Read my lips, twooooo weeeeeks! Then the same old bum I married popped up again and I've been unhappy ever since."

"You're not unhappy, and you know it."

"You try living with him then and see how happy you are."

"You're too funny, Tanya. What would I do without you?"

"You'd be lost and confused, just like you are now. Feminine side—please!"

"I'm serious."

"So being promoted brought this on?"

"Yes. He's been running into a lot of resistance at work and no one has been there to help him."

"And I'm sure you're going to tie all of this together..."

"So I turned him on to Dr. Mac, this business advice columnist in the newspaper."

"Oh, this is priceless. Go on."

"Well, it turns out this Dr. Mac has taken an interest in Justin and now they've been meeting weekly at the park and he's helping Justin with all his work problems."

"And that's it?"

"Basically."

"Pour me another cup of coffee, will ya? I can't believe what I'm hearing."

Megan continued. "Well, Justin is learning people skills through working with Dr. Mac. And probably the biggest thing he is doing differently is communicating. That's what I mean when I say he's developing his feminine side."

"Honey, I knew what you meant, but I'm still in shock. Don't get me wrong—I love Justin—but a communicator? This I've got to see."

"The down side is that he works longer hours and has started to bring work home with him—something he's never done before. He's even taking calls in the evening from Christal, his boss."

"And to think I almost slept in this morning," joked Tanya.

"Okay, it's only been two weeks. I don't blame you for being skeptical."

"Megan, you are my closest friend. My teasing is only out of love for you."

"I know."

"So let me ask you a serious question. Justin is a better communicator. But he is also working more and bringing work home. Is that better than the old Justin who rarely communicated but who was home all the time—of course, mostly on the couch, but that's another story."

"I'm not crazy about him bringing work into our relationship, but I must tell you, I'm really attracted to the new Justin. There is something about a man with drive and determination."

"Do you think some of that could wear off on Lamar?"

In between meetings

ANOTHER DAY, ANOTHER MISTAKE, another reprimand. This was starting to get old for Justin. *If I were a cat, I'd clearly be on my last life,* he thought to himself as he walked down the hall with Cynthia.

"I'm sorry things got so serious in there," she said.

"All I did was threaten to fire Charlie; I didn't actually do it. If I didn't know better, I would have thought I got caught stealing from the company or something. Was what I did that bad?"

"Justin, Melvin tends to err on the side of caution. He's always been that way and always will be."

"I guess. So, what's this meeting going to be like with Charlie?"

"I don't know. This is my first one of these."

"So I'm contributing to your professional development. See, I do serve a purpose here at DataDump."

"Now, now, Justin!"

"Cynthia, I finally stood up to Charlie. I can't begin to tell you how great that felt. In truth, that was the first moment that I truly felt like a manager. I commanded respect, and my staff knew I meant business. I understand that my choice of words was inappropriate—again—but a lot of positive things happened in that moment as well. I don't think its right to solely focus on the negative all the time. I feel like crap now. It's just not right."

"I'm sorry Justin. Look, I've got to go, but I'll mention what you said to Melvin. He really is a pretty good guy."

"I'm just hoping there is some support for me in that meeting. If I end up being the one called out on the carpet instead of Charlie, we'll be sending the wrong message."

"I'll talk to him. See you in an hour."

The moment Cynthia walked away, Justin raced down the stairs to his office. He needed to call Christal before anyone else could. It was critical that she heard about all of this from him.

The phone on his desk rang the instant he plopped himself down in his chair.

"Hello. Oops, I mean, this is Justin."

"Hi. Did you get my resumé?"

"Colleen?"

"Yes."

"Oh, hi. How are you?"

"You sound stressed."

"Not stressed as much as frazzled. Maybe that's stressed. I don't know."

"Well I don't mean to bother you. I just want to make sure you got the resumé and that you are still interested in having me come out."

"Of course. Hey, can I call you back? I'm in between meetings and would rather have a quality discussion with you instead of a hurried one."

"Sure thing, Justin. I'm looking forward to hopefully coming out there."

"Me, too, Colleen. Me, too."

Justin hung up and immediately called Christal's cell phone.

"Hello, this is Christal. I'm unable to take you call right now, but please leave a message at the beep and I'll call you back. Beeeeep."

"Christal, Justin. Look, I need to talk to you right away. Can you call me before 10:00 a.m.? It's urgent!"

As Justin put the phone down, he noticed that Amy was waiting for him just outside his office.

"Excuse me, Justin."

Oh great, just what I needed. "Yes, Amy, how can I help you?"

"Can I talk to you?"

Not sure what to expect, Justin could feel his guard go up. "Sure, what's up?"

"I understand that Colleen from Boulder is applying for your old position."

"Yes, she is one of the candidates. Why?"

"Well, this might sound like it's coming from left field but I was thinking about applying for her position in Boulder— that is if she gets your position. Anyway, I'm thinking a change might be good for me, and I'd love to be in Colorado."

Justin perked up. *There is light at the end of the tunnel yet.* "Wow, what brought this on?"

"It's nothing personal, I just don't think we're a good fit together."

"Really?"

"Come on, Justin! Where have you been the last two weeks? Oops, sorry. It's just that it's important for you to have a team around you that you feel comfortable with and that is equally comfortable with you."

"And you are not in that grouping?"

"Again, nothing personal."

"Amy, I'm not opposed to the idea. Let's just see how the interviews go. In the meantime, is there anything I can do right now for you?"

"Actually yes, there is. Could you talk to Claire and Christal? I'm going to need your support."

"Let me see what I can do. To be honest, I'm not convinced that you and I couldn't work things out here—I mean, we haven't even tried. Nevertheless, I also want to support you if transferring to Boulder ends up making the most sense. Why don't we talk next week? We should know by then if Colleen is coming out or not."

"Okay. But please know—"

Justin interrupted, "I know, I know, it's not personal."

Part Five

Charlie's Turnaround

The meeting of the minds

IT WAS JUST ABOUT TEN O'CLOCK and time for his meeting with Charlie, Cynthia, and Melvin. Justin never did hear back from Christal, making him wonder if she was aware of what was about to go down.

The phone rang.

Justin hesitated to answer it before realizing that it might be Christal. "Hello?"

"Don't think you're going to get Colleen without a fight!"

"Claire?"

"Oh, act surprised!"

"Hey, I have to go to a meeting with Melvin. Can I call you back later today? I promise you can abuse me all you want to then."

"Sweet!"

"Besides, I have something to talk to you about as well."

"That's cool. Call me back."

"Sweeeet!" said Justin.

"Justin, I don't know if you are cool enough to use my word."

"Later," laughed Justin, as he jumped out of his seat and hurried down the hall to Melvin's office. Given what had just transpired with Amy, the day was beginning to look a little brighter. *If only I can get through this next meeting without too much damage,* he thought as he entered Melvin's office.

"I'm glad you're feeling better," said Cynthia while staring at the speakerphone.

"Who are you talking to?" asked Justin.

Christal recognized Justin's voice. "Hello, Justin."

Justin smiled. *God, I love technology.* "Hi, Christal. I was trying to reach you earlier."

"Sorry, Justin, I must have been talking to Cynthia."

Across the room was Charlie, sitting by himself at the end of Melvin's conference table. He had a suit on.

Justin took a seat at the opposite end, feeling a little awkward. "Where's Melvin?"

"He'll be here," replied Cynthia.

The room was silent. Even Cynthia could sense the awkwardness as she tried to ease it with light conversation. "So, is anyone doing anything fun this weekend?"

No response, just forced smiles.

"Christal, what about you? How's California?"

"It's nice being out of the hospital and finally eating real food."

"How is it, living with your mom?" asked Cynthia.

"It's nice. In fact, we are talking about going to the flea market later today—that is if she's up for pushing my wheelchair. I still can't push myself very well."

"Just get well, Christal," yelled Justin in the general direction of the speaker phone.

"Thank you, Justin," replied Christal.

Despite the discomfort in the room, Justin was at least glad to see that there wasn't any tension between Christal and Cynthia. *That must be an indicator that she's not in any kind of trouble,* he figured.

Finally, ten long minutes later, Melvin walked into the room.

"Sorry everyone. Is Christal on the line?"

"Hi, Melvin," said Christal.

"How are you feeling?"

"I'm fine."

"Okay, then let's begin. Charlie, we understand that there are some issues between you and Justin and we wanted to bring the two of you together to see if we can clear them up."

Christal's voice shot out from the disc-like speakerphone on the table. "Excuse me, Melvin, could I say something?"

"Please do."

"I believe much of the misunderstanding here is my fault. Charlie, my intention was to sit down with both you and Justin to explain why I selected him over you for the position. Because I was unable to do that, you were both caught off guard. Then, when this whole hit-and-run thing occurred, it just made things worse."

Charlie spoke up for the first time. "It would have helped a lot if I had known what was going on and why."

"I understand," said Christal. "What you probably don't know is that Justin had no idea that I was considering him for the position and was as surprised as you the day I announced him as the manager. He had supported you all along to take the position."

"He did?"

"Yes. He even thought about turning it down, but we won't go there, right Justin?"

Justin perked up. "No, we won't, Christal."

"Then why Justin?" asked Charlie, looking confused.

"Because he has potential, and I see him as a better fit, in the long term, for your department. That's not a slight against you by any means. You already have the leadership abilities and I have other plans for you in the future. That's the part that I really wanted you to hear today. Just know that you were not passed over by any means."

The scowl on Charlie's face lifted for the first time in weeks. "What do you mean?"

"Well, what I'm about to tell you needs to stay in the room. J.W. has given me permission to share this with you but it must remain confidential. Do you understand what I'm saying?"

Charlie's eyes were now locked on the speaker phone. "Yes, what you are about to tell me stays in this room."

"Exactly. Charlie, I see you taking on a leadership role within the company, and not necessarily in the Orders Fulfillment Department. We've got some big projects coming our way and I'd like you to help manage them."

"Really, Christal?"

"Yes, really. And because we had that in mind for you all along, it only made sense to promote Justin now and give him some management experience."

"I never knew that either," said Justin.

"And I blame myself for that as well," replied Christal. "I should have never made the change in leadership in your department without getting both of you on board from the get-go. It wasn't fair to either of you or to the staff."

Charlie and Christal continued talking for a little while longer. Justin could see signs of the old Charlie re-emerge with animated gestures and his offbeat sense of humor kicking in again. In fact, it wasn't until that moment that Justin realized how much he had missed those traits.

The conversation between Charlie and Christal ended with both of them laughing together and agreeing to talk in more detail at a later date.

Melvin could see that what needed to take place had essentially taken place. Whatever the rub was between Justin and Charlie seemed to have been cleared up now, thanks to

Christal. "Well, is there anything else left for either of you to discuss here?" looking at Charlie and then at Justin.

"I don't have anything," said Charlie, now able to look at Justin.

Justin looked back at Charlie. "Are we okay?"

Charlie got up and put his hand out toward Justin. "I'm sorry. I'm really sorry."

Justin grabbed his hand and in an emotional moment, he and Charlie embraced right there in the conference room.

Cynthia was trying to conceal the tears in her eyes. Melvin nodded approvingly and walked over to the door, indicating that the meeting was over.

Justin and Charlie walked out together. "What do you say we go to lunch?" suggested Justin.

"I think that's an excellent idea," replied Charlie, as they walked out of the office.

Melvin turned back toward the speakerphone and said, "Christal, well done."

"Thanks, Melvin. I do see a lot of potential with both Charlie and Justin and could have prevented all of this from happening—"

Cynthia interrupted. "Christal, the important thing is that you were able to say what you said. You should have seen it— they hugged each other. And right in front of Melvin."

"Hey, I have a soft side too," cried out Melvin. "I just don't let either of you see it."

The three of them laughed together. It was a moment that they would remember for quite a while. So, too, would Charlie and Justin.

Like old times

LUNCH BETWEEN JUSTIN AND CHARLIE was just like old times. They laughed together, updated each other on their families and apologized to each other over and over again for allowing the misunderstanding to interfere with their relationship.

"Charlie, you were really mad at me, weren't you?"

Charlie nodded. "I can't lie to you Justin. I was convinced that you had been lobbying Christal for the position all along. I know that was wrong, but I'm being honest here."

"But Charlie, I told you guys on more than one occasion that I knew nothing about any of this."

"And I didn't believe you. I feel so awful for that. I guess I got so caught up in things that I wanted to make someone wrong for what happened. No, I wanted to make *you* wrong. I hated you, Justin. Can you ever forgive me?"

"Of course I can," smiled Justin. "You made my life a living hell, but at least I understand what was going on for you. I just wish we could have talked about this at the beginning."

"You tried, Justin. I just wasn't ready to listen."

"Well, it didn't help that neither of us actually knew what Christal was thinking. That is, until today."

Charlie nodded and then instantly smiled impishly. "Hey, let's play a joke on the office. Let's walk in and start yelling at each other."

Justin loved the idea. Things were too serious around the office, and the thought of stirring it up a bit made him laugh. "Okay, and let's involve the others somehow."

"Yeah! We'll really shake things up," replied Charlie.

The two of them came up with a plan as they drove back from lunch. Once at DataDump, they put their plan into action.

"You don't know what you are talking about," yelled Charlie as he and Justin entered the office.

Immediately Amy, Lee Ann, Will, and John's heads popped up from their cubicles, looking like a family of curious gophers peering out of their holes.

"You know what, Charlie, I've had it with you and your attitude. You can pack up your things right now and get the 'you-know-what' out of here!"

"Look at Mr. Tough guy over there. You really think I'm the problem?"

"You are the problem."

"Then maybe you should ask Amy."

Amy jumped up. "I didn't say anything. I swear, Justin."

Charlie continued. And let's not forget Will over there. He went straight to Melvin with his complaints."

I did no such thing!" insisted Will.

It was now Justin's turn. "Do you have any idea what John said about you, Charlie?"

John stood up with the others. "Charlie, you know I'm on your side. I wouldn't say anything bad."

"And Lee Ann over there called Christal personally to complain."

"What are you talking about?" replied Lee Ann, with a confused look on her face. "What's going on here, Justin?"

"Yes, what *is* going on here?" asked Melvin as he entered the office.

Charlie and Justin began laughing so hard that neither of them could stop.

Lee Ann was the first to catch on. "You guys!" and began laughing herself.

Melvin looked completely confused, but laughed just the same. Will was crouched up on the floor from laughing so hard. The rest quickly joined in. Employees from other departments were now gathering outside the Orders Fulfillment Department, wondering what was going on.

Finally Charlie spoke up. "We got you! We planned this at lunch and you all fell for it."

Melvin could only shake his head. "Well, I see things are all back to normal here. I just wanted to announce that we are closing early today. Sales are up and we wanted to acknowledge all departments, especially yours, for a job well done. You are free to go home at anytime. Have a great weekend, everybody."

The laughter turned into cheers as Melvin headed out the door. Justin looked across the room and saw everyone smiling. It was an instant that even topped the *sweeeet* moment in the Boulder restaurant. He had finally turned the corner with his own staff.

It didn't take long for the office to clear out. Once everyone had left, Justin sat down in his leather chair and pulled out his journal. He wasn't going to let today's insights get away.

Journal Entry # 9

a)   When planning a significant change (i.e., like a promotion), it's a good idea to talk to the people that will be impacted the most by that change before announcing it.

b)   Don't wait for relationship problems to escalate before addressing them. This is especially true for the people that really matter to me.

   c) Having a supportive boss is essential to my success.

   d) Sometimes a good practical joke is all a staff needs to lighten up.

Before leaving, Justin turned his journal to the page with his homework for Dr. Mac and updated the list.

Good Things	Bad Things
Charlie's back in the office	Amy's lack of support
Charlie's attitude	John's wishy-washiness
Will's support	
Dr. Mac	
Lee Ann's turnaround	
Journal writing	
Cynthia & Melvin's support	
Boulder Office	
Christal's support	
My confidence	
Colleen applying for position	

As he gazed over his newly revised lists, he remembered how lopsided it had been under the "Bad Things" column earlier in the week. Now, just four days later, it was lopsided under the "Good Things" column. He couldn't believe how much had happened in the past week. More importantly, he couldn't believe how much he had learned about being a manager.

"Knock, knock."

Justin looked up and saw Cynthia smiling at him in the doorway. "Wow, Justin, I was so impressed at how that meeting went between you and Charlie. And wasn't Christal amazing?"

"I think we all deserve a pat on the back," acknowledged Justin.

Cynthia nodded. "So why are you still here?"

"I was going to ask you the same question."

"Because I've been on the phone. Guess who I was talking to?"

"Who?" asked Justin, picking up on her excitement.

"Nice guess. I was talking to Dr. Mac!"

"About me?"

"It's always about you, isn't it," joked Cynthia. "Actually, that was part of our conversation. And guess what? Although he said he normally doesn't do management coaching, he said he would in this case. You are going to be tutored by The Dr. Mac! Excited?"

"Really?"

"Yep. He said you guys had met before."

"Oh, sort of."

"Well anyway, he said that he'd meet you at 3:00 p.m. on Monday and said that you'd know where. Is there something I don't know?"

"It's nothing. We met accidentally at a park bench once and I'm guessing that's where we'll be meeting again. He is such a neat man."

"I know. And guess what the other news is?"

"What?"

"Justin, you're supposed to guess. Forget it, you're no fun."

"Sorry. How about he's going to feature you in his next column?"

"Oh right! No, silly, he's agreed to be our keynote speaker for the all-staff annual meeting in January! I'm so excited. Melvin and J.W. are going to be so happy that I got him. Did you know that he's syndicated now around the country? We lucked out. I can't wait to tell everyone. Anyway, that's my excuse for still being here; what's yours?"

"I had a few loose ends to tie up, that's all. I'm on my way out now."

"Well, you'll have to tell me about your coaching session with Dr. Mac. We've got you signed up for four sessions. Did we do good?"

Justin nodded. "Between that and all that has transpired today, I'm feeling pretty fortunate. And you were a big part of that, by the way."

Cynthia flushed. "Please Justin, I'm just glad I could help. Watching you and Charlie embrace at the end of the meeting is the whole reason I do what I do. You have no idea how powerful that moment was for me. I'm getting emotional just talking about it."

The two walked out of the office together and gave each other a high five as they parted in the parking lot. When Justin got in his car, one word and one word only came to him that he just had to shout at the top of his lungs: "Sweeeet!"

Lamar's situation

IT WAS SATURDAY AFTERNOON at Skokie Playfield, and Michelle had her first flag football game.

"Go, honey!" yelled Justin, as Michelle caught a pass and headed downfield. "Run, run!"

Megan and Tanya were sitting in their lawn chairs over by the other moms. To no one's surprise, the men were more actively engaged in the game, pacing the field with the players and coaches. Granted it was only grade school flag football, but it was football just the same.

"Your daughter is a tiger out there," said Lamar, whose daughter was on the same team.

"Do you think we should send our girls to football camp?" joked Justin.

"Only if we can go with them."

Justin laughed. He enjoyed Lamar's sense of humor.

"Hey Justin, let me ask you a question."

"What's up?"

"Tanya was telling me..." And then in mid-sentence Lamar suddenly ran over to the sidelines to yell at the ref. "What do you mean she was down; she wasn't down!" He then turned back to Justin. "Oh man, those refs!" he said, shaking his head.

"Anyway, like I was saying, Tanya says you got yourself a promotion! Is that true?"

Justin modestly tried to downplay it. "Yeah. It came as quite the surprise!"

"Seriously, man, congratulations. Well deserved, well deserved. Tanya also said that you have some guy helping you out—giving you advice and all."

"Oh, she must be talking about Dr. Mac. He's a management consultant. He has a daily column in the newspaper called 'Ask Dr. Mac'."

Justin found himself a bit protective of his relationship with Dr. Mac and was reluctant to say much more.

"Man, I could use some advice. I've got a situation that's blowing my mind."

Justin nodded supportively. He didn't want to ask Lamar any questions for fear that he'd end up talking shop with him instead of watching their kids' first football game. "Look, Lamar, I suggest you check out his column and consider writing to him. He's responded to both my inquiries."

"That's cool, man."

As the halftime whistle sounded, Justin was feeling bad for not being more supportive of Lamar and reintroduced the topic. "Hey, if you want to talk tonight at your barbeque, I'd be happy to give you my two cents worth. I didn't mean to put you off."

"No offense taken. I would like your opinion. Let's talk while we're outside grilling tonight."

"You got it," replied Justin.

The initial pass that Michelle had caught ended up being the only time the ball was thrown to her for the remainder of the game. Because this was the first year of coed football at her school, Faith, Hope and Charity, the teams had twice as many players on the roster as in previous years. And even though Michelle was clearly one of the better athletes, she had to take her turn just like the other twenty-five kids on her new team.

As evening arrived, so did the colder winds off of Lake Michigan. The festivities for the anticipated fall barbecue had to be moved indoors.

With coats on, Justin and Lamar headed outside to put the burgers on the grill.

"Justin, isn't it interesting how the women do the talking, we do the cooking, and the kids do the cleaning up. What's wrong with this picture?"

"You know Lamar, the way I see it, we don't have it so bad. I can only handle about five minutes of talking about clothes, stores, and who's doing what to whom in the neighborhood."

"Yeah, I guess you're right, Justin. It's all good!"

"So, are you going to fill me in on what's going on at work or what?"

"Sure, man. Here goes. I think I've got an office romance happening and I'm not sure how to handle it."

"I could think of worse problems," said Justin.

"Maybe, but this is impacting other relationships and stuff. And the gossip around the office makes Tanya and Megan's conversations seem boring, if you get my drift."

"So who is it?"

"Nicole and Trevor."

"But isn't Trevor married?"

Lamar nodded. "Now do you see why it's causing problems?"

"Sure do. So what happened?" asked Justin curiously.

"Sam, the woman in accounting, apparently walked in on them after work one evening. They were in the mailroom and..." Lamar didn't finish the sentence but his eyes told the rest of the story.

"No way!"

"That was just the beginning. The next day, Sam and Nicole had a shouting match in the office. It was so loud that even I could hear it from my office, and I had my door closed.

"So what did you do?"

"Nothing. I know, I'm their manager and probably should have said something already but it just happened last week and I'm still trying to assess the situation before I talk to them. I don't even know for sure if *you-know-what* actually happened. Nicole's not saying anything to anyone and neither is Sam. But the tension in the office is getting unbearable. And everyone has a slightly different version of what happened."

Justin shook his head. "Huh! And I thought I had problems."

"So do you think your Dr. Mac could help me on this one?"

"Oh, I'm sure he can. He's pretty incredible."

"So what would *you* do, Justin?"

"Me? Well, if I were in your shoes, I'd probably talk to Nicole, Trevor, and Sam individually first to assess what did and didn't happen."

"And then what?" asked Lamar.

"Of course it would depend on what I found out. But let's say it did happen. Would you say that the incident has had an impact on the whole office?"

"The gossip alone has turned it into common news."

Justin was really enjoying this conversation. "Exactly, Lamar. So the question is, since the whole office has been impacted, shouldn't the whole office be involved in the resolution of the problem?"

"Now you're losing me, Justin. Why wouldn't I keep this between the three people involved? As an employee, I was always taught to mind my own business. Why would I include the rest of the office in the resolution?"

"Because they're all involved? I don't know for sure. I think that's more of a question for Dr. Mac. I'm just telling you what my gut feeling is on things."

"I hear you, man. I'm just confused, that's all."

"Lamar, have you heard the phrase, 'the elephant in the living room'?"

"You mean the issue that everyone knows about, but that no one is talking about?"

"Yeah, exactly. You've got the incident that happened that involved Nicole, Trevor, and Sam, right?"

"Right."

"Let's call that the 'primary' issue."

"I like that."

Justin paused for a second. "Wait. As I think about it, there are three primary issues here. There is the 'office romance' part. There is the alleged 'sex in the office' part and there are the dynamics between Sam, Nicole, and Trevor."

"I'm still with you."

"Great. The three primary issues need to be addressed with the people directly involved but don't necessarily need to be shared with the whole office."

"That's what I was saying," added Lamar.

"Okay, but there is still the gossip and rumor mill out there that has evolved into the 'secondary issue'."

"I feel like I'm taking a graduate class," joked Lamar.

"Sorry, I'm just thinking out loud. I guess it all goes back to the original question I posed. Does the whole staff need to be involved with the resolution of the 'primary' issue? After all, won't they be curious to know what happened? If they don't know, will the rumors go away or take on a life of their own? Do you see what I'm saying here?"

"I think I do, Justin. They may not need to know the specifics but they need to know that the problem was handled."

"Yeah. That's it. In fact, what they probably need to know is that a) the situation has been resolved, b) that there is an expectation that any problem that interferes with effective working relationship will be addressed, and c) that everyone shares in the responsibility to make their office environment a productive one."

"But how do I do that?" asked Lamar.

"I don't know exactly. I just know that you can't look at problems as isolated events and think you can solve them as isolated events. Sometimes the impact on others is greater than the actual problem itself."

"Man, I'm impressed. Where did you learn this stuff?"

"Believe it or not, from making mistakes." Justin paused. "Let me correct that, it's from learning from my mistakes. In fact, I need to follow my own advice and fill in my staff about the results of a meeting I just had with one of my employees."

"Well all I can say is *thanks!* I think I'll check out your Dr. Mac."

More analogies

THE NEXT DAY, Justin's mind was racing. He was beginning to spot management analogies everywhere. Even in the Bears game. It was third down and long with a minute to go before halftime and the Bears had the ball. A timeout was called. The coaches surveyed the situation, developed a strategy, explored the strengths and weaknesses of the other team, and communicated a play that they hoped would get them at least close enough to kick a tying field goal before the half.

The coaches were, in a sense, management and the players were the employees. The players knew the plays, their individual roles and expectations and everyone bought into a common goal—winning. *I had never looked at football this way,* Justin thought to himself.

"Honey, what was it you and Lamar were talking about last night?" asked Megan as she joined him on the couch.

"Oh, he wanted some advice on a work situation." Just then the Bears missed the field goal.

"Rats!" grunted Justin.

"You mean you two actually have a topic that you can discuss other than football?" she asked archly.

"Oh, aren't you the funny one," replied Justin, tickling her. "Say you're sorry."

"Okay, okay, I'm sorry."

"That's better. Seriously, it was nice to talk with Lamar about work for a change. We have been pretty one-sided in terms of how we relate to one another."

"I must say," said Megan, "he was certainly impressed with you. He kept telling Tanya how helpful you were. What was his situation at work?"

"Ah, honey, don't make me go there. Let's just say that I was able to shed some light on it because there were similarities that I had experienced. In fact, the more I learn, the more similarities I'm beginning to see in everything. Why, take the Bears for example..."

Megan jumped up from the couch. "Honey, I'm interested, but not that interested. Love ya." And she practically fled from the den.

Tommy ran in and dove on Justin. Their halftime wrestling match was now underway.

"No roughhousing," cried Megan from the kitchen.

Justin and Tommy looked at each other and laughed. "Sure, honey," yelled Justin as he put Tommy in a headlock.

"Sure, honey," mocked Tommy, as he grabbed Justin around the neck. It wasn't long before Sandy got into the fray and began barking.

"Daddy," cried Michelle, who was standing in front of them with a football in her hand. "Can we play catch outside? I'm playing quarterback next week and I need to practice."

"Music to my ears, honey, music to my ears." Justin got up from the floor with Tommy still hanging on his neck. "Let's go troops, outside it is!"

Suddenly the chaos in the den dissipated as Justin, Michelle, Tommy, and Sandy all ran outside.

Megan shook her head. *I'm so glad things are back to normal.*

Macology in the mornings

JUSTIN HOPPED INTO HIS CAR truly anticipating the week ahead. It was a feeling that he could not recall ever having before, especially on a Monday morning. *That's pretty sad,* he thought to himself.

As he drove down Maple, he found himself getting bored with *Bears Talk.* Even though the Bears had finally won a game, Justin wasn't interested in hearing the post-game analysis he previously couldn't live without. It was what usually got him through his Mondays.

Instead, he switched to the *Bobbie and Jay Show,* hoping to catch Dr. Mac, who had become a regular morning guest during the seven to eight o'clock slot. They now called that hour, *Macology in the Mornings.*

"Go ahead, caller," said Bobbie, trying to move the show along.

"First-time caller, man. Listen, I've got an office romance going on and need to know how to handle it. Is that something you can help me with?"

Justin's mouth dropped. *Wait a minute, is that Lamar?*

"Tell me what your question is and then I can tell you if I can help," replied Dr. Mac.

Jay and Bobbie weren't about to let this one go without a comment.

"Wow, wow, my man," cried out Jay. "With all due respect to Dr. Mac, we just happen to have an in-house expert right here on the matter. Bobbie, go ahead, tell the man what to do!"

"Me? What about the time you...wait, is your wife listening?"

"Alright you two," intervened Dr. Mac, "we still haven't heard the question. Go ahead, caller."

"Thank you. I guess my question is, do I have the responsibility to address this with anyone other than the people directly involved?"

"I guess that depends if you have incriminating photos," joked Jay. "Sorry, go ahead Dr. Mac."

"Sir, do you mind giving me your first name?"

"Lamar...I mean Lamont."

"Holy cow, it is Lamar!" cried out Justin. Not wanting to miss this exchange, he pulled off to the side of the road. DataDump was just two blocks away, and he didn't want to be sitting in the parking lot in his car where everyone could see him.

"Lamont, I take it you are the supervisor. Is that correct?" asked Dr. Mac.

"You got that."

"Lamont, without knowing the specifics, let me address your question generally and then you can ask me questions based on that."

"Sounds great, man."

"Do you have reliable information that this romance has happened or is happening?"

"Yes sir, I do."

"Do you have a policy at your company that forbids inter-office dating?"

"No sir."

"Are other people aware of this relationship?"

"Everybody is aware of it and everybody is talking about it."

"Do you oversee the two people in the romantic relationship?"

"Yes, I do."

"Are they aware that other people in your office know about this?"

"I believe so."

"Lamont, going back to your question, there are two tiers to this scenario. You've got the two people in the romantic relationship and you have the people who are impacted by these two people being in that relationship."

"Heard that."

"Obviously your first action needs to be in talking to the two individuals, either together or separately, and sharing your observations and potential concerns about the impact their romantic relationship could have on the office. Because you do not have any policy that inhibits such behavior, I would recommend that you emphasize two things to them. First, that the *romantic* part of their relationship needs to take place *outside* of the office. And second, that job performance and productivity are of the utmost importance and should never be compromised because of their relationship, and that includes their ability to work effectively with others. Make sure they also understand that if their personal relationship impedes their ability to do their job, then you will be forced to address that as a performance issue."

"Alright."

"Yeah but what about the other people in the office?" asked Bobbie.

"If two employees are violating a policy or behavioral expectation, then that is one thing. But since these two people are not breaking any rules, I would hope that just by talking to them they will adjust their behavior accordingly. By doing that, the gossip should die down, given that their personal relationship is not impacting anyone's ability to get their jobs done in the office. Hence, I would not make a bigger deal out of this than it needs to be, and wouldn't mention it to the office staff."

Jay couldn't hold back. "Notice how interested Bobbie is in this topic, Dr. Mac. Kind of makes you wonder?" He then quickly closed the show before Bobbie could respond. "Well, we've once again run out of time. Thank you, Dr. Mac! It's coming up on the hour and we'll be taking a break. Join us again tomorrow for more *Macology in the Morning.*"

Justin pulled away from the curb and headed down the street to DataDump. He couldn't help but smile at the realization of how similar his advice to Lamar had been to that of Dr. Mac's. The only real difference was whether or not to address the situation with the whole department or just the people directly involved.

I guess there is still a lot more I need to learn, he thought to himself. *Maybe I don't need to bring up what happened between Charlie and me to the staff after all.*

A change in momentum

WITHOUT QUESTION, COLLEEN HAD the edge over the other two candidates. With an excellent job performance record at DataDump already, plus glowing recommendations, it was essentially her job to lose, at least in Justin's mind.

"So Justin, how is this supposed to work?" asked Lee Ann, who was heading up the interview team.

Justin scratched his head. "How about this idea. First, you and the whole staff will interview each candidate separately. As I recall, we've got Mike this morning, Colleen this afternoon, and Sara tomorrow. Then, after you interview each one, bring them by my office so I can meet them as well."

"And how do you want us to make the decision?" asked Lee Ann, making sure she was clear on the plan.

Justin had actually not given any thought to the process since, in his mind, Colleen was the obvious choice. "Why don't you guys make a recommendation to me, and we'll go from there. How does that sound?"

"That's fine."

Justin could see something else was on Lee Ann's mind. "Is there anything else?"

"Well, sort of. What's going on with you and Charlie? What happened on Friday?"

Lee Ann's question convinced Justin that he probably should address that with the whole staff. "I apologize for not saying anything about that. Charlie and I talked with Christal, and we were able to clear everything up. It's all good now."

That was just what Lee Ann was hoping to hear. "That's so great, Justin. The joke you guys played on us Friday was too much! I thought you were really getting into a fight."

"Lee Ann, I can't begin to tell you how glad I am that we can start to joke with each other around here again. I've really missed that."

"Me too."

Lee Ann looked as if she was about to say something else. "What?" asked Justin.

Lee Ann began to blush. "I just want you to know that I really think you're doing a great job."

Justin smiled. "Thanks, Lee Ann. That means a lot."

Clearly there was a shift happening within the office, and Friday's meeting between Justin and Charlie was truly the turning point. Now the momentum was finally moving forward and no one was happier about that than Justin. And better yet, Colleen wouldn't have to come into a situation that was more dysfunctional than the one she was currently in. In fact, the only real question mark left for Justin was Amy.

The phone rang.

"Hello, this is Justin."

"Ah, you thought you were going to get away from me!"

"Oh hello, Claire."

"Hello. Have you hired Colleen yet?"

"No, her interview isn't until one o'clock...then we'll steal her away from you."

"Well, speaking about stealing, I got an interesting call from one of your employees this morning."

"You did? Was it Amy?"

"Yes. She said she was interested in transferring to our office, should Colleen be offered the position out there. What do you know about this?"

"Hmm. She did express to me her interest in going to Boulder. I'm a little surprised that she called you, however."

"She must really want to get out of there," said Claire.

"Why would you say that?"

"Because she's making her intent known even before we have a job posting."

"Yeah, you're probably right," replied Justin. "Off the record, she and I haven't been seeing eye-to-eye on things since I've become manager."

"Oh, I get it. I'm giving you my best employee and you are shipping me your worst. Is that it?"

"Claire, you know better. Amy is actually a very good employee. And I'm not shipping her to you. This was all Amy's idea, not mine."

"Okay, so tell me, if Colleen is offered your position and accepts it, should I go ahead and interview Amy for her position? How's that for putting you on the spot?"

Justin selfishly knew he'd be better off if Amy left and wanted to believe that a change in scenery would be best for her as well. "Claire, I think you should interview her. She has been a good employee. I would endorse her."

"I'm going to trust you on this," replied Claire. "Gotta go!" Click.

Justin hung up the phone feeling a little guilty for not telling the whole truth about his feelings about Amy. He wasn't quite sure if it was his place to share his biased opinion or not.

The interview

54

IT WAS HALF PAST ONE, and Justin was waiting to meet with Colleen. From the look of things, she was doing real well in her interview. He could hear lots of laughter and animated discussion coming out of the break room. That wasn't the case with their first candidate, Mike, who was not very impressive.

Lee Ann appeared outside Justin's doorway. "Colleen is ready for you; are you ready for her?"

Justin looked up to see Colleen smiling. He thanked Lee Ann and then escorted Colleen over to his conference table.

"So, how did you interview go with the staff," asked Justin.

"Pretty well. They are a great group of people."

"Colleen, since you already know the job and all the duties that go with it, I'm not going to focus on that. Let me ask you a different kind of question. Do you think you could fit in with this group?"

"Definitely. I like the fact that it is a larger staff, that it is a mixed group with males and females, and that you are in such a large office. You have no idea how difficult it has been working with four women in a cramped space. This is so much better."

"Well, I think you'd be a great addition to this group. Granted we've had our problems here, but we've made great progress as of late and having you here would only make us that much better. We need you here."

"Thanks for saying that. Can I be honest with you about something?"

"Of course."

"You never called me back on Friday like you said you would, and it bothered me. I really needed some reassurance from you that I was doing the right thing. When you didn't call back, I began questioning your resolve for having me come out."

"Oops! I'm so sorry. I did forget to call you. Colleen, if you only had an idea of what happened here on Friday, perhaps you'd understand."

"I kind of know, Justin. Nevertheless, you said you were going to call and you didn't. I need to know that you will keep your word with me."

"Colleen, I also get upset when people don't keep their word. You can count on me in the future. But please know that I'm also on a learning curve, just as you will be if you end up coming out here, and we need to be understanding of that for each other. My intention was to call you back, I swear. I screwed up and I'm sorry."

"Well I'm sorry too for making it a big deal."

"I'll tell you what, why don't I drive you to the airport when you're done and we can talk some more. I've got a three o'clock appointment and I know you have a few more people to meet with while you're here. How does that sound?"

"Sounds good. Again, I'm sorry for jumping all over you a minute ago. I'll meet you in the lobby at four."

"Colleen, you were right to hold me accountable."

"Thanks for understanding, Justin. I'm glad I came out."

Let the mentoring begin

JUSTIN WENT EARLY TO THE PARK so he could jot down his questions for Dr. Mac and review his homework before their meeting. He wasn't sure if their informal discussions would change any since DataDump was now formally paying Dr. Mac to coach him. He hoped not.

He wrote:

> 1) What's my obligation to Claire regarding Amy?
> 2) Do I owe my staff an explanation about what happened in my meeting with Charlie?

He then pulled out his homework, eager to tell Dr. Mac everything that had happened since they last talked.

"Well, well, there's my client."

Justin looked up from his journal and happily greeted Dr. Mac. "Hello, Dr. Mac. Heard you on the radio this morning—excellent advice as usual. Actually, one of my questions for you today ties into your comments this morning."

"Very good, but let's get the formality out of the way first. You know I don't take on coaching clients."

"Yes, that's what Cynthia said."

"But since it was you, I decided to make an exception."

"And I appreciate it. I know how busy you are, and I'm glad that you are getting paid for this. It makes me feel better for taking up your time."

"I don't mind the time," said Dr. Mac, "I enjoy talking with you and wouldn't be doing it if I didn't."

"Thanks, Dr. Mac. Hey, any chance we can keep these meetings on an informal basis like we've been doing? I didn't know if we had to change things since my company's gotten involved."

"I'd prefer to keep our meetings informal as well. In fact I told Cynthia that this would be more of a mentor relationship and to not expect a formal report or anything of the kind. I said you were a good man and that I would be happy to help out if I could."

"Dr. Mac, if you only knew how helpful you've already been. I've been picking up stuff from you in your column and now on your radio program—which leads me to one of my questions."

"Nice segue!"

Justin smiled as he opened up his journal. "By the way, this journal idea has been incredible. I can't tell you how it has helped me.

Okay, here's my question related to the advice you gave Lamar this morning."

"Lamar? Wasn't it Lamont?"

"Yeah, you're right. Anyway, you told him that he didn't need to talk to the office employees about the romantic relationship that the two employees were having. Do you remember that?"

"Well it was only this morning. I think I can remember. Boy, a man turns eighty-six and no one thinks he can remember anything," joked Dr. Mac, twinkling.

"Sorry, sorry. What I'm wondering is if the same logic can be applied to my situation with Charlie. He's the guy that I threatened to fire and you wrote me back in your Friday column telling me, essentially, how to fix the situation—great advice by the way."

"Stop kissing up!" teased Dr. Mac.

"Sorry again. Anyway, to make a long story short, we had the meeting and everything got resolved, thanks in part to our supervisor, who, for the first time, explained her rationale in promoting me and not him. That explanation did wonders in shifting our relationship back to where it was before all of this happened."

"O'Brien, I know there is a question in there somewhere."

"Here it is. I was planning on telling the rest of the staff about what happened between Charlie and me at the meeting, thinking they would want to know. After all, they've been impacted by my relationship with Charlie ever since I took over."

"So the question that you still have not asked me yet is?"

"Do I need to talk about my meeting with Charlie to the staff or not?"

"I don't know. What do you think?"

"Is that what I'm paying you for?" mocked Justin.

"First off, you're not paying me. Secondly, I'm here to help you, not tell you what to do. What kind of coach would I be if I just gave you my opinion on everything?"

"Alright, I get it."

"So?"

"So what?"

"So what do you think and why?"

"Hmm. Based on your advice this morning—"

"O'Brien, I'm not looking for a *correct* answer. Forget about what I said this morning. Tell me what you think and why."

"Okay, okay. The more I think about it the more I don't think I owe a response to the group. If individuals ask, I'd be happy to tell them. But in a way I'm just doing my job by handling problems. If I felt obligated to share every problem I have with the staff, we'd never get any work done."

"Bravo! Next question?"

"Cool. Here's my other question. One of my employees is applying for a job at our Boulder office and frankly she's been a pain in my side ever since I got promoted. She's had a bad attitude and has been pretty disruptive in meetings. I know, I know, get to the question! So my question is, do I have an obligation to tell my counterpart in Boulder all of my perceptions about this woman, which are mostly bad?"

Dr. Mac leaned toward Justin. "Put yourself in her shoes and tell me what you'd want to hear?"

"I'd want to hear the truth."

"O'Brien, you certainly have an obligation to be fair in what you say. Share the facts and your perceptions of those facts. Let your colleague decide what to do with it. More importantly, don't get in the habit of passing off your difficult employees to another manager. It's not fair to the other manager and it is especially not fair to the difficult employee. How are they supposed to grow and develop as an employee if the organization's response to their problematic behavior is to move them elsewhere within the company?"

"Wow, see you did have an opinion."

"Yeah, even I don't always follow my own advice."

"So can I show you my homework from last week?"

"Why?"

"I don't know. I figured since you assigned it that you might want to see it."

"I assigned it because I wanted to show you a methodology that can be very helpful in thinking through problems and making decisions. Sometimes something as simple as writing it down is all that is needed in order for us to see the problem or circumstance from a slightly different perspective. Do you know what I mean?"

Justin nodded. "Sort of."

"Well, the bottom line is that I'm not as concerned with solving your problems as I am with providing you with techniques to solve them yourself. So tell me, was it helpful?"

"Yes, extremely. And you'd be proud of me this past week. When I started, the sheet was heavily weighted toward what was not working and by the end of the week it had almost completely turned around."

"Bravo, again. Look, O'Brien, our time is up. Let's continue to meet here each Monday as long as the weather cooperates. Sound good?"

"Yes, sir."

"Oh, please, cut the formality! I'll see you next week, Desperate Dave."

"You got it," smiled Justin.

Not so sweet

JUSTIN HEADED BACK to the office in just enough time to pick up Colleen, who was waiting out front.

"Jump in. Where are you headed Miss?"

"To the airport, and step on it!" replied Colleen, playing along.

The traffic on the Edens Expressway was as expected, packed and slow moving. Fortunately, there was plenty of time for her to make her seven o'clock flight.

"So, what are your impressions?" asked Justin.

"Hmm. Well, since I'm technically still a candidate, I don't want to say anything that could possibly jeopardize my chances of being offered the job."

"Oh give me a break! I'm still your manager either way."

"That's right, you are. Tell me what you want to know."

"You suddenly sound like someone else I know."

"Who?"

"Never mind, long story," replied Justin. "So, give me your impressions of my staff members."

"Let's see, I was very impressed with Lee Ann. She was very helpful and sweet. We bonded immediately. Then there was John." Colleen paused to find the right words. "Interesting fellow. He was very nice as well. Seems to like to gossip."

"What do you mean?"

"He prided himself in telling me all the happenings in the office since you took over. In actuality, he seemed much more concerned with filling me in on office dynamics and much less concerned with interviewing me. It was more like I interviewed him. I don't think he asked me one question, now that I think about it."

Justin couldn't refrain from shaking his head in disappointment. He was reminded that John would be his next challenge...after Amy, that is.

"Then there was Charlie and Will. I liked those guys. They were funny and very knowledgeable." She paused. "Let's see, who have I missed?"

"How about Amy?" asked Justin curiously.

"Amy. She doesn't seem happy here. She clearly was more negative than the others and hard to figure out. I couldn't connect with her very well."

"You and me alike."

"What do you mean?"

"Oops, that wasn't nice of me to say." Justin had a troubled look on his face. "Is this conversation still confidential?"

"It better be!"

"Okay, something's been going on with her ever since I became the manager. We haven't exactly gotten along. In fact, she wants to apply for your job back in Boulder if you end up coming out here."

"You're kidding. Really?"

"That's what she said. She even called Claire this morning."

"Why?"

"I don't know. I'm guilty in the sense that I haven't made much of an effort to talk with her. I've been hesitant because she has been so negative, and attacks me in front of the group on a regular basis."

"Oh, and going to Boulder will help that?"

"Well, I still have to confer with Claire about that. I wasn't sure if it was my place or not to share that with her. Besides, her problem might only be with me. But now I believe I need to. After all, whether Amy's out in Boulder or Winnetka, she's still my direct report. Passing her off to Boulder doesn't really solve my problem. And in all likelihood, it could make it worse."

"Justin?"

"Yes. What is it?"

"I'm glad that you believe you should be up front with Claire regarding Amy. There is something else that you should know."

"Gee, this doesn't sound good," replied Justin, who was now bracing himself to hear what she had to say.

"Remember when you came out to Boulder?"

"Yeah, I thought it was a very productive trip. Why?"

"Well, don't get mad, okay?"

"I won't. Go ahead."

"We sort of painted a picture for you that we all get along. The truth is, we don't."

Justin's jaw hit the floor in shock.

Colleen continued. "Katie is a terror, and nothing has changed there. I was going to quit had your position not come open. And I know for a fact that Claire's not happy and Taylor isn't either. And it's not just Katie that's the problem. Claire pretty much ignores all the office dynamics."

"But, what about the norms we created? What about the evening at the restaurant and all the fun we had?"

Colleen shook her head to imply that none of that mattered. "I'm sorry, Justin. I thought about saying something to you then but it felt too risky."

"Wow. I'm surprised someone didn't try to sell me some swampland while I was out there. I was buying everything else!"

"I didn't want to tell you, but thought I should be completely honest with you as I expect you to be with me."

Justin's mind had drifted back to the Boulder trip. He had his game face on now—deep in thought and barely present.

"Justin, hello Justin?"

He snapped out of his trance. "I'm sorry Colleen. It frustrates me to know that I couldn't pick up on the real dynamics. I guess I have a ways to go yet before becoming a truly good manager."

"So you thought you would be perfect right out of the gate?"

"No, it's just a lot harder than I ever imagined. I feel like a racehorse that just can't seem to get in stride."

They were now at the airport and Justin pulled up to the United curb.

"Will you be calling me tomorrow either way?" asked Colleen.

"Definitely. I'm looking forward to having you here on staff."

Colleen gave Justin a quick hug as she got out of the car. "Me too."

As Justin pulled away from the curb, it began to snow ever so lightly. Shaking his head, he said to himself, *this is just too perfect. I got snowed in Boulder and now it's snowing here. Perhaps I need the constant reminder on the drive home.*

57

Q3 feedback

JUSTIN TOSSED AND TURNED all night. He was still in game-face mode when he woke up to the words of Megan.

"Honey, are you okay?"

Justin turned toward her. "What? Why'd you ask?"

"Because you were restless all night."

"I was? I'm sorry. Hope I didn't keep you up."

"What's going on? Is it work?" asked Megan.

Justin wasn't up to talking about Colleen's comments, at least not yet. "Oh, it's nothing. Just the trials and tribulations that go with being a manager."

"I see. So tell me, is that right up there with the trials and tribulations of being a husband and father?" Megan asked.

"Ah, sarcasm!" cried out Justin. "What you're really implying is that I've been a little preoccupied lately with work, right? Allow me to start over. Good morning, honey!" as he gave her a big hug.

"Better, but still a bit contrived," said Megan, pushing him away. "Have you considered acting lessons?"

Justin was grateful that Megan was keeping things light. "Why would I do that? I'm a natural! You've said so yourself."

"I've called you a lot of things, but don't recall ever using the word "natural" with you in the same sentence."

"Funny!"

"Seriously, it's my day to drive the kids, so we'll be leaving now. I let you sleep in a bit given that you got home late last night. Call me later, okay?"

"You got it!"

Justin jumped out of bed and raced into the shower. He actually was a little perturbed that Megan had let him sleep in. He had a big day ahead and was counting on some planning time before things got going. *So much for that idea!*

It was about eight-thirty when Justin walked through DataDump's front doors. To his surprise, he heard someone calling his name.

"Justin, over here."

He turned to see J.W., who was walking through the lobby with a client.

Oh no! The one time I come in late and J.W. sees me. That's just great! "Good morning, J.W. I took a candidate to the airport last night so I slept in an extra half-hour today."

J.W. ignored the comment. "Justin, I'd like to introduce you to Nicholas Larsh. He's with Megatronics out in Houston."

Justin put out his hand. "Hello, Mr. Larsh."

"Glad to meet you Justin; call me Nick."

"Nick, Justin recently took over the Orders Fulfillment Department and has been doing an exceptional job," said J.W. boastfully.

Justin scoffed. "A lot of people have been helping me."

"Nonsense," rebutted J.W., "quit being so modest. If *number two* says you're doing a good job, then you must be. He's my eyes and ears."

Twice I've thought Melvin was going to fire me, and now I'm getting compliments from him? "Thank you sir."

"By the way, son, we just reviewed the third quarter performance figures and the Boulder office is up for the first time. Nice job."

Justin tried hard not to look surprised as he thanked J.W. for the compliment. *Figures are up for the first time? Imagine that!*

Moments later as he walked into his department, he noticed that the room was completely empty. He did a double take and looked around the room again. Just then, a burst of laughter shot out from the break room, and Justin remembered. *Of course, they're all interviewing the last candidate.*

Shaking his head, he retreated to his office before it was his turn to meet the candidate. Between the good and bad news about Boulder plus Dr. Mac's advice and Colleen's feedback, he had plenty of new insights for his journal.

Journal Entry # 10

   a) It is important to always keep my word with my employees and empower them to hold me accountable when I don't.

   b) It's unfair to pass off a difficult employee to another department without being totally up front about what I'm doing. And even then, it's probably not a good idea.

   c) Productivity is not always an indication of how well a staff is working together.

Justin was still having a hard time understanding how the Boulder office was actually improving its productivity, given what Colleen had to say the previous night. Nevertheless, he'd take the compliment, especially from J.W.

Lee Ann popped her head in Justin's office. "Justin, I'd like to introduce you to Sara, who is applying for our order taker position."

Justin jumped up and shook Sara's hand. "Hello."

"Hello, Mr. O'Brien. I've heard a lot about you."

Gosh, I wonder who that came from! "Oh really, I hope it was all good."

For the next fifteen minutes, Justin and Sara talked about the position, his expectations, and her past experience. Although he had pretty much decided that Colleen would get the job, he couldn't help but notice how well qualified Sara was. *Too bad I don't have two positions open,* he thought to himself.

Another surprise decision

THE STAFF MEETING THAT FOLLOWED Sara's interview was supposed to have been a slam dunk in Colleen's favor. That was until Amy took it upon herself to announce to Justin the group's recommendation.

"Come again?' asked Justin, taken aback.

For whatever reason, Amy seemed to have assumed the role of spokesperson for the group. It was as if she were using this opportunity to personally *take on* Justin.

"I think," and then she immediately corrected herself, "I mean, we think that Sara is the best candidate."

"Over Colleen?" winced Justin.

"Yes, over Colleen. She brings more experience and, quite frankly, doesn't come with baggage."

"Baggage? What baggage does Colleen bring?"

"Let's face it, Justin, the Boulder office has been troubled ever since their existence. Even Colleen acknowledged that."

Given the conversation Justin had just recently had with Amy, he couldn't understand why she'd shoot herself in the foot by choosing Sara over Colleen. Meanwhile, Lee Ann was noticeably shaking her head over in the corner. He began to wonder if the group really was in alignment with Amy regarding their choice.

"Let me tell you something, Amy," said Justin, "this troubled group, as you say, has increased their productivity for the first time ever this quarter. And if you are implying that my trip out to Boulder was a waste of time, then you don't know what you are talking about."

Suddenly a familiar sensation came upon Justin. Here he was arguing with a staff member in front of other staff members again—a dynamic he'd sworn never to repeat. He refocused and tried to calm down.

"Look, I admit that Sara is a viable candidate. But Colleen already has a proven record with this company. In fact, she exemplifies the characteristics that this company stands for: dependability, quality, high motivation, and an all-around good person."

"And Sara doesn't have those qualities?" Amy shot back.

Justin looked around the table. "Why is this between me and Amy? I want to hear from the rest of you. Charlie, give me your take."

"Justin, I thought they were both equally good candidates. And to tell you the truth, I really don't know if the fact that Colleen is coming from the Boulder office is a good thing or a bad thing."

"So you are kind of in the middle?"

Amy glared at Charlie.

"Yes, for the most part. But with a slight lean toward Sara."

Justin kept going around the table. He was determined to find out who was leading this charge for Sara and why.

"I pretty much agree with Charlie," said John.

"You know what, John, you're not Charlie. I want to hear your own assessment, not a summary of what Charlie said."

John clearly struggled with Justin's directive.

Lee Ann chimed in. "Go ahead, John, I'd like to hear your perspective as well."

Now all eyes were on John. He began squirming in his seat. Finally he spoke. "Truthfully, I liked them both. I'm serious."

The group looked both amazed and perplexed. John had finally given his own opinion, albeit an ambivalent one. Nevertheless, he had just spoken up for himself for the first time.

Justin stayed focused on John. "Even though you're feeling undecided, I appreciate the fact that you gave your own opinion. You need to do more of that, especially in front of everyone else."

Amy's power was slowly diminishing as each person spoke up. Clearly there had never been a true group consensus, as least as far as Justin could surmise.

It was Lee Ann's turn. "I also liked them both, but I agree with you, Justin. I think Colleen would fit well here. She's nice, personable, and a hard worker. She gets my vote."

Now it was Amy who was squirming in her seat.

Justin was sensing some momentum. "Will, your thoughts?"

"I was split as well. I guess I'd like to hear your rationale, especially about the *Boulder factor*. You never really told us about what happened out there and your assessment of that group. If they are truly dysfunctional, then I'm not so sure we'd want Colleen over Sara."

"You're absolutely right, Will. The tension around here was pretty thick when I went out to Boulder and upon my return I stopped short of sharing my perception. I guess I was feeling that none of you really wanted to know."

"That's not true, Justin," asserted Lee Ann. "I think it would help if you shared your perceptions more. In fact, if I can be totally honest with you—"

"Please do."

"I know you've shared with me some things that you haven't shared with the group. I guess I'd like it if you were more open and forthright with the entire staff as well."

"You're also absolutely right, Lee Ann. I haven't always been forthright with the whole staff. Perhaps it's time I am."

Aside from Amy, who was uncomfortable with the changing focus of the meeting, everyone else nodded for Justin to go ahead.

"I didn't feel any support from anyone when Christal first selected me as manager, including Christal. Believe me when I tell you that my life would have been much easier if she had just selected Charlie. But she didn't. So there I was in this awkward position of trying to manage a group that didn't want me as their manager. So yes to your comment, Lee Ann, I tried to make headway with each of you on an individual basis instead of as a group. For some reason, the group dynamics have been much more difficult for me to handle. But that's slowly changing."

Will broke the sudden silence. "Is this where we sing "Kumbaya" together?"

A welcome laughter broke out in the room. Even Amy couldn't hold back. Justin felt greatly relieved.

"I just want to say one more thing if I may," added Justin. "Yes, the Boulder office has some personality difficulties. At the same time, I think it would be tough for anyone to be cramped up in a small room with three other people and be expected to perform at the same level that we have here. But probably the biggest thing they need over there, aside from a larger office, is more direct supervision from me. That is why I went down there, and that is why I'm going to be much more involved with them. And the fact that their productivity is on the rise tells me that I'm on the right track."

Justin looked at Will. "Does that answer your question?"

Will looked very satisfied. "Yes, it does. I would support Colleen."

Heads nodded in agreement with Will.

Justin knew that there was one more issue still looming large in the room. He hesitated before deciding to go for it. "Amy, can you support Colleen for the position over Sara?"

Amy was clearly upset and threw her hands up. "Apparently it doesn't matter what I think. Maybe you should hire both of them!"

"What's that supposed to mean?" asked Justin.

"It means perhaps Sara should take my job. I don't fit in here anymore!"

Making it official

EVERYONE LOOKED AT EACH OTHER with surprise as Amy abruptly left the break room. Justin was the first to go after her, but not before making sure they were all in agreement. "So we are going with Colleen, right?"

The group nodded their approval. He shot out the door.

"Amy, hold on!"

Amy stopped and turned toward Justin, trying to hold back her tears. "Justin, do you mind if I take the rest of the day off?"

"Of course not. Go home and let's talk tomorrow, okay?"

She turned, grabbed some things out of her cubicle, and headed out the door.

Justin called out one more time. "Amy!"

She looked back.

"I'm going to offer Colleen the position. I hope you're okay with that."

"Whatever, Justin." And out the door she went.

As Justin headed back to his office, he found himself still struggling over why Amy had decided to use the candidate decision to challenge him. But even more disconcerting was the fact that the rest of his staff had seemed so willing to go with her recommendation. *What was that about,* he wondered.

He then picked up the phone and made the call that he had been looking forward to making all along.

"This is Colleen."

"Yes, Miss, this is the Winnetka Police Department and we have a warrant for your arrest."

"Oh really?"

"Really. And you are summoned to appear at DataDump within the next two weeks in order to begin your restitution."

"Are you offering me the position, Justin?"

"Yes, I am."

"Hmm. Let me think about it." She paused. "Okay, I thought about it and I'll take it!"

They laughed. For the next few minutes they continued to talk and firm up logistics before Justin asked Colleen to transfer him to Claire. He figured now was as good a time as any to share the official news with her.

"Justin, do you mind if I tell her first. I know it's silly but I feel like I owe her that much."

Justin knew the minute she mentioned it that she was right. "Sorry, that was me trying to multi-task in one phone call. When should I call her?"

"Give me ten minutes."

"You got it, Colleen. Hey, I can't wait for you to get out here."

"Me either," replied a grateful Colleen. "Thanks again, boss!"

Coming clean

JUSTIN HAD BARELY EVEN HUNG UP the phone before it rang a second time. "This is Justin."

"Sweeeet!"

"Hello, Claire."

"So, what am I supposed to do now?"

"What, no 'Good morning, Justin,' or 'How is your day?'"

"Well, I know how your day is going," replied Claire, "because you've just added my best employee to your staff."

"That I did, that I did. Hey, I do have some things to talk to you about."

"As he quickly changes the subject," mocked Claire.

"This is serious. Regarding Amy, I didn't tell you everything when we talked yesterday. It is true that she is proficient in her job skills and all but—"

"But?"

"But there has been a little problem lately with her attitude here on the job."

"She doesn't like you, does she?"

"Why would you say that?" asked Justin.

"Ah, I just sensed it, that's all. I've talked to her a couple of times in the past week and there definitely was an edge to her. That's why I was pressing you to tell me what you thought of her."

"I see. Well, I guess I thought that if in fact I am the problem then maybe a fresh start in Boulder might actually work for her."

"So should I go ahead and interview her?"

"Yes. Why not," said Justin. "I've never had a problem with her work."

"Okay, then I'll handle it from here," reassured Claire.

Justin wasn't ready to let her get away just yet. "A couple more things."

"Sure, Justin."

"First is a compliment, via J.W. Boulder's productivity levels went up in Q3. Way to go, Claire! He was impressed, and he said it is the first time that that's happened. Is that true?"

"Wow, imagine that," said Claire. "I guess that's good, right?"

"Why do you say that? Of course it's good."

"Justin, things like productivity levels and customer satisfaction results usually went right to Christal. She never shared any of that, so we never worried about it. I always figured that she would say something if it was really bad."

"Hmm. Well, from now on I think we need to utilize all the data we can get. Once you're able to replace Colleen and get stabilized again as a staff, I'd like to have quarterly meetings and go over all the performance data that's available. I want you involved in that process."

"No problem, but why is this such a big deal suddenly?" Claire asked a bit defensively.

"Because I need more objective measures to assess how things are going out there. If J.W. relies on the quarterly reports to make his assessment, then I need to use them as well. Besides, this way I can better support and/or defend you guys to him, based on what the reports are saying. Does that make sense?"

Claire was a little suspicious. "Did Colleen say something to you?"

"Not directly. But I'm sensing that not a lot has changed there since I left."

"Hey, our figures are up, so something improved, right?"

Justin conceded. "Okay, I'll give you that one."

"Justin, you've known all along what the issues are out here. We were all honest in identifying what our problems were that day with you. Even the norms we created were exactly what we needed to do. But..."

Here we go. "But what?"

"But there is a difference between saying we need to do something and actually doing it. With all due respect, we've done the *norm* thing before. It unfortunately doesn't change personalities. Our problem isn't about getting the work done, it's about *how* we get the work done."

"Claire, is being the team lead too much for you to handle?"

"What's *that* supposed to mean?"

"Claire, I don't mean it the way it sounds. You are not a supervisor, yet here I am expecting you to not only manage the office but manage the employees as well. Do you think I'm asking too much of you?"

Claire paused to think about the question. "I don't know."

"So it is possible, then?"

"I guess."

"Okay, thank you. Now, was that so bad? Please know that it's not my intent to put you into a situation that you are not comfortable handling or that involves something that I should be taking care of."

Justin was still frustrated to find that he had to pry this omission out of her. "Claire, why couldn't you just come out and tell me?"

"Because, Justin, you went out of your way to empower me as the lead and I didn't want to let you down. But I guess I did."

"Look Claire, you need to understand something. The truth is, any problem can be solved. I just need to know what they are so I can help."

"So what do we do now?" Claire asked.

"First, from now on you have to communicate with me about *everything* that's going on out there. And I mean everything. Will you do that?"

"Yes."

"Okay. Let's talk weekly. How about every Friday?"

"I'd like that."

"Great. As far as what else, I'm not sure yet. Let me talk with Christal to get her thoughts."

"Justin, am I in trouble?"

"Why would you say that?" asked Justin.

"I don't know. I guess it feels like I'm getting reprimanded."

"No, not at all. We are just clarifying and refining our work relationship. If anything, I put you in a no-win situation. It's my responsibility to set you and your staff up to succeed. I haven't quite done that yet."

"Okay, well, thanks Justin. You really have been great."

"Thanks Claire, and yes, it's okay to say it."

"Are you sure?"

"I wouldn't feel complete without it."

"Here goes. Sweeeet!"

61

The boys

LATER THAT DAY Charlie and Will walked into Justin's office.

"J-Man, do you have a minute?" asked Charlie.

J-Man was Charlie's nickname for Justin. It was a welcome indication that things were getting back to normal.

"Boys," smiled Justin, "come on in."

Justin got up to join them at his conference table but they had already pulled a couple of chairs right up to his desk. He sat back down.

Charlie spoke first. "Hey, interesting meeting, huh?"

"I was a bit surprised. What was all that about?" asked Justin.

"I think it was a combination of things," answered Will. "Two pretty equal candidates, one local with a variety of experience and one with DataDump experience from Boulder."

"Yeah, and let's face it Justin," added Charlie, "we all know that the women in Boulder have had their problems working together."

Justin tried to finish the logic. "So let me see if I got this. Colleen came in with a strike against her because she was from our Boulder office?"

261

Charlie and Will nodded in agreement.

"Even though you both seem to like her and I know you can work with her?"

"I think we could have worked with Sara as well," said Will. "And no one knew where you stood, so we all went along with Amy's recommendation."

Justin had been wondering if he should have taken more of a leading role with these interviews or not, and now he could see that he should have.

"So what should I have done differently?" he asked.

"Here's my thought, in hindsight of course," said Charlie very sincerely. "First, we should have met as a group beforehand to identify the kind of person we wanted to hire. That way we could have discussed the *Boulder factor* then. Secondly, we never really knew what your role was in the process. Was this going to be your decision, our decision, or a group consensus? Were we just making a recommendation or what?"

Justin nodded. He had assumed that Colleen was going to be a shoe-in so he never gave much thought to the process.

"You're right, my bad!"

Charlie still had another point to make. "J-Man, there's more."

"Go ahead."

"When you heard our recommendation—"

"You mean Amy's recommendation," interrupted Justin.

"No, we may have been waffling, but it was our recommendation," added Will.

"You seemed to freak out," said Charlie

"Freak out?"

"It was obvious that you didn't hear what you wanted to hear, so you took on Amy and challenged the validity of the decision."

"Really?" asked Justin.

"That's how it appeared to me," said Charlie. "I'm not saying that that was your intent, but I think Will agrees that at that point it turned into a thing between you and Amy."

Will nodded.

Justin was confused now. "I thought that Amy was using this issue to take me on. She's been on my case ever since I got promoted."

"Nevertheless, Justin, I think she took it as a personal attack on her. It's why she got upset at the end," replied Charlie.

Justin leaned back in his chair, shaking his head. "Wow, I had no idea. That wasn't my intent. Now I feel like crap!"

"J-Man, just talk to her. Apologize or do whatever you have to do to get her back."

"Boy, where have I heard that before?" lamented Justin.

"Where?" asked Charlie.

"That's what everyone kept saying to me when you walked out."

Charlie smiled.

"I'm just glad we were finally able to talk with Christal and clear things up," acknowledged Justin.

"Me too," added Charlie.

"Wait a minute," cried Will, "what exactly happened in that meeting that turn things around between you two?"

"It was being able to talk with Christal together, wouldn't you say so Chas?" asked Justin.

"Certainly that helped tremendously. But you know what had an even bigger impact on me that day?"

"You missed hanging out with me?" teased Justin.

"Sorry, dude. It was Dr. Mac's column in the newspaper that morning. Have you ever read it before?"

Justin didn't know how to respond to that question so he downplayed it. "Oh, I've seen it. Why?"

"Well the column was about what to do with employees who have an attitude problem. I think the guy who wrote in called himself 'Desperate Dave.' He mentioned that he threatened to fire these two employees and was wondering if he could or not."

"Oh man, I saw that one, too!" cried Will. "That Desperate Dave guy has written in a couple of times."

Justin was amazed that both Charlie and Will were familiar with the column, let alone with the two letters he had submitted under his alias.

"So Charlie," asked Justin, "what did that have to do with our meeting last week?"

"Oddly enough, I found myself relating more to this Desperate Dave guy than to the two employees. Then it dawned on me that I was slowing becoming one of those employees with the attitude problem—the very thing I hated. Needless to say, by the time I was at that meeting I was ready to work through whatever issues we needed to fix."

"Even though you still thought I had been lying to you about applying for the position?" Justin asked surprisingly.

"Yep. I figured that it was time for me to be part of the solution instead of the problem."

Justin nodded as he got up to end the informal meeting. "I appreciate that Chas! And I guess I owe Amy an apology."

"Let us know if you need any more help, *boss-man*," smiled Will as he left the room.

Justin and Charlie looked at each other.

"Boss-man?" laughed Justin. "Oh well, an endearment is an endearment—right, Chas?"

Charlie pointed at Justin. "You're the man!"

Amy's resistance

As much as Justin appreciated the feedback and suggestions from Charlie and Will, it still was bothersome to him—especially the part about Amy. *Boy, I guess I was pretty hard on her.* He hated having a knot in his stomach and couldn't bear to wait until tomorrow before talking to her. He decided to call her now on her cell phone.

"Hi, it's Amy. Leave me a message! Beeeep!"

"Hello, Amy, Justin. Can you call me today if possible? I'd appreciate that. Bye."

Before putting the receiver down, Justin quickly called Christal's cell. He wanted to make sure he covered all bases just in case Amy decided to call her.

"Hello, this is Christal. I'm unable to take your call right now but please leave a message at the beep and I'll call you back. Beeeep".

Justin rolled his eyes. *Don't people ever answer their cell phones any more!* "Christal, this is Justin. Amy and I had a falling out in a meeting this morning and I need to confer with you about it. Sorry. Call me right away."

As he hung up the phone, he pulled out his journal so he could record his insights from his earlier talk with Claire as well as the feedback he received from Charlie and Will.

Journal Entry # 11

a)   Staff commitments (i.e., the Boulder group) work best when there is accountability around those commitments. As manager, it is my responsibility to ensure that happens.

b)   Before asking my staff to participate in future projects (i.e., the interview process), it's important that I spell out up front what the process is, what my expectations are, and how a decision will ultimately be made.

c)   Challenging decisions that I've asked my staff to make goes in direct opposition to asking them to make a decision in the first place.

d)   It's important to create a work environment where employees feel comfortable providing me with feedback about my performance.

As Justin put his pen down, the phone rang.

"Hello, Justin. You called?"

"Amy?"

"Yes."

"Look, it was unfair of me to challenge your recommendation. I apologize for that."

"So what are you saying?"

"I'm saying I'm sorry."

"What about Sara?"

"It's too late, I've already offered the position to Colleen."

"Would it really have made a difference, Justin?"

"What do you mean?"

"I mean it was pretty apparent that you already had your mind made up. Why did you even ask us for a recommendation if you knew there was only one correct answer?"

Justin had hoped that apologizing and acknowledging his mistake would cause Amy to back down a bit. Instead, here he was once again defending himself with her. "Yes, Amy, I failed to define the interview process and my expectations for the group. I didn't do it intentionally. My God, give me a break. I said I was sorry!"

"I just don't know, Justin. I feel like I personally had to pay the price for your latest mistake. It's not right. And now I have an interview in Boulder later this week and I'm worried that somehow this will be used against me in some way."

"Amy, you won't have to pay twice for my mistake. I told Claire that you deserve an interview. The rest will be up to you."

"I have to go now, Justin. I have another call coming in." Click.

Justin could only shake his head. He knew there was something else going on with Amy, but clearly she wasn't about to let him in on it.

Cynthia's help

JUSTIN HAD HIS FAMILIAR "lost puppy look" on his face as he peered into Cynthia's office.

"Come on in, Justin. What's up?"

"Ah, where to start."

"Did something happen…again?"

"Sort of. It's Amy."

"Tell me you didn't threaten to fire her!"

"No, of course not."

"So what happened?"

"Today or for the past three weeks?"

"Let's go with today."

"Well…" hesitated Justin, "we kind of got into it over the selection of my replacement."

Cynthia looked confused.

"You see, I told the staff to give me their recommendation on who they thought was the best candidate for the position. To my surprise, they initially selected Sara over Colleen."

"What do you mean *initially*?"

"I'm getting to that. I made the mistake of not spelling out how the interview process and ultimate decision would be made. So when Amy, who was leading the charge, told me that they selected Sara, I challenged their decision."

"Because you wanted Colleen?" asked Cynthia.

"Yes and no. It is true that I thought Colleen was the best candidate, but what bothered me more than their decision was the way they made their decision. It became obvious to me that they really didn't debate much among themselves and essentially allowed Amy to be the deciding factor."

"So then what happened?" asked Cynthia.

"It turned into a 'me against Amy' debate."

Cynthia nodded. "I think I can see where this is headed."

"There's more."

"I figured."

"Well, to make a long story short, everyone found the two candidates to be pretty evenly qualified and probably would have selected Colleen had she not been from our Boulder office. They referred to that as the *Boulder factor*."

"Oh, this is getting good. Tell me Justin, what's the *Boulder factor?*"

"There is a perception," and then Justin corrected himself, "I mean there *was* a perception among my staff that our counterparts in Boulder are pretty messed up."

"Messed up?"

"I know, they're not. But I had not communicated well enough to them about what's going on in Boulder and about what happened when I went out there. They still had an old perception of Claire, Katie, Taylor, and Colleen that was not very good. Let's just leave it at that."

"So you cleared all of that up?" asked Cynthia.

"Yes, and then people changed their vote in favor of Colleen."

"Except Amy, right?"

Justin nodded. "Except Amy. That's when she got so upset with me for altering the group's decision that she walked out."

"Is there more?"

"A little. I did go after her and ended up giving Amy the rest of the day off, *at her request*. I then called her later to apologize for how I handled that whole thing."

"And?"

"And she proceeded to unload on me some more."

Just then Cynthia's eyes lit up. "Hmm. I might have an idea for you."

"I'm open to anything," replied Justin.

"Let me think out loud here," said Cynthia. "There are two pieces that probably need to be addressed. Certainly you and Amy have some work to do on your relationship. But there is also a second component here as well. When is Colleen starting?"

"She starts in two weeks. Why?"

"I think your staff, with Colleen, should also do a team-building day together. The dynamics have changed enough in the last month that I think it would benefit all of you to do something like that."

Justin liked the idea. "It would also be a way to integrate Colleen into the staff!"

"Exactly. And it will help open up the communication channels between you and your staff as well. In fact, we've been using a guy named Walt, and I think it would be a worthwhile expense to have your department work with him for a day."

"Is that the breaking boards guy?" asked Justin.

"Yes, he does have a program where people come up and break boards. But that's not what I'm referring to when I say teambuilding. He'll customize a program for your group that builds cohesion, communication, and group synergy. He's great. As I said, we've used him before."

"Do you think this will also help with Amy?" asked Justin.

"I think it can only help, but I can't guarantee that it will address any issues she has with you personally. You are going to have to work that out with her separately."

Justin knew she was right and that the teambuilding would only be half the battle.

"When should we do it?"

"Let me see if I can set something up for the end of October."

"Thanks Cynthia. You know, I really am making progress with my staff."

"I know, Justin. I can tell you're doing a great job. I wish every manager here was as willing to improve as you are."

As Cynthia got up to walk Justin out of her office, she shook her head. "It's too bad about Christal."

"What? What are you talking about?" asked Justin.

"She's run into some complications and is back in the hospital. I'm sorry, I thought you knew."

"No, but it probably explains why I haven't heard from her. Is she going to be okay?"

"Yeah, I think so, but you may want to call her."

Amy's interview

AMY WAS PRETTY QUIET on Wednesday before leaving for her interview in Boulder the following day. Justin made sure to wish her luck, but decided against initiating any other kind of conversation until she got back. He didn't want to upset her or risk getting into another confrontation.

The next two *Amy-free* days were glorious for Justin. For the first time since he had become manager, the intra-office stress and tension that had permeated the place was absent.

It was Friday afternoon when Justin noticed he had an e-mail from Christal. She had not called him back in a few days and he was very concerned.

To: jobrien@datadump.com
From: cdeeds@datadump.com
Subject: Medical complications

Justin,

Thank you for your patience. I've had some medical complications come up and am briefly back in the hospital. At least my laptop is reliable, unlike my body these days.

I apologize for not calling you back and am not sure of my availability in the next couple of weeks. Hang in there and know that I'm thinking of you.

I understand that you have a departmental team-building coming up and that Cynthia has arranged coaching for you with Dr. Mac. It all sounds good to me. I will set you up with some management classes as well once I get back to the office. Again, sorry I'm not there for you.

Christal

Justin leaned back in his chair. He felt awful for what Christal was having to go through. *She's really a trooper,* he thought.

The phone startled him.

"Justin, Claire. I need to talk to you."

Justin's relaxed disposition suddenly shifted to a defensive mode. "This doesn't sound good."

"No, it's really not. I hate to ruin your upcoming weekend but we just completed our interview with Amy."

"And?"

"Man, what's up with her? She blasted you over and over again. It was weird at first but quickly got uncomfortable."

"You're kidding me!"

"No. Finally Katie, of all people, told her that she didn't appreciate it. It had become more of a gripe session than an interview. I don't know about you, but I've always been taught to never put down your own boss, especially in an interview!"

"That's common sense, isn't it?"

"I thought so. Anyway, it was pretty unanimous that we don't want her here. You can have her back."

"Oh, great. Did you tell her that?"

"I didn't have to. At the end of the interview Amy apologized for her anger and admitted that she was not in a good place right now to be interviewing."

"Really?"

"Yeah. We've all been there Justin! In fact, if she would have been as authentic during the interview as she was after the interview, we probably would have offered her the job."

"So was that it?"

"No. We all went out for drinks afterwards."

"You're kidding me!"

"No, we really like her. She's just not in a good place right now, just as she said."

Justin shook his head. "I've got to move out to Boulder. You guys really know how to have fun, regardless of the circumstances."

"You can always count on us for that, Justin."

"Thanks, Claire."

"Have a good weekend, boss."

Thinking things through

CLAIRE'S NEWS ABOUT AMY was disconcerting to Justin in many respects. For starters, Amy's attitude was already problematic for him; this latest rejection was sure to only make it worse. Secondly, she'd be working right next to Colleen, the woman she didn't choose for the Winnetka position and who didn't choose her for the Boulder position. *So much for my life getting any easier,* he thought to himself.

It was after five and everyone had gone home for the weekend—that is, except Justin. He was still in his office, pacing around while trying to come up with a plan or a strategy for dealing with Amy. Finally he stopped dead in his tracks, sat down, and pulled out his journal. He had an idea, and began writing down his immediate concerns.

> What's bugging me?
> 1. I'm concerned that Amy will come back with even greater animosity and will continue to make things difficult for me, not to mention the rest of the staff.

2. I'm concerned that Colleen will be impacted by Amy's negativity and regret taking the job.

Justin put his pen down and thought about each scenario. He then began flipping through his list of insights and pulled out the ones that offered him some guidance. Then he carefully wrote down how they could be applied to his present situation. They included:

Journal Entry # 1

c) It's always a good idea to think through both the process and what outcomes I'm looking for before confronting another employee. And that includes trying to view the concern from their perspective as well.

My initial thought: That is essentially what I'm doing now via this process. I must remember that Amy has a perspective that I need to consider as well.

Journal Entry # 4

a) It takes a lot of work to turn a "strained" relationship into a "supportive" relationship, but it certainly is worth the effort.

My initial thought: I need to make sure I've tried to salvage this working relationship before getting heavy-handed.

Journal Entry # 6

a) Supervision is about action. I cannot manage people by doing nothing.

My initial thought: I need to take action immediately instead of letting things simmer.

Journal Entry # 7

a) Sometimes asking the right question is a better intervention than trying to provide the right answer.

<u>My initial thought:</u> I need to ask questions with the intent of understanding her perspective before addressing my own concerns. Something has been up with her and I have no idea of what it really is.

Journal Entry # 8

b) Standing up for yourself and what you believe in is invigorating!

<u>My initial thought:</u> Ultimately, I'm captain of this ship, not Amy. I'll certainly work with her to get back on track but I need her to either get on board or get off the ship.

Journal Entry # 9

b) Don't wait for relationship problems to escalate before addressing them. This is especially true for the people that really matter to me.

<u>My initial thought:</u> Again, I need to move on this Monday morning.

Justin was already beginning to feel better. Reviewing his previous insights from his journal proved to be extremely useful in helping him think through what he needed to do in working with Amy. Now all he had left to do was to go back to his original two questions and create a couple of action steps for each before going home.

And then it hit him like a ton of bricks—he had forgotten about the time. Here it was after seven o'clock on a Friday evening and he had never called Megan to tell her where he was and when he'd be home. *Oops, I'm in big trouble,* he groaned. He called home.

"Where are you?" asked Megan, concerned that something had happened.

"Honey, the good news is that I'm working through an issue here at the office so that I can come home and not have to think about it over the weekend. The bad news is that I need another forty-five minutes or so."

"Justin, its Friday night! This has got to stop."

"Honey, can we talk about this at home? Arguing now will only prolong when I can get out of here. Give me forty-five minutes and I'll be on my way. Do you want me to pick up dinner on the way home?"

"Only if you're getting it for yourself," said Megan with a pinch of anger in her voice. "We've already eaten."

"Of course you have; it's late. Sorry. See you within the hour, I promise."

Justin knew he was in trouble with Megan, but he wasn't going to quit working until he laid out some action steps. Megan would just have to understand.

He went back to his two initial concerns.

> What's bugging me?
> 1. I'm concerned that Amy will come back with even greater animosity and will continue to make things difficult for me, not to mention the rest of the staff.
>
> Action: I will take Amy to coffee on Monday morning and use the Boulder interview as a way to get her to talk to me about what's really going on. Perhaps I can help her in some way. If it does come down to her concern with me as her manager, I'll ask her if she can find a way to work with me. If

she can't, then together we'll discuss her options. The most important thing is for me to focus on listening first and trying to understand what's going on with her. The second most important thing is for her to know that I want her here and am willing to do what I can to keep her here. And, should I get pushed into a corner, I need to be prepared to tell her that her attitude is unacceptable and will be addressed, if it continues, through the disciplinary process if necessary. Hopefully it won't come down to that.

2. I'm concerned that Colleen will be impacted by Amy's negativity and regret taking the job.

Action: I still have a week to resolve this with Amy before Colleen gets here. If Amy ends up still being a problem when Colleen arrives, I'll have to bring in Cynthia and Christal before committing to any specific action. I can only hope I don't have to go there. It's time for both Cynthia and Christal to see that I am capable of resolving my own issues, once and for all.

Justin jumped up and closed his journal. He was finally feeling back in control of his situation with Amy, and more importantly, he had done it on his own. *Now if I can only be as successful with Megan,* he thought to himself as he headed home.

66 Date night

MEGAN STRUGGLED WITH THIS ONE. As she told Tanya, Justin's promotion had brought out a passionate side of him that even he didn't know he had. That certainly was the upside. The downside was the added time his new position required. At first it was just an annoyance, but now it was starting to become problematic. For the first time since he'd accepted the job, Megan began wondering if it may have been a mistake after all.

"Honey, you don't like when I've got my game face on during the weekends," began Justin right after walking in the door, "but look at my face right now, what do you see?"

"I see a man that is overworked and who neglects his family."

"Funny. Point made."

Megan wasn't trying to be funny. "You know I would only be half as mad if you had the consideration to call and let me know that you were going to be coming home late."

"I did call you."

"No, you forgot to call and then suddenly realized at seven o'clock in the evening that you hadn't called. That doesn't count."

"Megan, I'm not going to argue with you. It was inconsiderate of me. I got so engrossed in solving a particular problem that I lost all sense of time and place. Guilty as charged."

"Is that another technique Dr. Mac taught you?"

"What are you talking about?"

"It's not like you to give in so easily. Don't think that's going to make me less angry!"

"This has nothing to do with Dr. Mac. I screwed up and I'm sorry."

Megan could hear the kids coming up from the basement and instantly worked them into her argument. "It's not just me, Justin. The kids were looking forward to spending time with you as well. You've also got them to answer to."

Tommy ran right up to Justin for his customary bear hug. Michelle, however, seemed to be holding back. "Daddy, where have you been?"

"Kids, daddy is so sorry. I was bad. I was working at the office and lost track of time."

"Can we go to the park tomorrow?" asked Tommy.

"Of course we can, tiger."

"Daddy, I wanted to practice throwing the football with you. You know I'm playing quarterback tomorrow," cried Michelle.

"I've got it," announced Justin, "why don't we throw the ball around tomorrow morning before the game instead. That way your arm will be warmed up."

Michelle smiled. That seemed sufficient to satisfy her.

Megan was shaking her head at how forgiving the kids were. "Don't think you can buy me off that easily, my dear."

Justin was all smiles as he turned back toward Michelle. "Honey, you know I wouldn't miss practicing with you on purpose for all the tea in China."

"Daddy, what's tea in China?" asked Tommy.

Justin laughed. "I'm guessing there's a lot of tea there...I don't know, ask your mother."

"Kids," interrupted Megan, "mommy and daddy are still talking. Why don't you go downstairs and play and we'll be down in a few minutes. Okay?"

Tommy bolted out of the room while Michelle reluctantly stayed behind.

"Michelle, that means you, too," said Megan.

"Can't I stay?"

"Honey," jumped in Justin, "the sooner we can finish our talk, the more time we can have together before your bedtime."

"Okay, daddy."

Justin smiled at Megan. "She's old enough now where giving her the reasoning seems to help."

That comment struck a nerve with Megan. "Justin, are you implying I don't do that?"

"No, I was acknowledging what just worked with her, that's all."

"Honey, you may be becoming an expert in management, but don't be so quick to ordain yourself an expert in raising kids."

"What are you saying?" asked Justin.

"I'm saying spend time with the kids first before philosophizing to me on how to talk to them."

"Whoa! Hold on," cried Justin. "You certainly have a right to be upset because I forgot to call you tonight, but don't take potshots at me."

"Then stop telling me how to talk to my own kids."

"I'm not!"

An uncomfortable pause followed before Justin spoke. "Megan, why are you really mad at me?"

"You mean besides forgetting to call or the fact that you have now become Dr. Spock and are telling me how to raise my children?"

"That's exactly what I'm asking. What's behind all of this?"

Tears began to well up in Megan's eyes. Her demeanor softened. "Justin, you hurt *me* tonight, more than the kids. I'm the one who is feeling neglected."

"Thank you for saying that, Megan. That was what I needed to hear. All that other stuff is peripheral and just creates arguments." Justin put his arm around her. "I don't mean to neglect you, honey."

Megan put her head down in disappointment. "I'm sorry. I shouldn't have said anything."

"No, no, I'm glad you did," replied Justin. "I have been neglecting you." And then suddenly he had an idea. "Wait a minute, I have an idea. What if we reserved one night a week just for the two of us?"

Megan quickly brightened. "You mean like a date night?"

"Yeah, a date night. It will be our time together. Just the two of us."

"Alright, I suppose. But what about the kids?"

"Ah, I'm sure Tanya and Lamar will help up out. Are you in?"

Megan smiled for the first time that night. "As long as you promise to always call in the future when you're going to be late."

"I promise."

"Then you've got a date!"

Justin put his arms around Megan and the two embraced for a good long time before joining the kids in the basement. The weekend was suddenly looking better.

More Macology

THE RAIN PRETTY MUCH DOMINATED the weekend and put most of the planned activities on hold, including Michelle's football game. Yet despite the bad weather, it didn't dampen the spirits at the O'Brien household, especially between Justin and Megan. In fact, the only thing that would have made it a *perfect* weekend, at least as far as Justin was concerned, was a Bear's victory over the Redskins. But wishful thinking was one thing and a miracle quite another.

It was now Monday morning.

"So is today your big meeting with Amy?" asked Megan as she put the cereal out on the table for the kids.

"Yep, it should be an interesting day, to say the least," replied Justin. "The good news is that I get to end the day with Dr. Mac. I think I'm going to really need him after dealing with Amy."

"Amy…Amy. Is she the reason you stayed so long at work on Friday?"

"Yeah, pretty much. She's a tough cookie and I needed to be ready for today's meeting." And then Justin smiled at Megan. "Although you got to admit honey, I did a pretty good job not worrying about her the rest of the weekend."

Megan kissed him on top of his head as she walked by. "You were great, honey."

Justin was proud of himself for not thinking about work over the weekend. Unfortunately, all this talk about Amy this morning had gotten him worked up enough that he quickly pulled out the cheat sheet he'd made Friday at the office. On it were four key reminders that he wanted to be sure to focus on when meeting with Amy today.

Remember:
- Focus on understanding and asking questions.
- Look for areas of agreement.
- Do not respond emotionally, no matter what.
- Seek out a commitment to better the relationship.

After reviewing the list Justin was amazed at how *centered* he felt. It was also a confirmation that he had done the right thing by preparing on Friday for his meeting with Amy today. Granted he should have called Megan, but the fact that he took the time to prepare himself for today was significant. It was something he never would have done in the past. But of course that was before his transformation into management. He also would have never listened to anything but *Bear's Talk* as he drove into work each morning—yet that had changed as well. Now he was regularly taking the longer route to work just so he could listen to *Macology in the Mornings*. And today would be no different. The show was already in progress as he headed down Wilson Street.

"Hey, Dr. Mac, why didn't you come in to the station this morning? Is it because of Jay's body odor?"

"Bobbie, the truth is I'm a little under the weather and didn't want to pass my germs on to either of you."

"Not to worry Dr. Mac," retorted Jay, "I believe Bobbie already has every germ imaginable."

"Now boys, don't make me come down there," joked Dr. Mac. "Should we take our next caller?"

"Right you are," replied Bobbie. "Listeners, it's *Macology in the Mornings* and we have Dr. Mac via remote.

Go ahead, caller."

"Yes, hello, my name is Jeanine. I hope you feel better, Dr. Mac."

"Thank you, Jeanine. How can I help you?"

"My question has to do with virtual teams. You see, I'm on a virtual team but have never met my other team members in person. We're pretty spread out around the world. Anyway, there are some communication issues evolving between a few team members and no one is sure what to do. When we brought it to our supervisor, he said that we needed to try to resolve it amongst ourselves first."

"And you don't know how to resolve it or where to start?"

"Correct. I mean, I really don't know these people, so I don't think I want to rock the boat, if you know what I mean."

"Jeanine, your scenario is fairly common," began Dr. Mac. "It sounds like you have a supervisor who is slightly removed from the group and your day-to-day activities."

"That would be putting it mildly," replied Jeanine.

"Then would you also agree that you have a virtual team whose focus is around getting the task done without much thought given to *how* the task gets done."

"That would be us."

"So what your team needs," summarized Dr. Mac, "is more leadership, direction, working norms, performance expectations, defined roles and responsibilities, and a better sense of knowing each other."

"Is it that obvious?" asked Jeanine.

"I'm afraid so, Jeanine."

"And your solution?"

"Ah, where to begin," replied Dr. Mac. "Let me address this from a virtual team perspective right now. We can talk about how to *manage up* with your supervisor on another occasion.

"Virtual teams work best when members have the opportunity to meet in person at the onset of their formation. Unfortunately, these face-to-face meetings are viewed as fringe benefits and often end up getting neglected. When that occurs, the team leader has the heightened responsibility to provide team members with the necessary leadership, guidance, direction, and communication deemed essential for the team to work effectively together. This ultimately creates a greater dependence on the leader and leads to a propensity for the members to become more of a virtual *work group* than an actual team. Add to that dynamic a leader who lacks the interpersonal skills to truly lead effectively, and you've got a potential disaster on your hands. Sound familiar, Jeanine?"

"Unfortunately it does."

"What I'm about to tell you, Jeanine, is more of a quick-fix solution for now. Given your situation, I'd suggest the following course of action. Set aside some time either at a meeting or one-on-one to do a team assessment. Ask team members to identify the following: First, what are the strengths of the team in working together? Second, what does the team need to be better at in working together? Third, what does the team need to do to improve? And fourth, what does the team need *more of* and *less of* from the supervisor in order to improve? Then tabulate the results and discuss the results as a team at another virtual team meeting and make sure your supervisor is a part of that meeting."

"Thank you, Dr. Mac. I know it doesn't solve the bigger problem, but I think it will get us moving in the right direction."

Justin was all smiles as he pulled into DataDump's parking lot. The process Dr. Mac suggested to the caller was very similar to the process he had used with the Boulder office. *Great minds think alike*, he mused. But his smile quickly vanished as he realized that Dr. Mac wasn't feeling well and probably would cancel their session today.

Once in his office, he noticed that his phone was blinking. *I bet it's Dr. Mac*, he thought as he retrieved the message.

"Justin, this is Amy. I have a week's worth of vacation time left and have decided to use it this week. I need the time to sort out a few things. I'll be in next Monday."

Justin sank down into his chair. In one sense he was relieved that he had gotten out of talking with Amy, but in another sense he was disappointed that he'd have to wait another week before talking to her. What's more, Amy would be coming back on the same day that Colleen was starting her new job. And, as if that weren't enough, their teambuilding session with Walt was at the beginning of next week. It was the exact scenario that he was hoping to avoid.

Frustrated Fran

J USTIN HAD TO RUN FROM the outer office to catch his phone. "O'Brien," said the hoarse voice on the phone, "Dr. Mac here. I'm a bit under the weather today and Daisy won't let me out of the house. Are you okay if we resume next Monday?"

Somewhat expecting the call, Justin tried to conceal his disappointment. "Sure, no problem. I heard you on the radio this morning and knew you weren't feeling too well."

"I'm sure it's just a cold or something. Should be fine by next week."

"Actually that's going to work out perfectly. I've got another disgruntled employee that I have to deal with on Monday and could use more of your advice."

"There's a lot of that going around. Check out today's column if you want to read a slightly different perspective on that. Got to go; the wife's calling. If you need me before then, you know how to reach me, Desperate Dave."

Justin smiled as he hung up the phone. Having Dr. Mac in his life was the best insurance policy a manager could ask for. Yet despite how fortunate he felt, he wasn't sure if it was better to keep his relationship under wraps or to openly boast about it. Was it cool to have a management coach or was it a sign of weakness? And would it make a difference that it was the popular Dr. Mac? Only time would tell which was the better position to take.

A few hours later in the day Justin took a break and headed over to Stella's. He wanted to look at the newspaper and see the letter Dr. Mac was referring to. Perhaps there'd be some new pointers he could use.

"Where you headed?" asked Charlie as Justin walked toward the door.

"It depends who wants to know," joked Justin.

"Well, it's my turn to watch you, so I guess it's me."

Justin laughed. It was nice to be back on joking terms with Charlie.

"I'm getting some coffee. Want to come?"

"Sure, I'm just pretending to work anyway," smiled Charlie, and then he whispered, "I've got something I think you'll want to see. I'll bring it along."

Justin watched him pull out the Daily newspaper. *Could it be the letter Dr. Mac had mentioned?* he wondered.

Once out the door Charlie pointed to the newspaper. "There's a letter to Dr. Mac that sounds like it may have come from this office."

"Really?"

"Let's just say it wouldn't surprise me."

"From whom?" asked Justin, now anxious to read it.

"Who do you think?"

"Amy?"

"That would be my guess."

"Why would Amy write to Dr. Mac? I didn't have the impression she cared at all."

"Don't know."

As they walked into Stella's, Justin grabbed the newspaper from Charlie. "Will you get me a hazelnut latte? I've got to see this."

"Sure thing, J-Man," smiled Charlie.

Justin immediately opened the paper to the *Ask Dr. Mac* column. Although there were three letters, it was pretty easy to spot the one in question.

Dear Dr. Mac,

You've talked a lot in your column about how to deal with an employee with a bad attitude. How about addressing what to do with an incompetent supervisor with a bad attitude?

My supervisor has been picking on different employees since being promoted and is now after me. He is unprofessional, lacks management skills, and frequently shoots his mouth off without thinking. Needless to say, not a good combination for someone who is supposed to lead a department.

The problem, as you can imagine, is that it puts the employees, namely me, in a very compromising position. Do I grin and bear it until he moves on to someone else or do I make a stink and risk losing my job? A fellow employee fought it and ended up in a closed door meeting with the company brass, probably getting his last rites read to him.

I don't want to quit, but I don't like the other options either. Need some advice.

Sincerely,
Frustrated Fran

Shaking his head in disbelief, Justin put down the paper just as Charlie brought over the two coffees. "I don't believe it!" he cried. "Why couldn't she come talk to me instead of resorting to this?"

Of course Justin knew full well that his last comment was a contradiction, given that he had written Dr. Mac on two occasions himself.

"I was surprised myself," said Charlie. "But there is one weird thing about the letter."

"What's that?"

"Correct me if I'm wrong, but it sounds like she doesn't want to leave."

Justin took a long look at Charlie. "You know something, you may be right. It's a cry for help more than anything."

"So what are you going to do?" asked Charlie.

"I don't know. What do you think I should do?"

"Hmm. Well, you don't know for sure if it was Amy who wrote this."

"Oh come on! Frustrated Fran! She didn't even try to throw us off." Then Justin panicked. "What if J.W. or Melvin see this? I've already got two strikes against me."

"Oh, please," reassured Charlie, "what do you mean two strikes? They've done nothing but support you."

"If you only knew, Charlie. There were several times I thought I was about to get fired."

"Well, I hope you know that I'm not after your job."

"That's only because Christal has bigger plans for you."

"That's still to be seen. Nevertheless, what are you going to do?"

"I don't know. She's gone all week and we have Colleen starting on Monday. In fact, most of my time on Monday will be in meetings. Oh, and I almost forgot, we have the department teambuilding with Walt on Tuesday. I'm afraid my hands are tied until then."

"Is there anything I can do for you, J-Man? I'm here if you need me."

"Probably not, but thanks, Chas. Oh wait! I never read what Dr. Mac said back to her. Give me that newspaper."

Charlie got up and tossed the paper at Justin. "Here you go. I've got to go make some client calls—especially now that you are tracking our client activity. When did you get so mean?"

"Just don't get on my bad side," snarled Justin as he whacked Charlie with the newspaper.

Charlie turned toward Justin before walking out. "Been there, done that!"

Justin shrugged. "Oh yeah, I forgot about that." He then opened up the paper again and carefully read Dr. Mac's response to Frustrated Fran.

> *Dear Frustrated Fran,*
>
> *The good news is that you do have options, as you mentioned. You could grin and bear it and hope that you'll eventually be left alone. You could complain to human resources or to your supervisor's supervisor and take your chances there. You could also seek out another job either within the company or elsewhere. But what I never heard in your letter was any consideration to talking directly to your supervisor. Sometimes we forget that direct communication is our best strategy, even though it is often perceived as the most difficult. In this case, you do have an obligation to talk with your supervisor before considering your other options. Anything else would be unfair to him, to you, and to your coworkers.*
>
> *Allow me to expound a bit. First, your supervisor needs the feedback. Granted, in a perfect world he would either ask for feedback or at the very least be able to read the signs that he's not being effective. But since that is apparently not happening, you need to fill in that void. Second, you are asserting yourself and asking for what you need. Third, you are role modeling*

effective communication to your coworkers. Fourth, you are helping your supervisor by participating in making him better at what he does. Fifth, you are demonstrating the behavior that you would expect in others, which is to address problems directly and in a safe and constructive way. And lastly, you would be developing the fine art of managing up. *Managing up is the ability to help your supervisor be more effective by making suggestions for him to improve that benefit not only him but the department as well. Hence, it's important in managing up to make sure that you emphasize the benefits to him and to the department when making your suggestion and/or request. Here is an example of a managing up suggestion:*

> *"Bob, it would be real helpful to me if you could spell out your expectations on the deliverables for this project. That way I could move forward on my own and wouldn't have to keep bugging you all the time. Is that something you could do?"*

In this example, Bob was not criticized for being vague or over-controlling. Instead the employee bypassed all of that anger and frustration and went right to what he/she ultimately needed most, which was for Bob to spell out his expectations. Bob hopefully will see this request as a win-win since it will make the employee more productive and provide him with more uninterrupted time. Although I may have simplified this too much, it gives you an example of how to manage up.

—Dr. Mac

Justin put down the paper and thought for a moment. *On one hand, Dr. Mac's advice was helpful in the sense that it encourages employees, namely Amy, to come talk to their supervisor directly with their concerns. Yet on the other hand, what if this advice is directed at me personally as her supervisor? Am I in fact incompetent? Am I picking on employees? Or is it in fact simply a cry for help on Amy's part?*

Either way, his stomach was feeling a bit queasy—and he knew it wasn't from the coffee.

In preparation for the teambuilding

THE REMAINDER OF THE WEEK went great. The staff was back to laughing and playing practical jokes on each other and Justin was finally able to focus on his own projects that had been put on hold ever since he'd been promoted. And to top it off, the department also received some great news from Christal. Not only was she back at her mother's home again and feeling better, but she passed on the latest customer survey reports which revealed that the Orders Fulfillment Department had received the highest customer ratings within the whole company. Yet, despite all the good things that were happening around him, Justin wasn't quite ready to celebrate. He was still bothered by Amy's letter to Dr. Mac and was having trouble letting it go.

The good news, he thought, *is that no one outside of Charlie has mentioned the letter. The bad news is that Amy was willing to take this issue public.* Why, just the thought of Melvin seeing the column made Justin cringe. *The last thing I need is any kind of public humiliation that could reflect negatively on the company.*

Justin spent the better part of Friday thinking through this dilemma before coming to the following conclusions. *First, I need to be mindful of not making any assumptions about Amy. It's possible that she didn't write the letter. I have to give her the benefit of the doubt, no matter what. Secondly, managing up is essentially talking to your manager about what you need but in a way that they can hear it. I want to know what my employees need from me. It's okay if they manage up. I want to know. Better yet, why even put them in that position. I need to just come out and ask them what they need from me, just as I did with the Boulder group.*

The more he thought about it the more he realized that their upcoming teambuilding could be the exact place in which to have this discussion. After all, his relationship with his staff as a whole was much better than it had been only a few weeks ago. Aside from Amy, he felt the rest of the staff could have a productive conversation about how they worked together and how he could best serve them. In actuality, it was the perfect time for this discussion.

Justin picked up the phone and called Walt, the teambuilding guru that they would be working with on Tuesday. He needed to make sure that they were on the same page.

"May I talk with Walt, please?"

"This is Walt."

"Hello, Justin here from DataDump."

"Hello Justin. I was about to call you."

"Great. I just wanted to touch base on our teambuilding next week."

"Me too."

"Walt, what exactly do you plan to do with us?"

"Thank you for asking, Justin. It's important that the teambuilding serves a purpose and meets the needs of your group. Let me begin with you. What outcomes would you like to see?"

Justin thought a moment. "Well, I want to integrate Colleen, our new employee, into the group for starters."

"Okay, what else?"

"I want to have fun and continue to improve upon our working relationships."

"That's great. Anything else?"

"Yes, I want to have the opportunity to solicit feedback from the group on how I can best serve them."

"Super. I wish more supervisors had that perspective."

"And I want to make sure we are all on the same page regarding my expectations around work functions."

"You've got it. In fact, why don't you start off the session by explaining why we are doing the teambuilding and what your expectations are from it? From there I'll take it and provide avenues for meaningful discussions, activities, and certainly some fun. How does that sound?"

"I like it. Oh, and one more question. Should I hang back a bit in the session? I don't want to inhibit comments from the staff."

"Absolutely not. You need to fully engage yourself. When supervisors back off, it sends the message that the teambuilding is more about their group and not necessarily them. Not a dynamic you want to get into, believe me."

By the time they hung up, Justin noticed that he felt much better. He liked it when there was a plan in place.

Not again!

IT WAS ANOTHER GREAT WEEKEND at the O'Brien household, full of family, fun, and, of course, football. But as had been the case lately, it didn't last long enough for Justin. Monday morning was already here and he had one thing on his mind—Amy. In fact, it was the second Monday in a row where Justin found himself thinking about her as he drove in to work. She was the one remaining wild card left on his staff and he wasn't sure what to expect from her. But what worried him even more was the fact that it was Colleen's first day. The same Colleen that Amy didn't want to hire and the same Colleen who didn't want to hire Amy. *This could get very ugly,* he thought to himself as he flipped on *Macology in the Mornings.*

"Yes, good morning Dr. Mac. My name is Linda and I have a question."

"Good morning to you, Linda; ask away."

Justin was relieved to hear Dr. Mac's voice sounding so chipper. Clearly, he must be feeling better.

"Well, I'm the volunteer coordinator at my organization, and my job is to oversee the volunteers and to coordinate their assignments. A couple of days ago one of our younger volunteers, maybe eighteen or so, came in with a very noticeable nose ring plus a rather large tattoo on the back of her neck. Now, don't get me wrong, I don't mind...."

Suddenly Justin could feel his hands perspiring and his heart beating faster and faster. Something was not right. This caller was beginning to sound very familiar—like the caller who called that very same day when he had first called the show. *Could it be they are repeating a previous show? Could it be they are repeating the show that I called in?*

No sooner had the realization hit him when he heard Jay say, "Dr. Mac, we've got a caller who wants your advice on whether or not he should take a promotion. Personally, I don't know why you'd ever turn one down."

"That's because you've never been promoted," joked Bobbie, the other host of the show. "Go ahead, sir!"

"Noooooooooo!" cried Justin from his car. "Not again!"

And then he heard his own voice come over the airwaves. "Ah...well...yes, I just wanted to know your thoughts on when it is a good idea to take a promotion."

"And your name is?"

"Just...um, just Paul."

"Okay "Just Paul," tell me a little more about your situation."

Justin shut off the radio. Sweat was coming down from his brow. *Why a rerun? Why this show of all shows! Now I have to cover it up all over again. This was not how I wanted to start my day!*

The moment Justin reached the front doors of DataDump, he quickly bolted for his office, making sure to avoid all eye contact with anyone coming his way. He could only hope that no one was listening to the program. He especially didn't want to have to lie about it again.

"Justin!"

Oh no! he thought as he looked up. To his surprise it was Colleen, who was waiting in his office for him.

"Oh hi, Colleen. Welcome!"

"Did I startle you?"

"More than you'll ever know," replied Justin, checking to see if anyone else was watching him.

As they exchanged a quick hug, Colleen pointed to her cubicle. "Did you decorate my cubicle, Justin?"

Equally surprised to see her cubicle decorated, Justin replied, "Let's just say it's our way of saying welcome." Just then he spotted Lee Ann winking at him from across the room. "But if you need to thank anyone," continued Justin, having solved the mystery, "it would be Lee Ann."

Colleen moved closer to him and whispered so only he could hear. "Is Amy okay with what happened in Boulder? I hope she's not mad at me."

"Oh, I wouldn't worry about it. I'm sure she's okay." replied Justin, willing to give Amy the benefit of the doubt.

As it turned out, Justin's hunch was correct. Amy seemed fine with Colleen, and even made a point to chat with her throughout the day. Unfortunately, the same could not be said for how she responded to him. If anything, she went out of her way to avoid him, making it very difficult for Justin to have his conversation with her. Finally, by mid-afternoon, Justin was able to corner her by the copy machine.

"Amy, how did your interview go?"

"You tell me, Justin. I'm sure you've already talked with Claire."

"You're right, I did talk briefly with Claire. But I think it would be important for us to talk. Can you join me for a cup of coffee at Stella's?"

"I'm really busy, Justin. I'll stop by your office in five minutes and we can talk then. But I really don't have much time to spare."

"I'll take what I can get, Amy. See you in five."

Justin was a little surprised by Amy's unwillingness to talk to him given that Dr. Mac had advised her in his column to come talk to him directly.

John approached him as he headed toward his office. "Justin, can I talk with you?"

"John, I don't have time to talk right now. Can it wait until tomorrow?"

"I guess so," said John, looking a little dejected.

Amy was only seconds behind as she walked into his office and immediately sat down. "What did you want to talk about?"

"Is everything okay, Amy?"

"I don't know what that means, Justin. Is what okay?"

Amy wasn't going to make this easy for him. He tried a different approach. "Amy, did I do something to you?"

"Not at all. Why?"

"It just seems like you've been unhappy here ever since I became manager. Would that be an accurate statement?"

Amy rolled her eyes. "Justin, Charlie should have been our manager, not you. I'm sorry but I don't agree with Christal's decision."

"Charlie's fine with it now, why can't you be?"

"In the first place, I'm not Charlie. And secondly, I don't believe that the manager's job should be a training ground for inexperienced managers."

"You're referring to the meeting when Colleen was selected over Sara, aren't you?"

"I'm referring to the meeting where you picked Colleen over Sara. But that's just the tip of the iceberg Justin. Is there anything else you wanted to talk about?"

Justin looked at his watch. It was almost three o'clock, and he was about to be late for his session with Dr. Mac. "No, that's it for now."

Amy's energy was noticeably low as she walked out of his office.

"Amy," cried out Justin. "Are you sure you're okay?"

"I'm fine, Justin."

Justin sped out the door and was at the park by 3:05 p.m. As he hustled to the bench, worried about keeping Dr. Mac waiting, he noticed that it was still unoccupied. *That's odd,* he thought to himself as he sat down, *Dr. Mac is never late.* He then remembered that *Macology in the Mornings* was a rerun. *Could it mean Dr. Mac was still ill?*

Justin looked down the walkway to the left and then to the right but saw no one. It wasn't until he looked straight ahead across the park that he thought he spotted someone. As the figure came slowly into focus, Justin could tell it was a little old man with a cane walking toward him. By the time the man got close enough, it was obvious that it was indeed Dr. Mac.

"O'Brien, sorry I'm late. Been waiting long?"

"No, Dr. Mac, I'm just glad you're here. I thought maybe you were still sick." Justin then looked at the cane. What happened?"

"My back's been giving me problems. Walking with a cane actually helps ease the pain."

"Have you seen a doctor?"

"You're sounding like Daisy now. I'll be fine."

Justin was truly concerned, but didn't want to push it. In many respects, Dr. Mac was like a father to him and he was beginning to feel more and more protective toward him.

"So, what's going on?" asked Dr. Mac.

"Well, I did read the letter from your column that you had suggested."

"And?"

"And, to be perfectly honest with you, I think one of my staff members may have written it about me."

"Why would you say that?"

"Because I have another disgruntled employee who is pretty upset with me."

"Tell me why, but from their perspective."

"What do you mean?"

"If this disgruntled employee was sitting here, what would he or she say your problem was?"

"You read her letter; just insert my name wherever you see the word 'jerk'!"

"Is that you or the anger talking?" asked Dr. Mac.

"Probably the anger." Justin took a deep breath to regain his composure. "I think she would say that I'm picking on her and that I'm incompetent. Essentially everything she said in the letter."

"How do you know it was a 'she' who wrote the letter?"

"I don't know for sure, but come on, *Frustrated Fran?* Call it a hunch?"

"People always use creative aliases—right, 'Desperate Dave'?"

"I can tell you this, Dr. Mac, I certainly don't have a bad attitude."

"Who said you did?"

"The letter started off by saying *I was...*I mean *the supervisor* was incompetent and had a bad attitude."

"And?"

"Well, sure, I may have stuck my foot in my mouth a couple of times, but I apologized. Truth is, she's never been supportive of me since I became the manager."

"O'Brien, it really doesn't matter whether or not this 'she' that you keep referring to wrote the letter. The fact is, you've got a problem with one of your employees that needs to be corrected, right?"

"Right. But you told her...I mean you told that person to go talk to their supervisor directly. I think you used the term, *managing up.* Well, she avoided me completely today, so I'm not sure she got the message."

"Again, let go of the letter."

"Oops. Sorry. So what do I do?"

"What do you think you should do?"

Justin smiled. "Why did I know you were going to say that?" He then pulled out his journal and opened to the page where he had addressed that very question. "Here's what I tried to do," and began reading.

> I will take Amy to coffee on Monday morning and try to get her to talk to me about what's really going on. Perhaps I can help her in some way. If it does come down to her concern with me as her manager, I'll ask her if she can find a way to work with me. If she can't, then together we'll discuss her options. The most important thing is for me to focus on listening first and trying to understand what's going on with her. The second most important thing is for her to know that I want her here and am willing to do what I can to keep her here. And, if I get pushed into a corner, I need to be prepared to tell her that a bad attitude is unacceptable and will be dealt with through the disciplinary process if necessary. Hopefully it won't come down to that.

Dr Mac smiled. "You didn't read that to her, did you?"

"No, of course not. But since I had it already written down, I figured it would be easier to read."

"I'm just teasing you. I like it. You sound like me when I was younger."

"Dr. Mac, I hope I turn out like you when I'm older as well... not that you are old or anything." Justin's face was turning red.

"Quit while you're ahead, O'Brien."

They both laughed.

"But it didn't exactly work out like I had planned," said Justin, returning to the subject.

"What happened, son?" asked Dr. Mac, realizing Justin was struggling with this.

"Instead of opening up to me, she loaded both barrels and pulled the trigger."

"And this upset you."

"Yeah. It was everything I didn't want to hear."

Dr. Mac put his arm around Justin. "I'm sorry."

"Thanks. I just wish that there was a different chemistry between us."

"O'Brien, my advice would be to let it go. By that I mean to stay supportive and trust that she'll come to you in time. Your conversation today is paving the way for future talks, even if it doesn't feel good right now."

"You're right as usual."

"It's not about being right."

"Okay, okay. But I do have one more question for you."

"Make it quick. Daisy's waiting in the car for me. She drove me here."

"She drove you here?"

"Yep. See that blue car over there? That's Daisy sitting inside. Wave to her."

Justin waved and, sure enough, got a wave back. "How come...oh never mind. It's none of my business."

"You want to know why Daisy has to drive me around?"

"Well, yes."

"My doctor doesn't think I should be driving, and asked me to stop. I have to tell you, it is the worst thing to have to come to terms with. You have no idea how much we count on our cars. I've never felt so restricted in my life." Dr. Mac could only shake his head in disappointment before changing the topic. "But that's about me, and we are here for you. What was your question?"

Justin knew there had to be more to that story, but didn't want to keep Dr. Mac. "Okay, real quick. How do I know when to make decisions on my own versus when to seek out consensus from my staff? I upset some of my staff when I overturned a decision they had made because I didn't agree with it."

"That's not good."

"So I've learned. Hence the question."

"Let me ask you this. Was it a decision that impacted your staff?"

"Yes."

"Was getting their buy-in important in carrying out whatever the decision was?"

"Yes."

"Then I'd say you blew it."

"That's insightful!"

"You asked! O'Brien, your mistake was not identifying the decision-making process up front to your staff. My guess is that you didn't know to do that. Now you do. But here's something that might help in the future. There's consensus and then there's *consensus with qualification*. Consensus means talking out a decision until everyone can support a given conclusion or solution. Consensus with qualification means that the manager will make a decision if the group cannot reach consensus within a given time period. The important thing here is to make sure everyone understands what will happen if a decision cannot be reached through consensus. The best part of this whole process is that—no matter what—you'll walk away with a decision."

Justin certainly saw the value in what Dr. Mac was saying but also realized that he had left out an important piece of the story. "That certainly will be helpful in the future. But as you were talking, I realized I forgot to mention my second mistake."

"Which was?"

"I didn't participate in the consensus discussion. I wasn't even there."

"You weren't there?"

"Nope. I showed up after they made their decision."

"I see. Well, so much for my lecture on consensus with qualification."

"I thought you'd better hear the whole story."

"O'Brien, do I need to ask you what you'd do differently should that opportunity arise again?"

"No, sir. As with everything else, I've learned the hard way how to keep this from happening in the future."

"Thank goodness for that," replied Dr. Mac as he got up from the bench. "Got to go; it takes a little longer to get around with this cane. See you next week, O'Brien."

As Dr. Mac hobbled away, Justin felt a sudden wave of sadness. Dr. Mac wasn't perfect after all. He was an elderly man whose health was starting to fail. What's worse, he realized that his mentor wasn't always going to be there for him.

Part Six

The Teambuilding Session

Too much energy

JUSTIN POPPED UP OUT OF BED. It was only four o'clock in the morning.

"Honey, what's going on?" asked Megan, still half asleep.

"Nothing, dear. Go back to sleep."

"Are you okay?"

"Yes, I'm fine. I'm just wide awake, that's all."

"What time is it?"

Justin looked over at the clock. "It's early."

"Alright dear, just don't wake the kids."

Before he could respond, Megan had dozed back off, snoring ever so softly. Smiling at how cute she looked, Justin gently kissed her on her forehead, got out of bed and headed downstairs.

His mind was racing. In just a few short hours he and his staff would be in their first teambuilding session together. Just thinking about it elicited two very different emotions. On one hand, he was excited about the possibilities that the day would bring. On the other hand, he was apprehensive about how the day would play out, especially with Amy. Yet despite the dual emotions, he knew that some kind of change would come as a result.

Justin paced around the kitchen for another ten minutes before deciding to go for a walk with Sandy. *I need to let go of some of this energy,* he thought, as he put on his walking gear. Minutes later he and Sandy were heading down Wilson Street. It was still pitch black out and pretty cold for a fall morning on the North Shore. Yet it was exactly what he needed.

The duo ended up going all the way down to the Village Green and back, but not before Justin stopped at the bench where he and Dr. Mac had their weekly meetings. Superstitious by nature, he touched the bench in hopes that some of Dr. Mac's magic would rub off on him for the day.

Back at the house, they were greeted by the smell of bacon, eggs, and hot coffee. Megan had gotten up and was cooking Justin's favorite breakfast. Realizing the significance of this day for Justin, she wanted to support him with a hearty breakfast.

"Wow! Honey, you are incredible!"

"Oh, please," replied Megan, "I was up anyway. How'd your walk go?"

"It was invigorating," replied Justin. "It was like we were the only ones left on the planet. We never saw a car, a person, or even a light go on in a house. It was eerie."

"Sure, I could see that," said Megan teasingly. "It's not too many people who decide to go for a walk at *four in the morning!* What'd you expect?"

"I don't know. I've never been up this early before."

"So where did you go?"

"We went to the park. I even sat on our bench for good luck."

"We have a bench?"

"No, not exactly. Dr. Mac and I have a bench."

"I see. You two have your own park bench now?"

"Well, sort of. It's where we sit for our sessions."

"Justin, you may not want to mention anything about the bench at your teambuilding session. Just a thought."

"Don't worry. It's between me, you, and Dr. Mac."

"Is he aware...oh never mind," laughed Megan, deciding to change the subject. "So what do you expect to happen today at your teambuilding?"

"I think, or at least hope, that we'll come together as a staff and have a lot of fun."

"Are you leading the teambuilding?"

"No, not at all. You see, that's the best part. This Walt guy is doing it. He's a professional team builder. All I have to do is participate. He's got the responsibility to orchestrate the day's activities."

"They have professional team builders? Is that something you go to school for?"

"Honey, I don't know. He does more than teambuilding. He's that guy who has people break boards in one of his programs. Do you know who I'm talking about? The Boulder staff all went through his program together."

Megan had never heard of this guy who breaks boards. "I'm not sure I see the connection. Did breaking the boards actually help?"

"I guess. But you're missing my point. I tried to lead the teambuilding in Boulder and it backfired on me. It actually would have been better had I participated instead of led that particular session, only I didn't know any better."

"I thought you said that went pretty well?"

"So I thought. Then Colleen tells me—"

"Is that your new employee?"

"Yes. Anyway, she tells me that it was all a front. They were all pretending that everything was okay."

"And you didn't know that?"

"How could I? I had to take everything at face value. I trusted that they were being truthful with me."

"So what does that have to do with today?"

"I'm getting to that. You see, it is very difficult to facilitate your own group's teambuilding when you are a part of the group dynamics yourself. I don't really think I saw myself as part of that group and thought there would be no problem leading their teambuilding. However, as I now know, I am a part of that group and probably would have been better off bringing in someone like Walt. Does any of this make sense?"

"Not really but I can see that it does to you."

"Actually, it's only now that I got that point. Boy, is this stuff interesting or what?"

"Well, regardless of what happens today, know that I'm proud of you and that I'll be thinking about you all day." With that, Megan gave Justin a big kiss and headed back up to bed. It was still too early to wake the kids up for school.

The teambuilding session

THE WINNETKA COMMUNITY HOUSE was on the corner of Lincoln and Pine. As Justin pulled up he could see someone out front setting up some boards on the lawn for some kind of activity. It had to be Walt.

"You must be Justin, hi. Looks like it's going to be a nice day today. I think we'll be able to do a couple activities outside."

"Great...I think," replied Justin apprehensively. "What are we going to do with those boards, build something?"

"Hey, that's a great idea. This place could use a new front entrance."

"Oh, okay, I see how this works. You're not going to tell me, are you?"

"And ruin the surprise?"

Justin shook his head. "I forgot, am I paying you for this?" he said jokingly.

Walt chuckled. "If not, I'm taking my boards and going home."

Justin liked being able to banter back and forth with Walt. It lightened the moment and even made him feel more relaxed. But what he especially liked about Walt was the air of confidence that he exuded. That, more than anything, made it easier for Justin to trust him and whatever plan he had for the day.

A few minutes later the staff began to trickle into the small conference room just off the front entrance to the Community House. Lee Ann was first to arrive, followed by Charlie and then Will. Colleen came a couple minutes later with her hair still wet.

"Sorry Justin, I overslept. It's the time change thingy."

"I'm just glad you're here," replied Justin.

John ran in just seconds before the eight-thirty starting time, grabbing one of the two remaining chairs.

Walt looked at the group. "Who are we missing?"

The group looked at each other before Lee Ann responded. "Amy's not here."

"Walt, why don't we go ahead and get started," suggested Justin, who was not about to let Amy dictate the start time of their session. "She should be here shortly."

Walt agreed and began by introducing himself. Then he called on Justin to share his reasons for initiating this team-building session.

"Thanks, Walt. I thought a teambuilding day would be beneficial for us for a few reasons. First, I wanted to continue improving on our working relationships with each other. Second, I want to make sure we integrate Colleen into the group. And finally, I wanted to make sure we're all on the same page regarding job responsibilities, expectations, and so on."

Everyone was nodding as Justin spoke.

"Would anyone like to add an outcome for today's session?" asked Walt.

Lee Ann raised her hand. "I particularly would like to have some fun today. We haven't done that very much and I think it's due."

Again everyone nodded.

"Anyone else?" asked Walt.

"I'd like to hear from Justin what his management philosophy is," said John. "I don't think anyone knows."

All eyes immediately turned to Justin, who looked surprised by the question. "I'd like to know, too. Do you know where I can get one?"

The group laughed.

"I think I saw the Cliff Notes at the bookstore," joked Will. More laughter.

As Colleen laughed she shouted, "Sweeeet!"

The room fell silent.

Colleen's face turned red. "Inside joke, never mind."

The group laughed again.

Even Walt jumped into the fray. "Wow, had I known you guys were going to be so much fun, I would have planned better activities."

By now the laughter became contagious, causing Will to accidentally fall off his chair. That triggered even more laughter. Charlie begged everyone to stop because his side was hurting so much.

And then suddenly it all stopped. It was as if someone had pulled the plug right out of the wall. The room was silent. All eyes turned to the figure in the doorway. It was Amy.

"Sounds like I missed something."

Walt was the first to welcome Amy and quickly caught her up to speed, while the rest of the group tried to regain their composure. He then asked Amy if she had any additional outcomes to add to the list.

"No, I don't," she said matter-of-factly.

"Then let's go out front for our first activity," said Walt, as he herded everyone outside and over to the boards that he had strategically placed on the ground in a "U" shape.

Once everyone was standing around the six-foot-long, four-inch-wide boards, as instructed, Walt explained the activity. "In order to achieve your objectives for today as a team, I want each of you to step up on the boards, one at a time, and provide a word that will represent how you, individually, need to be today in order to help this team achieve those outcomes."

Will was the first to jump up on the board. "My word is 'challenge.'"

"Will, tell me what that means within the context of how that will help you support this team today," asked Walt.

Will thought for a second before responding. "I tend to refrain from challenging the group and figured that that would be a way for me to help make our group better."

After Will, Charlie jumped up. "I'm going to steal Lee Ann's word, 'fun.'" I haven't been doing my part lately to maintain the fun and that's what I'd like to start doing."

Lee Ann stepped up next. "Since Charlie stole my word, I'm going to go with 'synergy'. I think we can be a pretty powerful group if we can learn to work together more effectively. I'd like to take that on."

Justin got up and shouted the word "student." "That's right, my goal for today is to be the student and learn how I can best serve each one of you."

The group cheered. "Nice one, Justin," acknowledged Walt.

Colleen got up on board next. "My word is 'connection.'" I'd like to connect with my new teammates today and let you all connect with me...or something like that."

The group laughed.

John looked over at Amy and got an approving nod to go next. "My word is 'respect.' I don't think we have enough respect for one another."

Walt intervened. "John, so how are you going to lead the charge today to create an environment of respect?"

"I don't know."

Lee Ann spoke up. "John, can I offer up a different word for you to consider?"

John welcomed the help. "Sure."

"How about 'assertiveness'? I'd love to see you assert yourself more in this group. You know, speak up more and give your opinion every once in a while."

"Okay. I'll try."

Walt thought about challenging John's *I'll try* comment but decided he'd better keep things moving. "Amy, I believe you're next."

Amy looked directly at Walt as she gave her word. "My word is 'cooperation.'"

"And..." asked Walt.

"And I will be cooperative."

Walt contemplated challenging Amy as well, but again held off. This first activity was about building trust and he didn't see any value in complicating things with an intervention this early in the program.

With the whole group now standing up on the boards, Walt asked them to rearrange themselves alphabetically, according to the word each person chose, without stepping off the boards. He then offered them a tip. "In order to succeed, you will have to formulate a plan and implement that plan by supporting each other physically so team members can get by one another without falling off the boards."

As expected, the next twenty minutes were pretty entertaining to watch. The group tried various approaches, from climbing over each other to jumping from one board to another. Eventually, they were able to use the corner areas of the U-shape boards to effectively rearrange themselves, which led to a loud cheer from the group. By now an audience of passersby was watching with great curiosity and cheering along with them.

Walt then asked the group to stay up on the boards for the debriefing. "I'd now like each of you to rate yourself on a scale of one to ten, with ten being the highest, on how well you personally demonstrated the word that you shared with the whole group."

One by one, each member shared their word and the score they gave themselves. Amy was the last to speak. "My word was 'cooperation,' and I give myself a nine."

Will seemed a little bothered and spoke up. "Amy, I'm not sure how you could give yourself a nine when you didn't say a word throughout this whole exercise."

Walt was about to intervene, but Amy cut him off.

"What's your problem, Will?"

The exhilaration that had engulfed the group was now giving way to an unwanted tension. Even the sun hid behind the clouds.

Will fired back. "You're the problem. You've been nothing but a bitch ever since Justin took over."

"Whoa, whoa, whoa! Hold on, Will," shouted Walt.

"No, let me finish," pleaded Will. "I said I needed to challenge, and that's what I'm doing."

Walt held off.

"For whatever reason, Amy, you have been preventing this group from moving forward as a team. You've been difficult to work with, mean-spirited, and unfair to Justin."

"Unfair to Justin! Give me a break," retorted Amy hotly.

Justin could only watch at this point, even though his name was being thrown around in the argument, like a ping-pong ball. This was between Will and Amy.

Walt intervened. "You guys, let's take this inside. I don't think we want to have this discussion out here."

"He's right," said Lee Ann. "There's an issue here that we've needed to address for a while now, and I think we need to take it inside and get it out on the table."

"Then let's go," said Charlie, as he led the slow procession inside. Everyone else was quiet. The tension was everywhere.

Walt pulled Justin aside. "Justin, I'm going to let this play out inside. Whatever is going on here, it's preventing this group from moving forward. Are you okay with that?"

Justin was so thankful to have Walt there. He had no idea what to do or how to handle the situation. "I'll leave it in your hands, Walt."

As everyone sat down in the chairs, which remained in a circle from earlier, Walt began by talking about safety in groups. He emphasized the need for some ground rules before talking about what happened outside. He also mentioned that conflict was a good thing and should only be viewed as an opportunity to better this group in their working relationships.

Interestingly, between the short walk to the room and Walt's talk on safety in groups, the tension seemed to subside a bit.

"I apologize, Amy, for using the 'b-word'," began Will. "I guess what I was trying to say to you is that I've seen everyone make an effort to support Justin as the manager, except you."

"I've been supportive," shot back Amy.

This whole confrontation was surreal for Justin. Here everyone was talking either about him or on his behalf as if he weren't in the room. Yet, he was overwhelmed by the support he was receiving.

Finally Charlie stood up. "You call writing that letter to the newspaper being supportive?"

"I have no idea what letter you are referring to, Charlie," returned Amy, her eyes welling up with tears. "And you're one to talk!"

Walt was monitoring the conversation closely, but was only going to intervene if he absolutely had to. He wanted to give the group a chance to manage this conflict themselves.

"Are you telling us you didn't write that letter?" asked Will.

Just then John said something that no one quite heard.

"Hold on, everyone," said Walt, firmly. "John was saying something."

Now all eyes moved to John. His face turned red and his voice trembled. "I wrote the letter."

"What?" cried Will.

"*You* wrote the letter?" inquired Charlie.

Amy had had enough. "I don't care about the stupid letter. I've had it, and I need to say something."

Now everyone was talking over each other.

"Just a minute," yelled Walt, "one at a time. Amy, go ahead and say what you were going to say."

"I'm done. I don't need this in my life. I'm out of here." She then stood up and began walking toward the door.

"Wait, Amy," cried Justin. "We need you here."

Amy stopped and looked right at Justin, "It's a little late for that, Justin. To tell you the truth, I've already written my resignation—it's on your desk. I merely came here today to say goodbye. But now I'm not even going to do that. You guys deserve each other!" And with that she stormed out of the room.

Walt was looking at Justin and Justin was looking at Walt. Neither knew what to do. Finally, it was Colleen, of all people, who got up and ran after Amy.

The rest of the day

THE GROUP TOOK A MUCH-NEEDED BREAK. Justin called Cynthia from his cell phone to give her a heads-up. Will, Charlie, and John were having an in-depth discussion out front. Lee Ann was with Colleen, who had just come back from an abortive attempt to have Amy rejoin the group. Walt was busy preparing his debrief of what had just transpired with the group. Everything had the look of a NASA control center that had just lost contact with its shuttle.

Eventually Walt called everyone back into the room. "Let's talk a bit about what just happened."

Colleen was the first to comment. "Walt, why didn't you intervene when things started to get bad? You just let it play out."

"Colleen, thank you for asking that question. My intention all along has been to support your group in becoming a team. One of the most effective ways to develop into a team is by learning how to successfully handle difficult situations together. Granted, it is not always pretty, but you need to do it yourself if you truly want to evolve as a team. Believe me, I was monitoring the dynamics and would have jumped in if I felt I needed to. But had I done that, the focus would have been on my intervention and you would have taken a step back as a team, not forward."

"But how is *this* taking a step forward?" asked Colleen.

"This discussion right now is the forward part. It is the ability to talk through a difficult situation and correct what needs to be corrected so that you can recommit to move forward as a team. That's right. I'm purposely using the word *team* in reference to this group. A team can only improve if it is willing to make mistakes and learn from those mistakes. Situations like today test the team's resolve. Are you going to embrace what happened and grow from it, or are you going to bury it and turn it into an unspoken topic? This moment, right now, can be a defining moment for this team. The question is, are you up for the challenge?"

Justin jumped from his seat. "I am!"

Will stood up next. "You can count me in!"

Charlie and Lee Ann stood up simultaneously. "You bet," shouted Lee Ann. Charlie pointed to Lee Ann. "Yeah, what she said!"

The group laughed.

Colleen stood up. "This is what I came out here for—to become a part of a real team."

Now all eyes shifted to John.

"John," said Justin, "I want to say something about your letter in front of the whole group."

John immediately apologized. "Justin, I wrote it when I was upset. I didn't mean what I said."

"It doesn't matter," replied Justin. "This is something I need to say to all of you. I'll be the first to admit that I wasn't prepared to be a manager. I have made a lot of mistakes that have impacted each one of you. I'm sorry for that. But you know what? I've also learned from my mistakes and it has made me better. I owe that to each one of you as well. So please know that I will make mistakes, just as I expect you will, but what will ultimately make us great is our ability to talk through these mistakes and learn from them, just as Walt said."

"Here, here," shouted Lee Ann as she led a group applause.

John looked over at Justin. "I'm sorry I didn't talk to you about it. That wasn't right for me to go about it the way I did."

"John, you did try to talk to me, and I blew you off," replied Justin. "I'm sorry for that and it won't happen again. And Walt, I have one more thing."

"This is your meeting," responded Walt.

"I wasn't going to share this, but since we are coming completely clean with each other—"

Charlie interrupted, as the group sat back down. "That was you on the radio with Dr. Mac, wasn't it?"

"You got me."

"Wait, who is Dr. Mac and what radio show are you talking about?" asked Lee Ann.

"He's some kind of business psychologist and he's on the Jay and Bobbie show every morning," answered Will.

"No way!" cried out Colleen.

"Yes, way," replied Justin. "Not only that, Dr. Mac is my leadership coach. I've been seeing him for a month now."

The group, including Walt, was in awe, and demanded to know the details. Justin obliged and proceeded to share the whole story from the very beginning.

The day continued with more activities and more team discussions and ended with a conversation about Amy and how to move forward after what had happened in the morning.

Will addressed the group. "I want to apologize to each of you as well for using the b-word with Amy this morning. I'm sorry. I also plan to apologize again to Amy before the day is over."

"I also owe Amy an apology," added Charlie. "In fact, I owe all of you an apology."

Surprised looks filled the room as Charlie cleared his throat.

"Some of this is my fault. You see, back when Justin got promoted, I convinced myself that he had covertly applied for the management position all along. Of course I know that's not true now but I got pretty upset over that and, as most of you know, became somewhat obnoxious. Well, during that time I confided in Amy about my theory and may have infected her with my bad attitude."

"But when things got better, didn't you and Amy talk?" asked Lee Ann.

"Not exactly," replied Charlie. "Shortly thereafter, she started distancing herself from me, and we've never really had a heart-to-heart talk since. That's my fault. I should have initiated a conversation."

The room fell silent.

Justin spoke up. "Thank you, Charlie, for saying that. I know it wasn't easy. Like you, I'm also guilty of not ever having insisted on having a real conversation with Amy. I felt like she didn't respect me anymore since I took the manager's position and instead of talking it out with her I pretty much avoided her. That's my fault."

"Don't beat yourself up," sympathized John. "We've all made mistakes."

Lee Ann's hand shot up. "Do you guys mind if I shift gears a bit?"

Everyone was relieved and nodded.

"Much of the work we did today as a team happened after Amy left. I don't want to lose sight of congratulating ourselves for what we've accomplished today."

The whole team applauded themselves.

Lee Ann continued. "Should Amy come back, we will need to integrate her back into the team."

Everyone nodded in agreement.

Walt then asked for any other closing comments.

Colleen asked to speak. "I just want to thank every one of you for embracing me as a member of this team. Today demonstrated to me that we all want to make this team better." Tearing up now, she finished. "It means so much to me to be part of a group that truly cares for each other. You have no idea."

Lee Ann and John, who were seated on either side of Colleen, each put their arm around her.

Then Charlie yelled out, "Group hug!"

Immediately everyone ran over to Colleen and began piling on top of one another. Between the laughter and Colleen falling over in her chair, the meeting ended as it had begun, with laughter.

The unexpected compliment

THE GOOD NEWS WAS THAT the teambuilding session did end up bringing the staff closer together. The bad news was that it was at Amy's expense.

As he returned to his office, Justin spotted Amy's resignation letter sitting on his desk. He opened it and began reading.

> Justin,
>
> This letter serves as my official notice that I am resigning from my position with the Orders Fulfillment Department and DataDump, effectively immediately.
>
> I apologize for the short notice but I have a pressing situation at home that needs my immediate attention.
>
> Sincerely,
> Amy Kerr
>
> P.S. I'm so sorry for my behavior the last few months. It wasn't fair to you and I hope someday you'll forgive me.

Justin read and reread Amy's letter a few more times. He was touched by her apology but bothered that it had to come in a resignation letter. *Why am I seeing a glimpse of remorse from Amy now, when it's basically too late,* he thought to himself.

Before Justin's analysis went any further, the phone rang. He hoped it was Amy.

"Hello, Justin O'Brien."

"You're there."

"Christal?"

"Yeah, it's me. How are things going?"

"Gosh it's great to hear your voice." Justin paused before answering her question with a question. "Did anyone talk to you yet about what happened today?"

"I have messages from you and Cynthia but I haven't actually talked to anyone. Why?"

"Well, do you want the good news first or the bad news?"

"I don't like the sound of this. What happened, Justin?"

"Well, we had the teambuilding session today with Walt."

"I know you did and I can't wait to hear about it. Did you like Walt?"

"Yeah, he was great. Anyway, to cut to the chase, there was an incident involving Amy."

"What do you mean, 'incident'?"

"Well, during one of the activities, Will said something to her about her attitude and Charlie kind of accused her of writing a letter to Dr. Mac, which was published in the newspaper."

"What letter?"

"Charlie was under the assumption that she had sent a letter to Dr. Mac in the newspaper complaining about me."

"Did she?"

"No, actually John did."

"John?"

"Yeah, but we cleared all of that up in the teambuilding session."

"Slow down Justin. John wrote a letter complaining about you to the newspaper?"

"Sort of. He wrote an anonymous letter to Dr. Mac's column."

"And is this something that I should be concerned about?" asked Christal.

"No, not about that. John and I talked, and we both agreed to check in with each other regularly from now on."

Christal was still confused. "So Amy walked out because of what Will and Charlie said to her."

"Yeah, I think so. But she didn't just walk out. She quit."

"How do you know that?"

"I've got her resignation letter right here."

"What did Walt do?"

"Nothing."

"Nothing?"

"I don't mean that in a bad way," replied Justin. "He said it was important for us to experience handling difficult situations as a team."

"I'm not sure I'd call Amy quitting as 'handling' the situation. Would you, Justin?"

"Actually, yes. Her resignation was on my desk before the teambuilding. Clearly she was on her way out already. I guess the incident with Will and Charlie just expedited things."

Christal paused for a moment before responding. "Have you talked to Amy since she left?"

"No, but I've left messages and I'll try again after we're done."

Christal's voice softened. "I talked to Amy a couple of days ago."

Justin's eyes widened. "Really? What did she say?"

"Unfortunately I can't go into it, Justin. She had asked me to keep the conversation confidential. However, what I can tell you is that there are some other things going on in her life that are weighing pretty heavily on her right now. I'm sorry I can't tell you more; hopefully she'll share those with you."

"Well that makes me feel better. I mean, not better, but up until today I wasn't sure if there were factors other than just me that were making her unhappy."

"Justin, if there was a problem with you, I would have addressed it with you."

"Thank you, but did you know that she was going to resign?"

"I had an idea."

"So, was there anything I should have done that I didn't do?"

"Justin, you are doing everything and more than I've asked of you. Productivity and customer ratings for both of your departments are well above average and you're making great progress with both of your staffs. I'm sorry about what happened in your teambuilding session with Amy but that doesn't take away from the fact that I'm very proud of you."

Justin wasn't expecting a compliment, given the nature of his call with Christal, but the fact that she said what she said had quite the impact on him.

"Thank you. That was nice to hear."

"You deserve it Justin, you really do. Oh, and promise me that if Amy doesn't end up talking with you about what's going on that you won't take it personally."

"Don't worry, I won't. And of course I'll do everything I can to help her through this transition."

Justin kept the phone in his hand after hanging up with Christal and called Amy's cell again.

"Hello, this is Amy. Leave me a message. Beeeep."

"Hi Amy, Justin. I wanted you to know again how sorry I am for what happened today. I also read your resignation letter and appreciated your comment at the bottom. It would really mean a lot to me if we could talk in person before you go. Call me when you get a chance. Thanks."

Justin wasn't sure if Amy would call him back or not, but he decided to wait around the office for awhile just in case she did. Besides, it would give him some time to write his latest insights in his journal.

Journal Entry # 12

a) Using Walt as the outside facilitator for the teambuilding session allowed me to fully engage in the process instead of being in charge of it. That was a good thing.

b) It's important to discuss safety in groups and establish ground rules before engaging a group in a confrontational discussion.

c) In order for working relationships to thrive, there must be an ongoing avenue available to talk and work through issues.

d) It only takes one staff member to create a tension-filled work environment. Don't ever let it get to that point again.

As Justin put down his pen and leaned back in his chair, he knew all too well that a critical shift had taken place within his department today. Although it didn't play out exactly as he had wanted or anticipated, it nevertheless happened just the same. With Amy leaving and John's issue getting addressed, the last of the resistance was now gone. He finally would have the staff that he needed to move forward. He had weathered the storm.

The rest of the story

AMY NEVER CALLED BACK, but was spotted the following day meeting with Cynthia in Human Resources. Justin hoped that she would come by the office to at least say goodbye.

The rest of the staff seemed to be doing very well. It was as if a burden had been lifted from the office, creating a welcome sense of serenity.

"John, how are you doing?" asked Justin, as he decided to check in with everyone one by one.

"Pretty good. I'm still feeling bad about writing that letter."

"Don't. You wouldn't have felt a need to write it if I had been communicating effectively with you and making sure your needs were being met. The important thing is that you asserted yourself. Promise me you'll keep doing that?"

"I will. I am glad you're not upset."

"No, not at all. Is there anything you need from me right now?"

"I think we're good now," replied John.

Justin then headed over to Colleen's cubicle. "Hi. Still glad you're here?"

"You have no idea. It meant a lot to have such open and honest communication with everyone. You should be proud, Justin. That was rare!"

"Colleen, it took a little time to get to this point and I truly believe that you were a missing piece of the puzzle. Thanks for being a part of this team."

Colleen teared up. "I promised myself that I wasn't going to cry."

"I'm sorry, I'm not trying to make you cry. I just wanted you to know that yesterday wouldn't have happened without you."

Colleen had a big smile on her face as Justin left her cubicle and stopped in to see Will. "How are you doing?"

Will shook his head. "I feel pretty crappy, to tell you the truth. I tried to call Amy but could only get her voice mail."

"Will, hopefully you'll get the chance to clear that up with her—but you know what? You were great yesterday. Don't beat yourself up over one comment. I found you to be supportive, assertive, and you did what you said you wanted to do—you challenged the group to be better. Yes, I too am sorry that the 'b-word' slipped out, but you were a lot more than that one comment yesterday and I was proud of you."

Will smiled, and then humorously replied, "Yeah, but I promised myself that I wasn't going to cry."

Justin gave him a playful shove. "Shut up."

Colleen came right over and looked at Will. "Are you mocking me, mister?" pretending to sound upset.

They laughed.

Justin headed over to Lee Ann's cubicle. "Hi. How are you doing?"

"I'm great, Justin. It's all good!"

"Thanks for all your support, Lee Ann. You have been so great."

"You're welcome...Oh, Justin?"

"Yes."

"I promised myself that I wasn't going to cry."

Just then the whole office broke out laughing as they joined Justin and Lee Ann.

"Never mind," shouted Justin. "Can't a guy get all touchy-feely these days?"

"It's only because we love you, J-Man," added Charlie.

As had been the case the previous day, the laughter suddenly halted as fast as it had begun. Amy had just walked in. "Justin, can I talk with you?"

"Of course. Here, or do you want to go across the street for coffee?"

"Your office will be fine."

Justin felt more of a sense of awkwardness than tension as he closed the door behind Amy.

"Did you get my message?" asked Justin.

"Yeah, I got it. I got Will's too...and Christal's...and Cynthia's."

Amy looked uncomfortable but much more reserved than Justin had seen her for weeks.

"Justin, I've been a wreck..." and she started to cry as she sat down.

"Amy, everything is going to be fine," said Justin, not sure what to say.

"No it's not. I have been a bitch. Will was right."

"Don't worry about it, Amy. Whatever it is, it doesn't matter. You've had a right to be frustrated with me. I have made lots of mistakes."

"Justin, it isn't about you, and truthfully, it never was. That was what I tried to say in my resignation letter."

Justin was hoping Amy would come clean with whatever had been bugging her. "Do you want to tell me? You don't have to if it's too personal."

"No, it's alright. My father has stage four cancer. I found out about it six weeks ago and just kind of blocked it out. I'm not ready for him to die." Amy was sobbing now.

"Can I do anything?" asked Justin.

"No. I'm sorry. It's not fair of me to put this on you."

"Amy, why couldn't you tell me this before?"

"I don't know. I got so angry. It wasn't really until last week when I went home to see my parents that it truly sank in."

"So how is he doing?"

"Not well. But my mom is much worse. She can't function without him and this whole thing is tearing her up."

"I'm so sorry."

"Well, the bottom line is that I need to be there with them."

"So then why...oh, never mind."

"No, go ahead."

"Why did you apply for the Boulder position?" asked Justin.

"The honest truth is that I just haven't been happy here for a while and I wanted out. Plus my dad's illness has really taken a toll on me. It's like my energy has been zapped for months. Frankly, I thought a change would be the best thing for me."

"And then you had to deal with me as your manager on top of that," added Justin.

"I'm sorry for how difficult I've been. I fully expected Charlie to get promoted and was obviously pretty upset with you and Christal when he wasn't. I'm still not completely clear on why that decision was made but I can see that Charlie has come to terms with it."

"Amy, I'm not sure why I'm not supposed to say what I'm about to tell you but it might help you understand why Christal did what she did. You see, all along she envisioned Charlie taking on another management role within the company and thought it made more sense to move me up in this department, thereby freeing Charlie up to take on whatever it is he will be taking on. Does that make sense?"

"I guess, but that should have been shared with everyone. Don't you think?"

"Of course I do. Charlie and I found out after the fact as well. And Christal couldn't say anything because some of that information was confidential at that time."

"Justin, none of that matters to me any more. I appreciate you telling me, but work is just not that important given what's going on with my father."

"I understand. I really do understand."

"Justin, I want you to know something, and I'm not just saying it because I'm leaving. I do think you're doing a good job as manager. I'm serious. I know that's a shock coming from me, but you need to know that. I didn't make any attempt to support you or acknowledge your efforts to make things better and that was wrong. I'm sorry about that."

"Amy, I'd be lying if I said your behavior didn't bother me, but now at least I understand what was going on with you. I only wish I had known so I could have been more supportive. And, to be totally honest with you, I was partially at fault here for not trying to talk to you about things. I guess what I'm trying to say is that I'm willing to let bygones be bygones and wipe the slate clean between us."

"Thank you Justin. I'm willing to do the same."

As Amy got up she gave Justin a very welcome hug goodbye.

"Amy, do you have any idea how much I've missed being able to talk to you like this?"

Amy began crying again. "I've missed it, too. I'm so sorry."

"Will you do me one favor?" asked Justin.

"Sure, name it."

"Will you be sure to say goodbye to everyone," as he pointed to the outer office. "You are still a big piece of this group and will be leaving us with quite a void. I know they all want to say goodbye."

Smiling now, Amy headed toward the door, "Okay, boss. It's time I'm honest with them as well about what's been going on with me."

As she entered the outer office, the rest of the staff merged toward her cubicle. Within seconds the whole group was congregating around Amy. Justin suddenly felt sad as he watched Amy hug each member of his staff, ending with Will. Some of them were holding back tears as the two of them embraced.

For Justin, it was one thing to add a new employee and an entirely different thing to lose one. Granted he'd been initially relieved when he found out Amy was leaving, but that was before he knew what was going on in her life. He suddenly felt closer to her than ever before, making her departure seem even more devastating.

Mutual mentoring

76

IT WAS THE FOLLOWING MONDAY and the first major snowfall of the season. Justin had already picked out their table in a very cozy corner at the Sweet Shop, a quaint little restaurant close to the park. He couldn't wait to tell Dr. Mac all about what had transpired during the past week.

"Dr. Mac, over here!" shouted Justin as Dr. Mac hobbled in, covered with snow.

Seeing Justin, he smiled warmly. "O'Brien, how are you?"

"I'm great, Dr. Mac. And you?"

"I'm okay."

"What do you think about this weather?" asked Justin. "It's hard to image that it's only October."

"I'm not quite ready for snow just yet. It's a little harder getting around at my age."

"Have you and Daisy thought about going somewhere warm for the winter?"

"Actually," replied Dr. Mac, "we have something lined up in St. Petersburg, Florida."

"Well there you go. You can go golfing by day and do your column by night."

339

Dr. Mac looked disappointed. "I don't think we're going now."

"Why not?"

"My doctor doesn't want me traveling right now. He says I have a 'condition'!"

"What kind of condition?"

"Not sure. He's running more tests—says he wants to keep an eye on me for a while."

Justin felt saddened by this news but didn't want to upset Dr. Mac any further. "Well, if there is anything I can do, just let me know."

Dr. Mac nodded appreciatively. "So enough about me, what's going on, my man!"

"Well," smiled Justin, wanting to lift Dr. Mac's spirits, "I believe I've finally turned the corner as a manager. Actually, it is probably more accurate to say that my department has finally turned the corner."

"Tell me all about it, O'Brien."

"Well, you knew we had that teambuilding last week, right?"

"I remember. You thought one of your employees wrote that letter to me."

"Yeah, exactly. Well guess what?"

"What?"

"Turns out she didn't write it. One of my other employees did."

"What?"

"I know this sounds a little odd, but it turned out that one of my quieter employees had written it. And it all came out in the teambuilding session."

"You're kidding!"

"Dr. Mac, it's all good...now at least. You see, some of my other employees accused the disgruntled employee of writing the letter. She denied it and then the quiet employee spoke up and admitted to writing it."

"And this is what you mean by 'it's all good'?"

"Exactly. I'm glad to see you're following all of this." Justin was having fun now telling the story.

Dr. Mac shook his head in confusion. "I'm getting a headache."

"The bottom line to all of this is that everything got put on the table. Granted it wasn't always pretty, but in the end, we have become a tightly knit group. And I owe much of that to you."

"Don't be bringing me into this circus."

"I'm serious. Your advice and support has given me enough of an anchor to keep me from floating away since becoming manager."

"So I'm a part of a boat now?" joked Dr. Mac.

"Look, quit trying to redirect my compliment. You have helped me more than you will ever know."

"Okay, thank you. I've told you a hundred times, I'm just an old man trying to be helpful."

"And I've told you a hundred times, you're more than that."

Dr. Mac's eyes watered up and he quickly became embarrassed. "Yeah, yeah, are we done with the touchy-feely?"

"Sure."

"So what did happen with your disgruntled employee?"

"She quit—but not because of me or the teambuilding session. Her father is very ill and she felt she needed to go home to be with her parents."

"So what did you learn from all of this?" asked Dr. Mac, trying to bottom-line the story.

"I learned that I need to check in with my employees on a regular basis and build enough of a rapport with each of them so that they feel they can both confide in me and provide me with feedback if there is something I could be doing better. When I think back about it, it was the two employees that I didn't develop much of a rapport with who ended up not communicating with me. I blame myself for that. They obviously didn't feel comfortable enough in talking with me and I should have noticed it and addressed it."

"O'Brien, you are going to make mistakes. The key is to embrace them as valuable learning opportunities. Sometimes it takes a mistake or a conflict coming to a head in order for an issue to even surface. You can't expect to be all things to all people all the time. You're human."

"Yeah, I know. I have to remember that."

"So where do things stand with both of those employees?"

"I ended up clearing the air with each of them and now our relationships are stronger than ever."

"And how does that make you feel?"

"Now look at who's getting all touchy-feely?"

"Just answer the question."

"I feel incredible. I feel content. I feel exhausted. I feel sad. I feel excited."

"You know what, O'Brien?"

"What, Dr. Mac?"

"I'm proud of you. You've weathered the storm and came out a better man. You are what leadership is all about. I'm terminating our coaching agreement."

"What? You can't do that!"

"I'm not ending our relationship; I'm just getting rid of the formal part. You may not believe this, but you've been my mentor as well through all of this."

"How so?"

"Your zest for life. Your willingness to learn and grow. You have been an inspiration to me and I refuse to receive compensation from your company for a relationship that is mutually beneficial."

"So what does this mean, Dr. Mac?"

"It means I'll see you at the bench next week, but I'm buying the coffee."

"Oh, okay, great. But in that case, how about a couple of donuts?"

"Don't push it, O'Brien. I've got a cane!"

Charlie's opportunity

THE NEXT FEW WEEKS WENT VERY SMOOTHLY for Justin and his Winnetka team. Work relationships continued to jell and productivity levels reached all-time highs. Amy's departure had opened up her position and this time the interview process went flawlessly. And, even more importantly, the staff was able to offer the position to Sara—the very same Sara that they had recommended in the previous go-around.

It was late in the afternoon when the phone rang.

"Justin, Christal."

"Hey Christal. Boy, you sound great. How are you feeling?"

"I'm doing much better, thanks. I'm finally able to walk a little bit each day. You have no idea how significant that is for me. I've been driving my mother crazy by requiring her constant care. Finally I can start doing some things on my own."

"When will you be able to come back to DataDump?"

"Not sure. As long as I can work from my mother's house remotely here in Redlands, J.W. said to take my time. He's been incredibly supportive."

"Amen to that," added Justin.

"Hey, got something I need to talk with you about."

"You mean about Boulder?" guessed Justin.

"Yeah, how did you know?"

"Well, I know that they have been short-handed ever since Colleen left and that they have been unable to find a qualified candidate to fill her position. Why, has something changed?"

"Sort of. I had a long talk with Claire this morning and she has decided to step down as team lead and move into Colleen's position."

"She did what?"

"She's taking Colleen's position. She wasn't comfortable being the team lead."

"But, but why didn't she say something to me? My God, I've been talking with her on a weekly basis for the past month. What's going on, Christal?"

"Justin, she feels like it's more than she can handle right now. This has been a very difficult decision for her."

"I certainly can understand that. I guess I'm disappointed that I didn't know this was going on. Christal, I would have worked with her on this had I known."

"I know, Justin. She really was using me more as a sounding board. Remember, I was the one who put her in that position in the first place. But know that she plans to talk with you directly about all of this in the next couple of days."

Justin sighed. "Okay, I'm sorry for sounding upset. It's just that I've been working so hard on getting my staff comfortable enough to come talk with me about these kinds of things. I thought I was making pretty good progress."

"Justin, see this as an opportunity to support Claire instead of focusing on what did or didn't happen. She's going through some difficult times right now and needs your help and support."

"Point taken. I was focused more on me than on Claire."

"But you know what?" asked Christal rather excitedly.

"You've got something up your sleeve, don't you?"

"Actually I do. What I'm about to tell you needs to be kept confidential for now. Can I count on you?"

"You didn't even need to ask," replied Justin.

"Okay, good. I'll start with what you already know. We are planning on expanding our product line and services by next year."

"Yes, you've mentioned that a few times."

"But what you probably didn't know is that we plan to take over a whole building in Boulder as part of that plan."

"Really? I guess that's not a surprise considering how fast we've been growing."

"That's right. And here's how it relates to what we've been talking about. We are going to need a manager out in Boulder to initially oversee *all* the departments that we bring out there."

"Okay, now I see where you are going with this. You're talking about taking Charlie away from me."

"His time has come. I have talked with J.W. and Melvin and we all agree that Charlie would be the perfect person to fill that role for us."

"It makes sense. You had mentioned that you had plans for him," said Justin, trying to cover up his disappointment.

"Yep, only we had not planned to move on this until late first quarter of next year."

"So what's going to happen, Christal?"

"I think we need to move him out there now to be the team lead and then move him into the managerial role once we are ready to expand. I don't think we have any other option."

"Does he know yet?"

"No. I wanted to talk with you first. What do you think?"

"Aside from the fact that it's in Boulder, I think Charlie will be very happy."

"No Justin, what do *you* think?"

"Selfishly, I don't want to lose him. Our staff has really come together and everything is finally working well. I hate to break up the chemistry." He paused. "Yet, at the same time, Charlie is clearly leadership material and needs to be in a leadership role. I know that, he knows that, and so does everyone else. I guess it was just a matter of time."

"I couldn't agree with you more, Justin. Given that, would you like to be the one to present this to him or would you like me to?"

"Christal, I'd like us to do it together. It only makes sense to me to do it that way."

"You got it. Call him in and put me on speakerphone."

Leaving Winnetka?

CHARLIE POPPED HIS HEAD in Justin's office. "J-Man, what's up?"

"Charlie, have a seat. I've got Christal on the phone and we want to talk to you."

"Hello, Charlie," came the voice from the speaker phone, "how are you?"

"I'm great, Christal. More importantly, how are you?"

"Much better, thank you."

Charlie was looking directly at the speakerphone now as he talked. "Hey, is this that conversation that we were supposed to have but haven't had?"

"Yes, finally. I'm so sorry to have kept you hanging like this."

It was now obvious to Justin that this was really Christal's conversation to have with Charlie. "Christal, why don't you go ahead and tell Charlie."

"Okay, thanks Justin. Charlie, you still there?"

"Are you kidding? I wouldn't miss this for the world."

"Great. I'm excited...I mean, *we* are excited to tell you that we have an incredible opportunity for you. What I'm about to tell you has been in the works for a while and now it's time to bring you aboard."

"I'm all ears!"

"Keep in mind this is highly confidential. Outside of your wife, you must not say a word to anyone until an official announcement has been made."

"Got it."

"Okay, here goes. We are going to expand our services and product line next year and along with that will be expanding our office in Boulder. As a result, we are going to need someone to manage the whole Boulder operation and we'd like you to be that person."

Charlie had the same shocked look on his face that he had the day Justin was named manager of the department instead of him. It was probably a good thing that Christal couldn't see him at that moment.

"Charlie, hello. Are you okay?"

"Wow, I'm sorry. That was a lot to swallow. You want me to oversee operations out in *Boulder*?"

"That's right. I told you I had something good for you."

Charlie was still trying to get his hands around the concept. "So, you want me to move to Boulder then, is that correct?"

"Yes, you'd need to be out there. Is that a concern for you?"

"Not sure, but I have to talk with my wife. It certainly is an incredible opportunity."

"Why don't you do that and get back to us by the end of the week," replied Christal. "Can you do that, Charlie?"

"Oh, sure," replied Charlie, now deeply in thought. "Tell me exactly when I would need to be out there?"

"That's the other part of this. You see, originally this wasn't to take place until the beginning of next year. However, Claire has stepped down as team lead and is taking over Colleen's position. So now we need someone out there right away to take over Claire's position as team lead.

Here's the way it would work. You would initially take her role as team lead and then we'd move you up to manager once we are ready to begin the expansion plans. It's that last part that we want to keep under wraps for now."

"Wow, that's real quick. Let me talk to my wife and kids. I'm sure I'll have a lot more questions after that."

"Justin, anything to add?" asked Christal.

Justin looked right at Charlie. "You've got to admit, this says a lot about how you are thought of around here at DataDump. I hope we can make this work. As much as I would hate to lose you, the company, especially our department, would benefit greatly by having you in charge out there."

After Christal hung up, Charlie pulled his chair closer to Justin's.

"J-Man, I can't go out there! It took everything I had to relocate back here to Winnetka, including a cut in pay. There's no way Mallory will go for it—promotion or not!"

"Charlie, do you want my advice?"

"Of course."

"Look, even though my promotion didn't involve a move, there are still some striking similarities to your situation."

"Like?"

"Let's cut right to the bottom line. Is advancing your career something you want to do?"

"Yes, of course."

"Okay, is DataDump the kind of company you'd like to stay and grow with?"

"This is a great place."

"So you want to advance and you'd like to advance at DataDump. Is that correct?"

"Yes."

"Do you honestly think DataDump will come back to you in the near future with another promotional opportunity if you end up turning this one down?"

"Maybe they would."

"When, Charlie? This company is about expansion, and I'm not talking about here in Winnetka. I'm talking about the western and eastern parts of the United States and then eventually overseas. That's where the new manager positions are going to come from, not here in the home office."

"So what are you saying?" asked Charlie.

"I'm saying that the only realistic way to move up in DataDump is by taking the position that has been offered to you and move out to Boulder. That way you stay with the company and get a great promotion. It would also be a feather in your cap, assuming you end up doing a great job, which I have no doubt that you would."

"Hmm. Do you really believe that?"

"Yes, I do. The truth is, my job is the only one here in Winnetka that you are suited for and I don't have any plans to leave. The way I see it, you have three options. You can take the Boulder opportunity. You can pass on Boulder and wait for another opportunity to come up here in the home office. Or you can start applying for management positions at other companies here in Winnetka. But notice that only the Boulder option is a sure thing."

Charlie was impressed. "When did you get so smart, Justin?"

"Like I said, I had to think about the same kinds of things when my opportunity came."

"So what was the deciding factor for you?"

"It was something Dr. Mac had said to me."

"Don't keep me in suspense. What did he say?"

"I can tell you exactly. He said, *'The key is not to wait for opportunities but to create them. Leadership isn't about timing, it's about stepping up to the plate when called upon.'*"

"Wow, Justin, you sounded just like him."

"That's the best compliment you could ever have given me."

Charlie's announcement

CHARLIE LOOKED A LITTLE SAD when he addressed the staff the following week. "An opportunity has come my way that I really cannot pass up. The best part is that it's within DataDump and I'll still be part of this organization. The other part is that the position is in Boulder and I'll be moving out there right away."

The room became quiet. No one knew which emotion to acknowledge, happiness for the promotion or sadness for losing Charlie.

Colleen finally broke the silence. "Is there something going on in Boulder that we don't know about?"

"Yes, there is another piece to all of this," replied Justin. "Claire stepped down the other day as team lead and has chosen to take your former position, Colleen."

"You've got to be kidding me," screamed Colleen.

"Afraid not. So, we've asked Charlie to take over Claire's position. This way all the Boulder spots are filled and we've got an experienced manager going out there to help get things running smoothly."

Will looked over at Charlie. "Chas, I'm not sure how to say this—"

"It's okay," said Charlie, "ask me anything."

"Well, it's just that I know how much it meant to you to move your family back to Winnetka. Is Claire's position enough of a bump up to warrant giving all of this up?"

Charlie looked over at Justin, not sure how to respond.

"Let me address that," injected Justin. "That position will become a manager's position in the near future. I can't really expound on that at this time but can tell you that the company thinks enough of Charlie to present this opportunity to him."

That response seemed to satisfy the group.

"When do you leave for Boulder?" asked John.

"Next week."

"Next week!" cried Lee Ann. "What about your family?"

"For now they are going to stay here and I'll commute on weekends. It's too much to even begin to think about moving just yet."

"Justin," asked Sara, "when is the company going to share with us what's going on?"

"Sara, that's a great question. I believe they are waiting for the all-staff meeting in January. They plan to present it so that everyone hears it together and at the same time."

"That's actually a good thing," added John.

Just then Charlie stood up. "I do want to say one more thing," as he turned to face Justin. "J-Man, I owe you. You have been nothing but supportive of me from the day we both started working at DataDump. You even supported me during that difficult time when Christal first promoted you. I just want you to know that it's been an honor to work by your side all these years and it will be an honor to move forward with you in our new relationship."

Justin got up and walked over to Charlie.

Will shook his head. "Oh no, here we go again. Don't hug each other. Please don't hug!"

But it was futile to try and stop the two old friends from embracing for one last time.

"I knew that was going to happen!" Will groaned.

John stood, looked at Will, and yelled, "Group hug!"

Immediately everyone, including newly hired Sara, ran over to Will and started hugging and piling up on top of him.

"I guess the meeting is over," laughed Justin.

It always works out

"**S**O IT'S A GOOD THING that Claire stepped down?" asked Megan later that night at the dinner table.

"That's an interesting question," reflected Justin. "You know, I think it was. I mean, at first all I could see was the negative side of it. The fact that I didn't know she was struggling; the fact that she didn't feel comfortable talking to me, not to mention the fact that I had to hear about this from Christal. To be quite honest with you, I was pretty upset."

"With whom, Justin?"

"Mostly with myself, but I'd be lying if I said I wasn't a little upset with Claire."

"So what changed?"

"My perspective for one. What I failed to see at the time was the impact that this would have on everything else. Instead of seeing possibilities, I was seeing gloom and doom. You know, the *poor me* syndrome."

"Yes I do know. You were being selfish and narrow-minded."

"I don't know if I'd go that far," retorted Justin.

"Well, weren't you?"

"I guess. But now I see it so differently. I'm actually thankful things happened the way they did."

Michelle popped her head into the kitchen. "Mom, you said we could have dessert at seven and it's already ten after."

Megan was so fascinated by this conversation that she told Justin to keep talking while she fixed dessert for the kids.

"Okay, I was narrow-minded," continued Justin, "you're absolutely right. Now that I think about it, Claire was always struggling with being the team lead. She couldn't handle Katie any more than anyone else could. Even Colleen said that. Yet it never even occurred to me to put someone else in that position—I never even knew it was an option."

"It seems so obvious now, doesn't it?" commented Megan.

"That would be an understatement. I really need to look at the bigger picture when it comes to these things."

"You need to put something about that in your journal, honey!"

"You are so right. I think I'll retire to the den and do just that."

"Just keep the television off," joked Megan. "Your brain turns to mush when you watch sports!"

Justin laughed all the way into the den and then turned the television set on. *I'll show her I can do both*, he mused to himself. But instead of taking out his journal as planned, he picked up the phone and called Claire. He had been bothered by the fact that she couldn't tell him she was stepping down, and he wanted to smooth that over somehow—even if it meant talking to her on the weekend.

"Justin?"

"How did you know it was me?"

"I have you on caller ID. Why are you calling me on the weekend?"

"I'm sorry, it couldn't wait."

"What's up?"

"I wanted you to know that I'm not upset that you stepped down."

"Oh my God, I can't believe that you are calling me to tell me that. You are so sweet."

"Christal said you didn't feel comfortable telling me. I blame myself for that."

"Justin, it wasn't you. You believed in me and went above and beyond the call of duty to help me. I've never had someone who has done that before. That's why I felt like I was letting you down. I'm sorry; I should have talked to you about it."

"Don't worry," consoled Justin, "we're talking now, right? Besides, I truly believe it will all work out for the best in the end."

"So you're okay then?"

"Definitely. Of course it's cost me my best employee."

"Touché," laughed Claire. "I guess that makes us even now, doesn't it?"

"Bye, Claire."

"Bye, Justin."

As Justin put the phone down, he felt a tinge of sadness. Between Claire stepping down and Charlie's new opportunity out in Boulder, his relationship with two of his key people had instantly changed. *I feel like I'm losing them both,* he thought to himself as he pulled out his journal to write his latest insights, *even though I know I'm not.*

About a half hour later, Megan walked into the den and found Justin sound asleep on the couch with his journal lying open on his chest. It made her smile. She then carefully removed the journal and placed it on a nearby table, trying her best not to look at his latest entry. But then curiosity got the best of her and she did look—and she was glad she did. In those written words she saw a man who truly cared about others and about bettering himself.

Journal Entry # 13

a) *Within every problem lies opportunity. Never lose sight of the big picture.*

b) *Change is constant no matter how good or bad things seem.*

c) *It's important for me to regularly check in with my employees (in both departments) in order to keep communication channels open and available on both ends.*

She never felt so in love with Justin as she did at that moment.

"Sweet dreams, honey," she whispered, as she gently kissed him on the forehead, placed a blanket over him, and turned the lights out. "You deserve it."

Part Seven

Two Months Later

A time of reflection

I<small>T WAS THEIR USUAL</small> M<small>ONDAY AFTERNOON MEETING,</small> but that was where the similarities ended. It also happened to be the day before New Year's Eve and "the boys," as Megan now referred to them, had decided to spend the afternoon reflecting on the past year. It was a ritual that Dr. Mac had been doing for years and one that he wanted to share with Justin.

"So do you want personal highlights or work highlights?" asked Justin.

"Give me the top five for each," replied Dr. Mac.

Justin began with his personal highlights, which all revolved around his family and ended with what he saw as the most important highlight of them all—date night.

"Date night?" asked Dr. Mac.

"Yep. Megan and I pick one night each week to spend together without the kids. It's a time to reconnect and just be there for each other. Dr. Mac, I can't begin to tell you how much that one weekly event has done to improve our relationship."

"That's great."

Justin was getting embarrassed and quickly moved on. "Okay, now for the top five work-related highlights. Ready?"

"Go for it."

"This was actually easy for me since I've been journaling this whole time. I have you to thank for that."

"It's helped, hasn't it?" replied Dr. Mac.

"More than you know. Anyway, the first highlight was of course my promotion. I am a different person today as a result. And, I wouldn't have met you!"

"There's a reason for everything."

"The second highlight was the transformation I had to make in order to turn a difficult situation into what is now a positive one. Remember when I was contacting you twice a week out of sheer desperation? Now when I think back on it, I'm so amazed that I survived. I had my whole staff against me at one point."

"I must admit," added Dr. Mac, "the odds were clearly stacked against you. You sounded so scared that time you called the radio station."

They both chuckled.

"My third work highlight was the teambuilding session. It was the first time that I truly felt support from my staff. In fact, it was that event that truly brought us together as a unit."

"But didn't you end up losing one of your staff members that day?" asked Dr. Mac.

"Yes and no. This takes me to my fourth highlight—Amy. You see it was Amy, the last of my disgruntled employees, who ended up quitting that day. She was the one that I thought had written a letter to you, but it actually turned out to be another one of my employees."

"Okay, I remember now." And then Dr. Mac suddenly looked puzzled. "So losing Amy was a highlight?"

"No, of course not," replied Justin. "The highlight was that we ended up getting her back! Her father's health took a miraculous turn for the better and we were able to coax her to come back after Charlie left. I'm sorry, I thought I had told you all of that."

"You probably did. I don't retain things like I used to."

"Which brings me to my fifth and most significant highlight of the year—you."

Dr. Mac's eyes widened. "Me? Oh, please!"

"Now, now, Dr. Mac, you are the reason that I even have work highlights from this year. I owe you so much."

"O'Brien, I'm just—"

"I know, you're just an old man trying to be helpful—and you have been. So much in fact that I asked to be the one to introduce you before you speak at our annual company retreat. And it's also why I got you this little gift."

Justin pulled out a beautiful hand-tooled pocket watch and handed it to Dr. Mac. On the back of the watch were the words,

> To Dr. Mac, my mentor and friend.
> —Justin

For the first time in their relationship, Dr. Mac seemed to be short on words, but certainly not emotion. With a hint of sadness in his eyes, he thanked Justin profusely for the gift. It clearly had touched him deeply.

"Daisy hates it when I get all emotional," lamented Dr. Mac, as he quickly turned the tables. "Now it's my turn to give you something."

"Oh no, Dr. Mac, you've given me more than enough already. Besides, you haven't shared your highlights yet."

"I will, but this is more important." He then opened a fairly large, dusty old bag that he had brought with him and pulled out what looked like an old book.

"O'Brien, I've never shown this to anyone, including my wife." He paused and brushed off the cover before handing it to Justin. "This is *my* journal. It goes back over thirty years. I want you to have it."

Justin was stunned. He couldn't believe Dr. Mac was actually handing over his own journal to him.

"You can't be serious, Dr. Mac," he protested. "Why would you part with this?"

Dr. Mac searched for the right words. "Daisy and I never had any children. But if we had, I would have wanted to pass this on to them. Justin, you've been like a son to me these past few months and it's important to me that you have this."

At that moment the two embraced, like father and son. Nothing else needed to be said.

A reunion of sorts

THIS YEAR'S ANNUAL COMPANY RETREAT promised to be much different than what employees had come to expect in past years. Instead of the day being taken up almost entirely by long-winded speeches from the various department heads, J.W. had invited Dr. Mac to deliver the first annual keynote address. It was also widely anticipated that J.W. would use this occasion to officially announce the company's future expansion plans.

In addition, the company retreat provided an annual opportunity for the two divisions of the Orders Fulfillment Department to get together. Although normally not a big deal, this year promised to be very special in that regard. The Boulder staff, now headed up by Charlie, was coming out today, a day early, so that the two groups could spend some quality time together. Given all the changes and the swapping out of each other's employees over the past few months, this get-together was more like a reunion than an actual business meeting.

For Justin, this day represented a culmination of lots of hard work. In many ways it was the final piece of the puzzle coming together—two staffs merging into one. He couldn't wait for the moment that Charlie, Claire, Katie, and Taylor walked through the door. And then suddenly, at that exact moment, he heard shouting from the outer office.

"Sweeet!" He looked up just in time to see Colleen and Claire embracing each other in one corner and Charlie and Amy in another. Soon it became a free-for-all as both staffs greeted each other warmly. Justin quickly joined in.

It wasn't long before the whole group was one cohesive unit. The remainder of the day consisted of some fun team-building activities led by Charlie, followed by a strategic visioning session facilitated by Justin.

But that was just the beginning. The group went to dinner together and eventually found their way to a karaoke bar where they very quickly became the entertainment. It went something like this: First Claire, Colleen, Taylor and Katie started off the festivities with their rendition of "I'm So Excited." Then Amy, Lee Ann and Sara performed a couple of popular country western songs. But the ultimate highlight of the evening was when Will, John, Charlie and Justin performed "YMCA" by the Village People.

By the end of the evening everyone was exhausted from laughing and vowed to make this a regular event to coincide with the annual company retreat. After goodbyes were said, Justin and Charlie headed out for a late-night cup of coffee together at Stella's. They still had some catching up to do.

"It was so great to see all of you again," said Charlie. "How is everyone? I really miss you guys."

"We are all doing great," replied Justin. "And Sara has been a welcome addition."

"I figured as much."

Justin leaned in. "So Charlie, how is it working with Claire, Katie, and Taylor?"

"J-Man, I knew you were going to ask me that," smiled Charlie. "You know, it's not bad at all. What really stinks is that room that they call an office. We're more like rats in a maze up there."

"Well at least you'll get to move into a real office this coming year," sympathized Justin.

"Yeah, I suppose so."

"Charlie, what's the matter?"

"I don't know. I love what I do and I particularly love where the company is headed. But frankly, I want to be in Winnetka. Mallory is still resistant to moving to Boulder. The kids love their school out here and don't want to move either. It's making me the bad guy."

"So what are you saying, Charlie?"

"I'm just saying that I don't know if it's going to work out, that's all. Please don't say anything to Christal. I'm being honest."

"Don't worry, I won't say a word. But what are you going to do?"

"For now, not a thing. Maybe time will help. I'm not ready to make any decisions yet. How about you?"

"Me?"

"Yeah, are you happy?"

"Very much so. Granted, the excitement has died down a little since I'm not fighting to keep my job anymore, but I'm sure the next challenge is right around the corner."

"That's cool, J-Man. Hey, I was hoping to finally see Christal. Do you know when she's coming back?"

"I was hoping she'd come back for the annual company retreat but obviously that's not happening. It feels like something's going on but no one's saying anything."

"I sure hope she's okay," said Charlie.

Justin nodded. "Me, too. I really miss her."

A day to remember

KATIE HAD ASKED FOR BOTH DEPARTMENTS to meet together the following day just prior to the start of the company retreat. The break room was abuzz in anticipation of what she had in store.

Both Katie and Taylor got up in front of the group. Katie began, "Taylor and I thought it would only be appropriate for us all to represent to the company that we are a unified department, regardless of whether we are in Boulder or here in Winnetka."

Taylor brought over a big box and opened it up in front of the group. "So we made these shirts for all of us to wear today."

Katie raised a shirt to show the group. On the front it had the initials, "OFD" for Orders Fulfillment Department, and on the back it had, in rather large letters, "SWEEET."

Katie then proceeded to explain the significance of the word *sweet* to the group but by this time everyone was already up and grabbing their shirts from the box.

Within a couple of minutes the Orders Fulfillment Department looked more like an *Up With People* cast with their brightly colored shirts and rosy glows on their faces.

It was now time for the company retreat to begin.

J.W. started off the meeting with a welcome and then proceeded to ask the Orders Fulfillment Department if they were planning on performing later. Although no one in Justin or Charlie's group was sure if he was referring to the shirts or their karaoke adventure the night before, it was still pretty funny. The rest of the DataDump employees seemed to appreciate the barb as well. J.W. then spent the next hour and a half going over the company's annual report, bit-by-bit, piece-by-piece. Had it not been for the fact that it had been DataDump's best year yet, half of the eighty employees in the audience could easily have fallen asleep. The truth is, J.W.'s speaking style was more similar to a meditation tape than to an Anthony Robbins seminar. It could be brutal at times.

After a long-awaited break, Melvin took over the meeting and unveiled the company's future plans, particularly focusing on the expansion of the Boulder office. As the excitement in the room began to increase, Melvin seized upon the momentum to name Charlie as the new manager, effective immediately.

There was a long applause.

Justin leaned over and winked at Charlie. Charlie, knowing that everyone was watching him, just smiled and waved his hand. Meanwhile, Claire, Katie, and Taylor all had grins on their faces a mile wide. It was the first they had heard of the expansion plans and they were overjoyed at the news that DataDump was going to purchase an actual building.

After lunch the crowd started buzzing again in anticipation of the upcoming keynote address. What made this even more special was knowing that they had a nationally syndicated columnist—not to mention guest host of one of Chicago's most popular morning radio programs ever—as their speaker. They had Dr. Mac!

Justin walked up to the podium. Although honored to have this opportunity to introduce Dr. Mac, he would gladly have parted with the trembling and sheer fear of speaking in public that seemed to join him at the microphone. He pulled out his notes.

"It's an honor to be here today to introduce a man that we've all come to know as Dr. Mac. He has helped people around the country through his business-savvy advice, commonly referred to as 'Macology.' Yet despite his fame and fortune, only those of us residing here in Winnetka can truly call him one of our own. Please join me in welcoming our neighbor and one of the world's greatest advice columnists, Dr. Mac!"

Immediately, all eighty-plus employees stood to give Dr. Mac a standing ovation. Although most of them had never seen him before, they immediately figured out that the older gentleman walking up to the podium with the aid of a cane was in fact Dr. Mac.

"Good afternoon, DataDump! Thank you for having me here today and thank you, Justin, for a wonderful introduction. It's true; we are neighbors. And as president of the homeowners association for this neighborhood, I must inform you that it's your turn to host the next block party!"

The room roared with laughter and cheers. Dr. Mac knew how to work an audience.

Justin glowed as he watched his mentor and friend dazzle the crowd with his wit and humor. By the end of the keynote, people were begging the old man for more stories, anecdotes, and advice. It was Macology at its finest.

Melvin jumped up to the microphone before the loud ovation ended to thank Dr. Mac and to present him with a gift. He then asked Dr. Mac to stay up front for two awards they were about to give out.

"This has been a wonderful day," began Melvin, "and a time for us to thank all of you for your dedication and commitment to DataDump. We owe all of our success to each and every one of you. Thank you!"

The whole room was standing now in anticipation of what was coming next.

"But success doesn't happen without a few champions, and there are a couple of those among us who particularly stepped up to the plate this year to perform above and beyond the call of duty."

The cheering became so loud that Number 2 had to yell over the PA system in order to be heard.

"There are two employees that we'd especially like to recognize here today. It's my pleasure to introduce the first recipient to you. If there ever was a person who exemplifies commitment, dedication, courage and passion, it is this employee..."

Suddenly the room went completely quiet.

"She has risen to every challenge put in front of her and succeeded. On September 14th, she had to face her toughest challenge yet when she was struck by a hit-and-run driver. Bedridden for months with a broken pelvis, broken ribs, and a punctured lung, this employee stayed strong and never once gave up. Ladies and gentlemen, I give you a woman who is everything Dr. Mac talked about and more, and, I'm happy to say, once again one of our own, I give you Christal Deeds!"

The room literally went crazy as Christal walked up, without any assistance, to join Melvin and Dr. Mac at the podium. There wasn't a dry eye in the room. It had been well over four months since that awful day Christal got hit by a car, and now she was finally returning home. She had become a heroine of sorts to everyone in the company.

It took all of five minutes before the room quieted down. Christal stepped up to the microphone, with tears in her eyes, and proceeded to thank everyone for their incredible support, prayers, and unyielding belief that she would in fact recover from her terrible setback.

She continued. "We have one more award to give out. I don't know if you've ever been in a situation where you were thrust into something that you didn't think you could do, didn't want to do, didn't know how to do, didn't have any experience to draw from; and virtually didn't have any help in doing. I can tell you this: there are not a lot of people who would take on such a challenge. There are even fewer people who could take on that challenge and find a way to succeed."

Justin still hadn't fully recovered from the shock of seeing Christal and couldn't understand why people were beginning to look at him as she talked.

"There is nothing worse than wanting to help someone but being unable to do so. I promoted our recipient on a Monday and then got hit by a car on Tuesday. He was left to completely fend for himself and to survive in what must have seemed like the most difficult of difficult situations he could ever have imagined. Yet he did. With the help of people like Dr. Mac—and through his own determination—he was able to turn the Orders Fulfillment Department, and I'm talking about both the Winnetka and Boulder offices combined, into one of the most efficient, productive, and well-run departments of the whole organization."

Justin's heart began pounding. *She's talking about me!*

"So it is my pleasure to introduce you to one of our own. I give you Justin O'Brien!"

What happened next would remain a little unclear to Justin. He remembered walking up to the front of the room and embracing Christal. He remembered embracing Dr. Mac. But he didn't remember embracing Melvin, which apparently he did as well. Needless to say, that generated a lot of laughter.

The retreat ended with a barrage of activity around Christal and Justin. It was easily one of the greatest days in Justin's life and he didn't want it to end. But like everything else, it did. And after saying goodbye to Charlie, Taylor, Claire, and Katie, Justin headed over to Dr. Mac. "You about ready for me to drive you home?"

"O'Brien, did I ever tell you how proud I am of you?"

"Yes, many times. I was proud of you as well today. I think we both did pretty well."

As they walked out, Dr. Mac turned to Justin. "I think it's time I share something with you."

The devastating news

THE DRIVE TO DR. MAC'S HOUSE only took about ten minutes, yet it would end up seeming like the longest ten minutes of Justin's life.

"Dr. Mac, you're kind of quiet. Are you okay?"

"O'Brien, there's been something I've been meaning to tell you for awhile now, but the timing has never seemed right."

"Is it good, I hope?" asked Justin, starting to get concerned.

"When I told you I was proud of you, I truly meant it."

"I know you did, Dr. Mac. That meant a lot to me. This has been one of the greatest days of my life, if not the greatest, and I'm so thankful that you were here to share it with me."

"Me, too, son. Me, too."

"Then what's going on? This isn't good, is it Dr. Mac?"

"I'm afraid not."

Justin could feel a surge of anger overtaking him as he pulled the car in front of Dr. Mac's house. "Why is it that every time things finally go right for me something bad has to happen? Every time!"

Dr. Mac now had tears in his eyes. "I'm sorry that happens to you."

"It's just so frustrating, Dr. Mac!" Justin then took a deep breath to regroup. "Forgive me... here I am selfishly thinking about myself when you haven't even had a chance to tell me what you were going to tell me. You're moving away, aren't you?"

"No son, I'm dying."

Justin's face went rigid. His stomach tightened so much that he was finding it difficult to breathe. "You didn't just say what I think you said, did you?"

"I'm afraid so, son. I've been sick for a while—have barely had any energy to write, let alone continue with my radio program. At first I thought I was working too hard, so Daisy and I took a vacation. But it only got worse. About a month ago I finally went in to see a doctor and was diagnosed with cancer."

"But can't they do something about it? Did they catch it early? You're going to be alright, aren't you?"

"The cancer has spread into my liver, my lungs, and there are even traces of it in my brain. In other words, there is nothing they can do at this point. It's progressed too far."

"So what are you saying, Dr. Mac?"

"I'm saying that our relationship as we know it is going to end. I've been given three months, maybe four."

Justin felt completely numb. He was having trouble comprehending what he was hearing. "Is that why you gave me your journal?"

Dr. Mac nodded. "I wanted it to be in good hands."

"But you seemed okay today. Your speech was great. Maybe you're getting better."

"I'm actually getting worse by the day. I didn't feel well at all when I was up there. But I didn't want to let you down so I gave it everything I had. That was my last speech."

Justin was shaking at this point. "So, can we still meet?"

"I'm not going to be able to come meet you anymore. I'm too weak. You can come by the house, but you'll have to coordinate that with Daisy. She's in charge now."

After an emotional goodbye, Justin felt saddened at the thought of losing the man who'd literally changed his life. He couldn't begin to imagine his life without his mentor, his friend—not now, not ever.

He drove off in a rage. The heaviness of the last half-hour had now become overwhelming. For what had been one of his greatest days ever had quickly become his worst. It was more than he could handle.

As he pulled up in his driveway and got out of his car, he noticed one of Tommy's baseballs lying in the grass nearby. Without a second's hesitation, he picked up the ball and heaved it as hard as he could at the garage door. The large glass window portion of the door shattered as if it had been hit by a rocket.

The front door slammed open. "What happened!" cried Megan, running out toward Justin.

Justin fell to his knees and started sobbing uncontrollably. He couldn't hold his feelings in any longer.

Family time

MEGAN KNEW INSTANTLY what had happened the moment she saw Justin crying. Without saying a word, she put her arms around him and held him tightly.

"Mom, is daddy okay?" asked Michelle as she popped her head out from the back door.

"Honey, daddy's fine. We'll be right in," said Megan, beginning to feel the cold for the first time.

"I'm fine, sweetheart," Justin called out. He then turned to Megan and kissed her on the cheek, "Thank you."

By dinnertime Justin had regained his composure and entertained the family as he shared the day's events, moment by moment. Although Tommy and Michelle didn't understand everything, they always enjoyed hearing their dad tell work stories. They especially enjoyed the part about Christal, a name that they had heard before.

Justin ended the storytelling portion of the evening by showing the kids the framed Certification of Appreciation he received from the company. He had planned to stop the story there—that is until Tommy spoke up.

"Daddy, why did you break the window?"

Justin nodded to Megan to let her know that he felt okay to respond. "Son, it was an accident. I was angry and threw the ball at the garage and accidentally hit the window. It was wrong for me to do that."

"Are you going to pay for it from your allowance?" asked Tommy.

Justin and Megan laughed simultaneously.

"No, stupid," replied Michelle, "daddy doesn't have an allowance."

Megan immediately intervened. "Michelle, that's not how you talk to your brother."

"Yes, son, I'm going to pay for it. That was a bad thing for me to do and I will get it fixed."

Fortunately for Justin, that was as far as that conversation went. He wasn't quite ready to articulate *why* he threw the ball.

As the kids left the table, Megan went over and put her arms around him. "Honey, why don't you go to the den and relax. I'll take care of the kitchen and putting the kids to bed. You deserve a break."

Justin nodded and thanked her for her understanding. Normally he would jump at the idea of having some alone time in the den, his favorite room in the house—but this night would be different. He was feeling hesitant to be by himself.

"Are you okay?" asked Megan, wondering why he was still sitting at the table.

"I'm good," replied Justin. "Are you sure you don't need any help?"

"I'm fine, honey," said Megan, sensing that he wasn't. "Do you want to talk later?"

"I'm alright—really I am."

Justin then heated up a cup of hot tea and headed to the den, where he plopped himself down on his favorite recliner. Seconds later he was joined by Sandy, who also enjoyed the recliner, especially when she could sit on Justin's lap. Together, they sat in total silence. For the first time in Justin's adult life, watching *SportsCenter* just didn't seem important.

Part Eight

Endings and Beginnings

The final goodbye

THERE WAS NO QUESTION that having Christal back in the office provided Justin with the added support and guidance he needed to better his skills as a manager. But not even Christal could begin to replace the special relationship that he had with Dr. Mac.

A couple of months had passed since Dr. Mac had given Justin the devastating news. Since then, his health had rapidly declined, forcing Daisy to limit his visitors to immediate family and a few selected friends. Justin, gratefully, had made the short list. He knew that he'd get to see Dr. Mac at least one more time, never knowing if it was to be his last. Cancer was such a cruel disease.

The mood in the office was back to business as usual. The novelty of Christal's dramatic return had since dissipated, leaving a department that once thrived on crisis and chaos left to find meaning in the relatively mundane day-to-day activities of order taking. But the biggest difference was with Justin. Ever since the annual retreat, his disposition had become more sullen and his smile had become a forgotten commodity. With Charlie now out in Boulder, many turned to Justin to keep the humor and occasional practical jokes alive. But lately, even those went by the wayside.

Amy knocked on Justin's door. "May I come in?"

"Of course. How's it going?"

"I was going to ask you the same question."

"It's all good, Amy, it's all good," lied Justin.

"Is it really?"

"Why do you say that?"

"Hello, Justin. This is me, Amy. I know you and I know something is bothering you. Is it Dr. Mac?"

"Is it that obvious?" asked Justin.

"I'm afraid so."

"I'm sorry. I can't seem to shake this. It's so overwhelming."

"What do you mean, Justin?"

"Everything is going so great in my life. Work couldn't be better. I have the best staff any manager could ask for. Even my home life is fantastic. Yet I've never been so depressed as I am now. What's wrong with me, Amy?"

"Justin, I know what you're going through. My dad got worse before he got better. We thought he was going to die and we prepared ourselves for it. It was the absolute worst time of my life."

"But how do I deal with it? It's so consuming."

"Justin, this might sound weird but I'm going to say it anyway. You have to live each day as if it were your last. You owe that to yourself, to Dr. Mac, and to all of us. The truth is, anyone of us could get hit by a car tomorrow—ask Christal. That's why you have to live your life with a sense of urgency today. Waiting for Dr. Mac to die doesn't give you an excuse to put off living today. You can't control what happens to him, but you can control the quality with which you live your life."

Just then Justin's cell phone rang. Before answering, he apologized to Amy for taking the call. "I'm sorry, it could be about Dr. Mac."

Amy gestured for him to take the call.

"Hello Justin, this is Daisy. Ken asked to see you. I'm afraid he's not doing well at all. You need to hurry!" Click.

Justin looked up at Amy as if he had just seen a ghost.

"Go, Justin," urged Amy, knowing the call was about Dr. Mac. "Go now!"

Justin raced out the door and jumped in his car. He was shaking as he struggled to get the key in the ignition. Finally his car started and he sped down Maple. Within ten minutes he pulled in front of Dr. Mac's house. He ran to the front door.

There a tall man with a shiny bald head opened the door. "Hi. Can I help you?"

"Yes," said Justin, a little frustrated that this guy was blocking his way into the house. "I'm here to see Dr. Mac. I'm Justin O'Brien."

Daisy yelled from the stairway. "It's okay, Ryan; you can let him in."

"I'm sorry, Mr. O'Brien. Please come in. He's upstairs."

Justin turned toward Ryan. "And you are?"

"Oops, sorry again. I'm Ryan and I'm with hospice. We're here to assist Ken and his loved ones with the dying process."

Justin didn't know too much about hospice but knew enough to know that they wouldn't be there unless Dr. Mac was in the final stages of dying.

Daisy waited for him at the top of the stairs. "Thank you for coming, Justin. Ken wanted to see you. He can barely talk, so you are going to have get real close to him."

Justin squeezed Daisy's hand and headed into the bedroom. There, lying on the bed under a blanket was Dr. Mac. His eyes were closed. Justin was relieved to see that he was still breathing. In fact he looked very peaceful as he lay there.

Just then Dr. Mac's eyes opened up. He immediately smiled as he recognized Justin.

"O'Brien," whispered Dr. Mac, "I'm so glad you could come."

Justin pulled up a chair right next to him and leaned in as he spoke. "Just being with you makes my day, Dr. Mac."

Dr. Mac was clearly struggling to get each word out. "How are you?"

Here Dr. Mac was dying and all he cared about was how Justin was doing. "I'm fine, Dr. Mac."

Justin paused before recanting what he just said. "No, I'm not. I miss you so much."

Dr. Mac held out his hand, his arm shaking just from the exertion of extending it. Justin grabbed the hand and held on to it tightly.

"O'Brien, I need two favors."

"Anything, Dr. Mac."

"First, promise me that you'll live each day as if it were your last."

Justin did a mental double take. That was the same thing Amy had said to him just a few minutes ago.

"Of course I'll do that, Dr. Mac. What else?"

Dr. Mac's breathing was almost nonexistent now. "Don't give our bench away. Let's continue to meet there."

Tears were now welling up in Justin's eyes. The moment he dreaded was now upon him. This was his goodbye. He squeezed Dr. Mac's hand. "You will always be with me, old man."

Dr. Mac smiled as he closed his eyes.

Justin called out for Daisy.

As he switched places with her, he looked at Dr. Mac for one last time before leaving the room. Dr. Mac and Daisy were holding hands, both weeping quietly. It would be the last time Justin ever saw Dr. Mac alive.

The memorial service

EACH STRIKE OF THE CHURCH BELL penetrated right through Justin, ripping away, little by little, at his protective exterior that was masking his deep pain and sorrow over the loss of Dr. Mac. He couldn't believe how emotional he was becoming, and the service hadn't even begun.

The church was completely full and there were still a line of cars waiting to get into Faith, Hope and Charity's parking lot. Mixed in with the crowd of mourners was the *who's who* of Chicago's media organizations, including all of the television, radio and newspaper executives. Even J.W. and Melvin were there.

"Boy, I hope I can get half as many people at my memorial," whispered Justin, trying to lighten the moment.

"Don't worry, honey," smiled Megan, "I'll make sure everyone brings a friend."

Before Justin could respond, the large wooden doors in the back of the church slammed shut and the music began. Daisy, along with Dr. Mac's brother and sister and their respective families, were then escorted up to the front row. The service began with Father Thinnes, a longtime friend of Dr. Mac, telling a heartwarming story about a time he and Dr. Mac went on a camping trip together. The crowd tearfully laughed with every word. Then Dr. Mac's favorite song, "What a Wonderful World" sung by Israel Kamakawiwo, came over the sound system. After a couple more testimonials from family and friends, the service ended with a bone-chilling rendition of "Amazing Grace," performed by a single bagpiper.

It was one of the most touching services that Justin could ever remember.

Afterward, Daisy invited Justin and Megan over to their house for a "small gathering of friends," as she called it. On their way over, they listened to WKBT, which was airing reruns of *Macology in the Mornings* as a tribute to Dr. Mac.

Megan turned down the radio and looked over at Justin. "Honey, it just occurred to me that you never told me what Dr. Mac said to you the day he died."

"I'm sorry," replied Justin, "I thought I had told you."

"Nope, you never did. Do you feel comfortable telling me?"

"Of course. He said two things. First he offered me a piece of advice— to live each day as if it were my last."

"Really, wow!"

"What made that even more interesting was the fact that Amy had said exactly the same thing to me earlier that day. It was eerie. Almost like the universe was sending me a message through both of them."

"And what was the second thing?"

"He said, and I quote, 'Don't give our bench away. Let's continue to meet there.'"

"He did?"

"Yeah. Those were his exact words."

"So what do you think he meant by that?"

"I'm not sure. What do you think?" asked Justin.

"Honey, I think he wants you to keep going to the park bench. Don't you?"

"I guess. I'd probably do that anyway, but now it will even be more special."

All of a sudden Megan's eyes lit up. "Justin, I've got it!"

"What do you mean, you've got it?"

"A lot of the benches at the Village Green have little memorial plaques placed in front of them. Maybe you should put a memorial plaque in front of your bench for Dr. Mac!"

Justin suddenly looked as if he had just won the lottery. "That's it! Megan, you're incredible. What a great way to memorialize him."

"I'm so excited for you, Justin. What would you put on the plaque?"

"Oh, I don't know. But it would have to be something good."

Megan was happy to see Justin enthusiastic again. "Wait one minute," said Justin. "I've got it!"

"Got what?"

"The plaque. I know exactly what to put on it."

"Don't tell me."

"What? Why not?"

"Because I want it to be a surprise."

"Okay, but you're going to love it."

The reception

THE GATHERING AT DAISY'S HOUSE was a fitting celebration of her husband of fifty-seven years. Although Justin didn't know many of the people there, he was honored to be included with this group of close friends and colleagues. Megan, equally honored, was in the kitchen, helping Daisy.

"Excuse me, are you Justin O'Brien?" asked a tall and distinguished-looking man.

Justin immediately put out his hand, just happy to have someone to talk to. "Why yes, I'm Justin."

"Justin, I've heard all about you. I'm Steve Landon, managing editor of the *Daily Tribune*. Ken talked a lot about you."

Justin wasn't sure if the man was pulling his leg or not. "Really, what did he say?"

"Justin, a lot of people who write in to the column are complainers. Now don't get me wrong, we're pleased that so many people are writing in and reading the column. But Ken knew you were different. He often commented that you were one of the rare ones who clearly was destined to be a leader. He was a very insightful guy. You should take that as a compliment."

"Oh, I do. I just didn't know that you guys talk about that kind of stuff."

"Ken and I conferred on all the letters. Perhaps sometime we can meet for lunch and I can fill you in on how all of that worked. It's pretty fascinating, actually. Would you like to go to lunch next week? Say Wednesday?"

Justin was surprised that someone of Steve's stature would be inviting him to lunch. Nevertheless, he was curious to know more about his working arrangement with Dr. Mac and agreed to meet with Steve the following Wednesday.

A few minutes later Megan walked out of the kitchen toward Justin. "Are you about ready to go, honey?"

"Yep, I do have to get back to work. Let's go say goodbye to Daisy."

"I just did, honey. You go, and I'll meet you in the car."

Justin walked into the kitchen and spotted Daisy talking with some people. "I'm sorry to interrupt, Daisy, but we have to get going."

Daisy smiled, "I've got something for you, Justin. Follow me."

She excused herself from the others and led Justin into the bedroom, the same room where Justin last saw Dr. Mac. It made him feel a little uncomfortable.

"Daisy, do you want me to wait out here in the hallway?" asked Justin, hoping that she'd say yes.

"No, come on in."

She then grabbed an object off the dresser and put it in Justin's hand. It didn't take more than a second for Justin to recognize it. It was the gold pocket watch that Justin had given Dr. Mac as a gift a couple of months ago.

"Ken asked that I give this to you. It meant a great deal to him and he was hesitant to part with it."

"Then why did he?"

Daisy looked right into Justin's eyes. "Because he knew he was dying and he thought that it was only appropriate that you have it."

"Wow, I'm so honored."

Justin and Daisy embraced before he headed out the front door, not sure if or when he'd ever be back.

Megan was already in the car with the engine running. Justin got in and then immediately got out.

"What are you doing?" asked Megan.

"I forgot to do something," replied Justin as he headed back into the house. Minutes later he came out smiling.

Megan was curious now. "What was that all about?"

"Oh, nothing, really. I just shared the idea about the park bench with Daisy and got her blessing."

"Very cool. Okay, now you can tell me what you're going to put on the plaque."

"Nope, it's too late. You're just going to have to wait."

Megan hit Justin in the arm. "Sometimes I hate you."

The unexpected offer

"**J**-Man, I'll tell you what," said Charlie, "why don't you come out here and take over the Boulder operation, and I go out there and take over your job. You like Boulder."

"Chas, I love Boulder but you've got to give it more time. You're not just managing the Orders Fulfillment Department out there, my man; you are overseeing the whole expansion project. It's not every day that an opportunity like that comes your way."

"I know, I know," said Charlie, "but Mallory wants me to stay only until the new building is up and running. In other words, she's not willing to move out here with the kids."

"I'm sorry, Chas. I had no idea that staying in Winnetka was so important to her."

"It's important to me, too. This promotion has been a bittersweet thing."

Justin looked at his watch and realized that he needed to get going if he was to be on time to meet Steve Landon for lunch. "Chas, I know you think I don't do anything anymore around here since you left, but I actually have a lunch meeting I have to get to."

"Alright, J-Man. Hey, how are you doing since Dr. Mac died? I'm sorry I wasn't there for you."

"I'm better. Thanks for asking. Oddly, the guy I'm having lunch with was Dr. Mac's editor at the *Daily Tribune*. And get this, he asked me to lunch."

"No kidding. Why? I mean, not that you aren't worthy."

"Look bud, you should have quit while you were ahead." They both laughed and hung up.

Justin hurried out to his car. He didn't want to keep the chief editor of the *Daily Tribune* waiting, even if he had no idea why they were meeting.

At the restaurant, Justin spotted Steve Landon seated at a corner table, waving him over.

"So, how have you been?" asked Steve, making Justin feel like he was the most important person in the restaurant.

"I've been fine. I miss Dr. Mac."

"Who doesn't? He was such a great inspiration to us all. He and I had coffee here every Tuesday morning."

"Really?" replied Justin. "And here I thought I was the only special one who had a weekly meeting with him!"

Steve laughed. He seemed to be enjoying himself. "Justin, I mentioned last week that Dr. Mac used to talk about you."

"Yeah, that still surprises me a little."

"Well it's true. In fact, and this might also surprise you, he and I had a conversation about a month ago about the future of his column."

"But he was pretty ill and in bed a month ago."

"I know. And despite that, he was the one who initiated the conversation. I tell you, the guy just never stopped." Steve shook his head in amazement. "Anyway, I'll get right to the point. Justin, Ken suggested that we continue the column. He felt strongly that it was serving a purpose. Quite frankly, I couldn't agree more."

Justin still had no idea why Steve was telling him all of this.

"And Justin, are you ready for this? Ken thought you should be the one to take over the column."

"Me? No, no. Surely there must be a mistake. First off, I know hardly anything about solving management and employee problems. In fact, I'm the one who usually creates them. And secondly, my degree is in marketing. You must have misunderstood him."

Steve smiled. "Do you know what Ken's degrees were in?"

"What?"

"Math!"

"Math?"

"Math. He was a very perceptive guy who cared greatly about people. That's what got him into this business, not his degrees."

"That's amazing. I always thought he was a doctor of psychology or organizational development."

"Not even close. He certainly developed an expertise in management over the years, but that was not what made him successful. It was his altruistic caring for others coupled with his ability to communicate. Keep in mind, Justin, Ken had a staff of researchers as well as business consultants with whom he regularly conferred. What people saw was Dr. Mac, but what they didn't see were the people around him who helped make Macology a reality."

Justin had no idea that Dr. Mac had a staff, let alone started out without any experience. Nevertheless, he couldn't see himself trying to fill such large shoes. Surely he needed to convince Steve of that.

"Besides, Steve, I've got a job that takes up most of my time. I wouldn't be able to find the time to read all the letters, let alone respond to any."

"Justin, we are talking about a full-time position with the newspaper."

"But, but, I thought that was a part-time thing. Didn't he also work for the radio station?"

"He did that on the side. He also spoke around the country as well. All of that was in addition to being a columnist at the *Daily Tribune*."

Steve seemed to have an answer to every comment or question that Justin could ask.

"I'll tell you what, Justin, just think about it for a couple of days and then let's get together again. It's a great opportunity and perhaps a way to pay tribute to Dr. Mac. After all, it was his idea to keep the column going and it was his idea to have you replace him. I believed so much in the man that I'm willing to take his word on all of this."

"Steve, don't get me wrong, it's an honor to even be having this conversation with you…but I haven't been in management for even a year. How could I help anyone?"

"We wouldn't throw you in with the wolves, Justin. You and I would write the column together until you felt ready to take it over. Plus, don't forget that there is an experienced staff ready to help as well. The column practically writes itself. Please consider it."

"I will, I will," replied Justin, still very much in denial. And just then his curiosity got the better of him. "Just for kicks, Steve, what kind of salary are we talking about?"

Steve smiled. "I was waiting for that question." He then took his napkin and wrote a figure down and passed it to Justin.

Justin opened the napkin and quickly looked up at Steve, trying to conceal his smile. It was $15,000 more than his current salary.

"And Justin, that doesn't include a possible radio contract and speaking fees," added Steve.

Justin had to pinch himself to make sure he wasn't dreaming. "Can I ask you one more question?"

"Of course."

"What are you thinking of calling the column?"

"We wanted to stay with *Ask Dr. Mac*. It's important to stick with a heading that people have come to recognize."

Their conversation ended with a commitment to talk in a couple of days. The shock of the offer was slowly sinking in for Justin. He couldn't wait to see what Megan would say.

A more difficult decision

"YOU'RE LYING!" cried Megan.

"I swear, he wants me to take over Dr. Mac's column—me, Justin O'Brien. The same guy who almost got himself fired on more than two occasions since becoming a manager!"

"Honey, are you telling me all of this so we can discuss it or have you already made up your mind?"

"Megan, I'm not going to make the same mistake I made the last time I was offered a position. Yes, I want to discuss this and get your opinion."

Megan hugged Justin. "I'm so excited for you. How much is he willing to pay you?"

"It's all about the money for you, isn't it?"

"Come on honey, tell me."

"He offered me $15,000 more than what I'm currently making at DataDump."

"Oh my God, Justin!"

"Yeah, and that doesn't include a possible radio contract or speaking fees."

"Yes, I think you should take it."

"That's it? That's the extent of our discussion?"

"Honey, why wouldn't you take it?"

"For starters, I'm not the least bit qualified."

"Quit saying that Justin! You said the exact same thing when Christal offered you the manager's position and look what you did with it. You took it to a whole new level and got an award for it to boot. When are you going to start believing in yourself?"

"Okay, I guess now we're having that *discussion*," replied Justin.

Megan moved closer. "What was it Dr. Mac told you that day you called his radio show?"

"I can't remember...something about jumping on opportunities that don't come around very often?"

"Exactly. Honey, I don't understand why you are struggling with this. What's going on?"

"Do you want the truth?" replied Justin.

"No, I want you to lie to me. Of course I want the truth!"

"Megan, what if I fail? What if I give some advice that backfires? There are real people out there with very real problems. This isn't pretend anymore. I'd be impacting the lives of others. Do you have any idea what kind of pressure that would be for me?"

"Honey, think about what you just said. You would have an opportunity to help real people with real problems. Isn't that what it's all about? You have a chance to truly make an impact on the lives of others. Why wouldn't you take that on?"

Justin knew Megan had a point but was still resistant to the whole idea. The responsibility of taking over the column seemed so overwhelming to him.

"With all due respect, babe, I need to get more input. I'm calling Christal."

"That's a good idea. I know she'll agree with me."

"That's fine if she does. I just want a second opinion," replied Justin as he dialed Christal's cell phone.

"This is Christal."

"Oh good, you're there."

"Justin?"

"Yeah, it's me. Hey, I need your help and guidance again."

"Now?"

"Yeah, it's kind of important."

"Okay, what's going on?"

"Are you sitting down?"

These weren't the kind of words Christal liked to hear. "Oh no, what happened?"

"No, it's good...well, sort of."

"Who's quitting?" Christal asked, nervously.

"No one. Then again..."

"Justin, just come out with it."

"Alright, I've been offered a job at the *Daily Tribune*. They want me to take over Dr. Mac's column."

Christal broke out laughing. "Ah, that's a good one, Justin. You had me going for a second. Is Charlie on the line with you?"

"I'm serious. And no, Charlie's not on the line."

"Really, you're serious?"

"I wouldn't have called you after hours if I wasn't. Remember, that's your rule."

"Okay, let me see if I got this right," clarified Christal. "They want you to take over Dr. Mac's advice column? Justin, you're a great manager, don't get me wrong, but giving out management advice? Shouldn't that be left to the experts?"

"That's actually what I thought. But it turns out Dr. Mac wasn't an expert either. Did you know his degrees were all in math? Besides, Steve says he'll co-write with me until I get the hang of things."

"Justin, who exactly is Steve and is he the one who asked you to take over for Dr. Mac?"

"Steve Landon is the managing editor," replied Justin. "But actually, it was Dr. Mac who recommended me. Apparently they had a conversation a few weeks before he died."

"So are you seriously considering it?" asked Christal, now becoming concerned.

"Yes—and Megan's all for it. But you two are the only ones I've talked with so far."

"Justin, can you tell me what he offered you?"

"Yes, it was $15,000 more than what you are paying me. And he said that didn't include a possible radio contract and speaking fees."

"Speaking fees?"

"I know, that sounds funny. Can you imagine me as a speaker?"

"To tell you the truth, Justin, I'm having trouble imaging all of this. Are you sure this isn't a dream?"

Justin laughed. "If it is, I'm going to be very disappointed when I wake up."

Christal knew she needed to do something. "Justin, do me a favor and don't tell anyone else about this right now—not until we talk again. I'll call you back tonight, okay?"

"Sure, Christal, but I'd like to figure this out by tomorrow. Steve's waiting on an answer."

As Justin hung up the phone, Megan walked in and sat down right in front of him. She had been eavesdropping just outside the door. "What did Christal have to say? Tell me everything."

Justin affectionately put her in a headlock. "You were listening outside the door; you tell me what she said."

"Come on, honey," cried Megan as she pulled his arms away, "I couldn't hear a thing."

Justin thought about teasing her some more but decided to answer her question. "By the time she realized that I was serious, she said she'd call me back. I think I threw her off."

"So what now?" asked Megan.

"I think I'm going to go out and get a cup of coffee."

"Why? What about dinner?"

"Sweetie, I just need some alone time to sort things out. Don't worry; I won't make any final decisions without you."

"Okay, but don't be gone long. You still have to talk to Christal."

Justin kissed Megan on top of her head and grabbed his journal on his way out the door. *This would be as good a time as ever to write down some thoughts,* he said to himself. And then another idea came to him—an even better idea. He went back to the den, reached up on the top shelf, and grabbed another journal that had been sitting up there for the better part of three months. It was Dr. Mac's journal. For whatever reason, Justin had been reluctant to open it. But perhaps this was the time.

The 91 counteroffer

THE SWEET SHOP WAS QUICKLY becoming Justin's home away from home. This was where he and Dr. Mac met when it was too cold or snowy to go to the nearby park. He loved this place and the memories that came with it.

"Justin, here's your nonfat, hazelnut latte," said Amber, who knew him well enough to call him by name. "By yourself tonight?"

"Amber, when you think about it, are we ever really alone?" teased Justin.

"Oh, please!" chuckled Amber. "I think you've had too much caffeine already."

Justin smiled as he headed toward his table. Seconds later a cell phone went off in the restaurant. Immediately everyone reached for their phones. Justin laughed at how funny that looked until he realized that it was his own phone that was ringing.

"Oops. Hello."

"Justin, Christal. Where are you? I can barely hear you."

"I'm at the Sweet Shop."

"Can you hear me?" shouted Christal.

"Yes, I can hear you just fine. What's up?"

"Justin, I just got off the phone with J.W. and Melvin and they have asked me to meet with you tomorrow to see what we can do to keep you at DataDump. Would you be willing to do that?"

"You're kidding, right?"

"No, I'm perfectly serious. Why? You haven't made your decision yet, have you?"

"No, I'm still thinking it through," replied Justin, somewhat surprised that DataDump was willing to fight to keep him. "I just wasn't expecting anything like a counteroffer."

"Believe me, it's not something we do very often. You are obviously worth it, Justin. So, tomorrow at 9:00 a.m.?"

"I look forward to it. Thanks, Christal."

As Justin hung up the phone, he couldn't help but wonder what Megan's reaction would be to this new development. After all, it wasn't every day that a company was willing to fight to keep a fairly new manager from leaving. That certainly would have to impress her. But fortunately or unfortunately as the case might be, he was in a slightly different position now than he had been just a short time ago. Now he would have to choose between two offers instead of deciding on just one. His decision had become much more difficult.

Justin opened up his journal and proceeded to make two lists, *Stay at DataDump* and *Take over Dr. Mac's column.* Under each heading he jotted down whatever came to mind:

Stay at DataDump	**Take over Dr. Mac's column**
• I like what I do now.	• It was Dr. Mac's wish.
• I have an excellent staff.	• It's an exciting & new opportunity.
• My job is comfortable.	• There's little or no room to fail.
• I know what I'm doing.	• It would require new skills like
• Sr. Mgmt is willing to make a commitment to me.	writing & speaking.
	• I could impact thousands of people.
• My job is predictable.	• It's more money.
• I like stability.	• There are a lot of "unknowns."

404

He then stopped and evaluated both lists. What he noticed was surprising. The "Stay at DataDump" side was more about comfort, security, predictability, and stability. The "Take over Dr. Mac's column," side, on the other hand, was more about risk, challenge, accountability, reward, and growth.

What does this mean? he pondered.

Then he glanced over at Dr. Mac's journal. Without hesitation, he pulled the journal in front of him and flipped to a random page. *Whatever page I open to will be the page I'm supposed to read,* he said to himself before looking down at the journal entry in front of him. Little did he know the significance of what he was about to read.

November 11, 1985

I've worked hard to get to where I am today. By most people's standards, I'd be considered successful. I have a good marriage, a nice home, and I like my job in data analysis. My life is comfortable, predictable, and secure.

Then why am I feeling so unfulfilled?

The answer is becoming increasingly clear to me. I've become ordinary. And in so doing, I've lost my passion.

Justin couldn't believe the coincidence. The irony was both haunting and insightful. It was as if Dr. Mac was in the room, speaking to him directly.

Immediately, he jumped up, grabbed his journals and walked out of the restaurant. He was suddenly feeling a lot of emotion and needed a different venue to sort this out. He needed to go to the park bench.

It was cold outside and beginning to snow as Justin trekked down the slippery hill to the park. Although many wouldn't venture out on such an evening, let alone on foot,

Justin felt more and more invigorated with every step as he headed toward his destination. He was on a mission.

Once at the bench he sat down and closed his eyes. He remembered all the good times he'd had at this very spot with Dr. Mac—all the laughter, all the talks, and all the tears. He missed the man terribly. And then he recalled Dr. Mac's final words to him before he died. "Don't give our bench away. Let's continue to meet there." With tears rolling down his face, Justin stood up and began talking out loud, as if he were talking to his mentor and friend.

My pattern all along has been to take the road "most" traveled. I work hard so that I can create a life that is comfortable, easy, and manageable. I don't like to rock the boat and I want things to always be neat and orderly. And I don't like conflict, challenge, or change.

He was now pacing around the bench, looking more like a professor lecturing to his students.

At the same time, I've never grown so much as I have in the last six months. I've never felt so alive! Was it the job that created that? No. It was who I had to become in order to take on the job that did it. In fact, to be totally honest, it was the relationship building that meant so much to me during the past six months, not the work. My true passion comes from helping people and creating empowering relationships. That's what gets me up in the morning; that's what makes me feel like I'm contributing. And that's what makes me feel alive!

Justin was smiling now. The answer had come to him. He would follow his passion and take the road *less* traveled. He was going to accept the *Tribune* position and take over Dr. Mac's column. This would be a night he would never forget.

Coming home

IT WAS LATE BY THE TIME JUSTIN got home that evening. Megan had fallen asleep on the couch watching Jay Leno. Justin went over and nuzzled her cheek. She rolled over and opened her eyes.

"Honey, are you okay?"

Justin had a glow on his face. "Couldn't be better."

"Did Christal call you back?"

"Yes, she did. She asked me to come in tomorrow so we could talk...but I don't think that'll be necessary any more."

"Why?" Megan was now smiling and she sat up, knowing what Justin was going to say next.

"Because I've decided that you were right all along. I want to take over Dr. Mac's column. What do you think?"

Megan jumped off the couch and into Justin's arms. "I think you are doing the right thing. I'm so proud of you!"

Sharing the news

THE NEXT DAY DIDN'T PROMISE to be any easier for Justin. Now that his decision was made, he would find himself spending the better part of the day defending it. He was not looking forward to his meeting with Christal.

Helen waved at Justin from down the hallway. "Christal called to say she's running late. She said to go ahead and have a seat in her office."

"No problem, Helen," smiled Justin, as he walked on by and into Christal's office. He was glad to see that things were getting back to normal.

Christal's office was now fully decorated. She had artwork up on the walls, pictures of her family on her desk, and a couple of comfortable chairs over by the window. As Justin looked around the room, he noticed that he was feeling a bit sad. For the first time since coming to DataDump nearly six years ago, he was preparing to leave.

"Good morning, Justin. How do you like my new digs?" asked Christal, as she walked in.

Justin smiled. "I was wondering where the fitness center will go."

"I'll have to take a wall out to do that but I don't think Melvin will mind, do you?"

They both chuckled. There was a slight awkwardness in the air.

Christal pointed over at the two comfortable chairs. "Shall we go sit by the window?"

"Of course, but I've got to tell—"

Christal raised her hand to interrupt. "Justin, promise me you'll hear me out first."

"Okay, but..."

"Justin." Christal's face suddenly softened as she took a deep breath. "You've already made up you mind, haven't you?"

"I had an incredible revelation in the park after I talked to you last night."

"At the park? But it was snowing out!"

"I know. It was great."

"So do I want to hear the rest of this?" asked Christal.

"I'll get right to the point. My revelation was that I need to follow my passion—and my passion is more in helping people than in managing them. As much as I love DataDump, my staff, and especially working with you, I owe it to myself to pursue this opportunity with the *Tribune*. If I don't at least try, I may regret it down the road, and I don't think either of us would want that."

Christal looked at Justin with admiration. "It's refreshing to see such passion. Of course you should pursue it. The opportunity that awaits you is much greater than anything we could have offered you here." She then leaned over and gave him a congratulatory hug. "But boy am I going to miss you."

Before Justin could respond, there was a loud knocking on Christal's door. "Excuse me, Christal," said Helen, as she popped her head through the cracked door, "but you have a ten o'clock with J.W."

Christal smiled at Justin and looked at Helen. "Please tell J.W. that we'll need to reschedule."

"Are you sure?" asked Helen, as if Christal were making a mistake.

"I'm sure, Helen."

Seconds after Helen closed the door, both Justin and Christal broke out laughing.

"I can't believe you just did that!" exclaimed Justin.

"I can't either," replied Christal. "I may be joining you at the *Tribune*."

After their laughter subsided, Christal asked Justin who he thought would be a good successor.

"I already thought of that. In fact, there is only one person who would be a perfect fit for the manager position."

"Will?"

"Nope."

"Lee Ann?"

"Nope."

"Then who?"

"Charlie."

"Charlie? You're joking. Why would he give up the opportunity he has in Boulder?"

"Christal, Charlie would kill me if he knew I was going to tell you this, but given the circumstances, I feel like I'd be doing him a disservice if I didn't. Charlie wants to come back to Winnetka more than anything right now. As you may recall, he took a step down in coming to DataDump just so he could be here in his hometown. Well I know for a fact that that hasn't changed. And Mallory has told him that she will not move out to Boulder and uproot the kids."

"You're kidding me. Boulder is such a great place to live."

"Yeah but Winnetka is her hometown, too. And like Charlie, she has friends and family here and simply doesn't want to leave."

"So why didn't Charlie come talk to me?" asked Christal.

"Because he loves being with DataDump and didn't want to pass up an incredible opportunity to advance in the company. Plus he didn't want to let you down."

"Let me down? Oh please!"

Christal leaned back, shaking her head. "So you think he would take your position?"

"I know he would," replied Justin.

The frown on Christal's face slowly softened before transforming itself into an outright smile. "Then let's call him!"

"What?"

"Let's call him right now. I'm not about to lose both of you."

Justin's face lit up in anticipation of Charlie's reaction. He pulled Christal's office phone over and carefully pressed each number of Charlie's direct line so as to not make a mistake. After the first ring, he hit the red speakerphone button.

"Hello, this is Charlie."

"Hello, this is Justin."

"Hey J-Man, what's up?"

"Chas, I have Christal here with me and we have some news for you."

Charlie's tone suddenly became serious, as if he was expecting something bad. "Okay. Tell me."

"Charlie, Christal. We were wondering if you would be interested in coming back to Winnetka to manage the Orders Fulfillment Department?"

There was a pause on the other end before Charlie responded. "You're kidding, right?"

"We're not kidding. Justin is leaving us and we both feel that you would be the perfect person to step into his job. If I can get approval for this, what would you say?"

"Wait a minute. Justin is leaving?"

"Charlie, it's Justin again. You won't believe this but I've been asked to take over Dr. Mac's column at the *Tribune* and I have decided to do it."

There was no response on the other end.

"Charlie, are you still there?" asked Christal.

Still no response.

"Charlie?"

After a few more seconds a choked-up Charlie replied, "I'm sorry, I needed a moment to take all of this in. You want me to come back and be the manager of the Orders Fulfillment Department?"

"Of course that's assuming you'd be willing to leave Boulder," added Justin.

"Are you guys playing a joke on me? 'Cause it would be an awful one if you were."

"Charlie, I wish it were a joke because that way I'd still have both of you heading up two of my most important areas," replied Christal. "But it's not. I need you here in Winnetka. If I can get this approved, will you come back?"

Charlie barely let her finish. "Of course I'd come back to Winnetka!"

Justin and Christal gave each other approving nods.

"Charlie, I'm going to call you the minute we have official approval. I'd like to put you on the speaker phone when we announce it to the staff," acknowledged Justin.

"No problem. Thank you both so much. I won't do anything until I hear back!"

After hanging up, Justin turned toward Christal. "Isn't it great how everything has a way of working itself out?"

"Justin, everything hasn't worked itself out yet—at least for me. I've got to get approval for Charlie to take your position and then go through the whole process of filling his position out in Boulder. I just hope I'm not in too much trouble for doing what I just did. I never told you that I was reprimanded for hiring you without going through an official interview process, did I?"

"I was wondering about that. I guess I wasn't much help this time by insisting that Charlie be the one to take my place."

"Justin, I appreciated what you said about Charlie. I feel bad that I didn't know and clearly need to do a better job in understanding what's going on with my direct reports."

"That haunted me as well," added Justin.

"What do you mean?"

"For quite a while I didn't know what was going on with John or Amy and was even more removed from the Boulder staff."

"I can relate to that. I never quite got the hang of it myself."

"Christal, don't take this personally, but was that why the Boulder women felt neglected by you?"

"You are just full of good news today, aren't you, Justin."

"I'm sorry, I thought you knew."

"Actually, I did. I was just giving you a hard time. But when I think back on it, I never took the time to get to know the ladies in Boulder individually or as a group. I constantly threw Band-Aids at them in hopes that it would help enough until we could get a manager out there on a permanent basis. Had I known that it was going to take well over a year for that to happen, I would have been much more responsive. That was my fault. It's also probably why I was so resistant to you going out there."

"Because I was doing something that you thought you should have done but never did?"

"Something like that. You know, you might not be so bad with Dr. Mac's column after all."

"Thanks. I'm going to need all the help I can get."

"Justin, can I give you a little advice?"

"Please do."

"Always believe in what you are doing and never lose focus, especially through the ups and downs. I call it *trusting the process*. I can't begin to tell you how many times I wanted to throw in the towel while lying in the hospital. I thought I'd never get better."

"But you stuck it out."

"I did, but it wasn't easy. It never is. But then one day I came to realize that I wasn't going to get any better by feeling sorry for myself. I had an obligation to the people around me, including you, to get better. It's funny how we can think the world revolves around us and us alone, as if no one else matters."

"I know exactly what you're saying!" replied Justin. "So what did you do?"

"I recommitted myself to getting better. Then I had to establish realistic goals so that I could start seeing some results."

"You mean like walking?"

"No, I mean like being able to sit up in the bed. Walking came much later."

"Wow, I had no idea."

Christal got up from the table, "I'm sorry, I didn't mean to get into all of that. This is a big day for you and here I turn the focus to me."

"No need to apologize. I was so lost in my own world when you were in the hospital that I was oblivious to what was going on in yours. I'm sorry for that."

Christal put her arm around Justin as she walked him out of her office. "You know, I'm sorry we didn't get a chance to work with each other more than we did. This is going to sound a little weird, but I feel like the mother who missed seeing her child grow up."

"Christal, you maybe didn't see it, but you certainly did your part to make it happen. You saw something in me that I didn't. For that, I will always be grateful."

As Justin walked down the hallway, he realized how much he was going to hate saying goodbye to this place. *This day is not going to get any easier,* he said to himself.

The last staff meeting

"STAFF MEETING AT ELEVEN O'CLOCK," yelled Justin as he entered the department. Although he was still waiting to hear about Charlie's approval, he knew at the very least that he'd share his news.

"Where have you been?" asked Lee Ann, looking concerned. "Is everything alright?"

"A lot has been going on, to tell you the truth. I'll fill you in with everything at the staff meeting."

"Okay then." Lee Ann had known something was up before even asking the question.

Justin headed into his office for some reflection time before the meeting and promptly closed the door. He pulled out his journal and began to write.

Journal Entry # 14
   a) Discovering my purpose and passion means nothing if I'm not willing to follow it.
   b) Trusting the process means having an unyielding commitment to a desired outcome, regardless of what's happening around me.

c) For every ending lies a new beginning...but only if I remain open to possibilities.

Justin couldn't believe how philosophical he was getting. *I'm actually beginning to sound like Dr. Mac,* he laughed to himself. And that thought immediately triggered another. *Oops, I still need to accept the job!* He dialed Steve Landon's number.

"Mr. Landon's office, can I help you?"

"Hello, this is Justin O'Brien. Is Steve—"

Lori, Steve's secretary, didn't wait for Justin to finish. "Hello, Mr. O'Brien. Steve has been expecting your call. Hold on."

"Justin!" said Steve, "I was hoping you would call today."

"Hello, Steve. How are you?"

"I'm better now that I'm talking to you. But more importantly, how are you?"

"All is well. And yes, I'd love to come work for you and the *Tribune* and take over Dr. Mac's column. Is the position still available?"

"Oh that—no, we filled it yesterday...not true!" Steve was a kidder, too. "Of course it's yours! When can you start?"

Justin loved Steve's energy. "Is four weeks okay? I want to help my successor with the transition process here and it might take a few weeks before he can even get here."

"Four weeks is fine. We've got a backlog of letters and responses that we can post until then. I'll let Susan and Chuck know."

Justin was confused. "Susan and Chuck?"

"They are your crack research staff. Susan is a human resources expert and Chuck is an employment law attorney. Both work on a part-time basis for you, Justin...or should I call you *Dr. Mac?*"

"Wow, that sure makes me feel better to know I have a research staff. But that brings up the other thing I wanted to ask you."

"What's that?"

"I don't feel right assuming Dr. Mac's name. Can we change the title of the column?"

"Justin, I can appreciate your concern, but we are talking about much more than a title here. Dr. Mac's advice has become an institution. It takes years to create that kind of credibility, let alone name recognition. Do you know how many different writers there were for the *Dear Abby* column?"

"I see your point, Steve, I guess the best way to let his legacy live on is through his column."

As Justin hung up the phone, he spotted John trying to get his attention outside his office, pointing to his watch.

Justin looked up at the clock and saw that it was after eleven. *Yikes!* He shot up out of his chair, and bolted out his door.

"Hey, slow down buddy!"

Justin turned around and spotted a familiar face smiling at him. It was Christal.

"Mind if I join you?"

"Hi, Christal. Sure, come on in with me," replied Justin, wondering if she had some good news to report. "Have you heard anything?"

"Yes I have," said Christal. "We're good to go."

"Really? That was fast."

"I've gotten pretty good with my persuasive skills," chuckled Christal.

"Super," said Justin, "now we've got two announcements to make."

Just then both Justin and Christal looked at each other in amazement.

"Does it feel like we've done this before?" asked Christal.

"I know," cried out Justin. "Isn't this ironic?"

Christal could only shake her head as they both entered the break room together, just as they did the previous September under slightly different, but very similar circumstances.

"Sorry for being late," announced Justin, "but we've got some important information to share with you today."

"You're taking Christal's job?" joked Will.

Everyone laughed.

Justin looked around at all the eager faces staring back at him, anxiously waiting to hear whatever it was he had to say. In that moment he also realized how much he was going to miss being their manager.

Just then the light on the phone in the room started beeping, indicating that someone was calling in.

"Should I answer it?" asked Sara.

Justin looked over at Christal, wondering if she had called Charlie.

"I would," said Christal, with a big grin on her face.

Justin winked back. "Put it on speakerphone, Sara."

Now everyone looked curious.

"Charlie, are you there?" asked Justin.

"Hello, everyone." replied Charlie to the whole group.

John led the group in a unified, "Hello, Charlie," by moving his arms up and down like a symphony conductor.

Justin began. "I invited Charlie here for our meeting so I could formally introduce you to your new manager!"

Blank looks and open mouths circumvented the group. The room was silent.

"That's right. I'm going to be leaving DataDump in four weeks and we've talked Charlie into coming back to Winnetka to take over my position."

No one moved or said anything. Most figured it was another practical joke and waited for a punch line or something...but none came. Finally Lee Ann asked, "Are you serious?"

Justin nodded. "Yes, very."

Charlie then went on to tell the group about all that had transpired for Justin in the past twenty-four hours.

It took the staff quite a while before they began to accept the news. As expected, everyone was excited to get Charlie back but sad to see Justin go. Needless to say, there was lots of laughter and lots of tears left between the walls of the break room that day—quite a contrast to what had happened in that room the last time the announcement of a new manager was made.

Epilogue: The Memorial Bench

IT WAS EARLY SPRING and Justin and Megan were walking hand-in-hand down the street.

"Don't you just love the spring, Justin...the smell of the flowers and the little tiny leaves budding on the trees?"

"I love it, I absolutely love it," replied Justin.

"So are you going to tell me where we're going, or do I have to tickle it out of you," demanded Megan.

"Honey, we're just going on a walk, that's all," replied Justin, steering her steadily toward the park.

Once they got there, Justin led Megan over toward the park bench that he now considered to be Dr. Mac's. As they sat down, he put his arm around her.

Megan knew something was up and began looking around, expecting something unusual to happen. And then she noticed it. On the ground and right in front of the bench was a plaque. It read:

> Live each day as if it were your last.
>
> Celebrating the life of Dr. Mac

Megan hugged Justin. "Honey, you did it! I'm so proud of you."

"He told me not to give the bench away so we could continue to meet." Justin paused as he looked up to the heavens. "Well, Dr. Mac, I'll see ya here on Monday at 3:00 p.m. We've got some catching up to do."

Justin's Insights Journal

Journal Entry # 1

a) If I can't say something nice, or at least say it in a supportive and constructive way, then I'm better off not saying it at all.

b) I need to take my concerns to the person I'm having the concerns with directly. Anything else would be disrespectful.

c) It's always a good idea to think through both the process and what outcomes I'm looking for before confronting another employee. And that includes trying to view the concern from their perspective as well.

Journal Entry # 2

a) Managing by way of assumptions only gets me into trouble. I need to have my facts straight before drawing any conclusions.

b) Never, ever confront a staff member in front of his or her peers. It only makes things worse and requires twice as much repair work.

c) Apologies are difficult but necessary to do when I make mistakes.

d) It's important to role model the behavior I wish to see in others.

Journal Entry # 3
a) I need to manage both the Winnetka and Boulder departments equally and respond to either when needed. And if they continue to see themselves as separate entities from each other, then I have not done my job.
b) Don't opt to use a consultant to do the work that I should be doing.

Journal Entry # 4
a) It takes a lot of work to turn a "strained" relationship into a "supportive" relationship, but it certainly is worth the effort.

Journal Entry # 5
a) Always support my employees in front of senior management, even when they are being difficult.
b) Don't be afraid to use humor to lighten up an uncomfortable situation.

Journal Entry # 6
a) Supervision is about action. I cannot manage people by doing nothing.
b) It's a lot easier to manage tasks than people but my ultimate success depends on being able to do both effectively!

Journal Entry # 7
a) Sometimes asking the right question is a better intervention than trying to provide the right answer.

- Three good questions to periodically ask the staffs I manage:
    1) What are your strengths?
    2) Where do you need to improve?
    3) How can I (your supervisor) help?
  b) It's important for a staff to think through how they want to handle conflicts <u>before</u> they have a conflict. That way they have a process already in place.

Journal Entry # 8

  a) The easiest way to learn from a mistake is by owning up to it. Granted it may be difficult in the moment, but it certainly is better in the long run.
  b) Standing up for myself and for what I believe in is invigorating!
  c) The key to an effective relationship, whether at work or at home, is open and honest communication. Of course that's easier said than done, but critical just the same.

Journal Entry # 9

  a) When planning a significant change (i.e., like a promotion), it's a good idea to talk to the people that will be impacted the most by that change before announcing it.
  b) Don't wait for relationship problems to escalate before addressing them. This is especially true for the people that really matter to me.
  c) Having a supportive boss is essential to my success.
  d) Sometimes a good practical joke is all a staff needs to lighten up.

Journal Entry # 10

a) It is important to always keep my word with my employees and empower them to hold me accountable when I don't.

b) It's unfair to pass off a difficult employee to another department without being totally up front about what I'm doing. And even then, it's probably not a good idea.

c) Productivity is not always an indication of how well a staff is working together.

Journal Entry # 11

a) Staff commitments (i.e., the Boulder group) work best when there is accountability around those commitments. As manager, it is my responsibility to ensure that happens.

b) Before asking my staff to participate in future projects (i.e., the interview process), it's important that I spell out up front what the process is, what my expectations are, and how a decision will ultimately be made.

c) Challenging decisions that I've asked my staff to make goes in direct opposition to asking them to make a decision in the first place.

d) It's important to create a work environment where employees feel comfortable providing me with feedback about my performance.

Journal Entry # 12

a) Using Walt as the outside facilitator for the teambuilding session allowed me to fully engage in the process instead of being in charge of it. That was a good thing.

b) It's important to discuss safety in groups and establish ground rules before engaging a group in a confrontational discussion.
c) In order for working relationships to thrive, there must be an ongoing avenue available to talk and work through issues.
d) It only takes one staff member to create a tension-filled work environment. Don't ever let it get to that point again.

Journal Entry # 13
a) Within every problem lies opportunity. Never lose sight of the big picture.
b) Change is constant no matter how good or bad things seem.
c) It's important for me to regularly check in with my employees (in both departments) in order to keep communication channels open and available on both ends.

Journal Entry # 14
a) Discovering my purpose and passion means nothing if I'm not willing to follow it.
b) Trusting the process means having an unyielding commitment to a desired outcome, regardless of what's happening around me.
c) For every ending lies a new beginning...but only if I remain open to possibilities.

Dear Dr. Mac (with Justin as Dr. Mac)

Dear Dr. Mac,

I'm very new to supervision and was wondering what advice you have for how I can best develop my people skills.

Greenie Boy

Dear Greenie Boy,

The first piece of advice I'd have is for you to discuss this very question with your immediate supervisor. He or she needs to partner with you to ensure that you get the classes, the resources, and the necessary experiences in order to learn and practice the people skills component of your job.

Secondly, know that one of your best teachers in this process will be your ability to learn from your experiences. In other words, continually be in student mode as you evolve into supervision. This means asking the right questions, being open to others' feedback, and admitting mistakes when you make them. Frankly, that's why keeping a management journal can be so beneficial. It provides a forum where you can record your inner dialogue and think through things in a reflective way.

Lastly, find a mentor. I'm talking about someone like Dr. Mac—someone with whom you can really talk about things and who will provide you with some helpful advice.

—Dr. Mac

Dear Dr. Mac,

I keep hearing people throwing around the term "mentor" and "coach" interchangeably. What's the difference, and is one better than the other?

Sincerely,
Confused Carla

Dear Confused Carla,

There certainly is an overlap between the role of a mentor and the role of a coach. And no, one is not better than the other. It really depends more on what you need from such a relationship.

Typically, the role of a mentor is to serve as a resource—providing guidance, support, and advice when needed. They usually have a wealth of knowledge and experience in a given area and are more than willing to share that with you. The role of a management coach, on the other hand, is to help you develop your own solutions, direction, and actions needed to move forward. Rarely will they interject their own opinions or advice since their focus isn't about teaching you as much as it is about helping you discover your own solutions.

—Dr. Mac

Dear Dr. Mac,

How would I find a mentor?

Lost and Lonely

Dear Lost and Lonely,

Probably the first place to look is within your own organization. Basically, you are looking for someone who has management experience, is well respected, and who can provide you with the right kind of guidance and advice that helps you understand and maneuver through the organization.

Keep in mind you can have more than one mentor. Personally, I have a handful of colleagues and advisors who at any one time can serve as a mentor to me. So even though I don't have a "formal" mentor relationship with any particular individual, I know I can go to any of them whenever I need some help.

—Dr. Mac

Dear Dr. Mac,

I like the journal idea but I am not sure if I'm a journaling kind of person. Your thoughts?

Thanks.
Can't Write a Lick

Dear Can't Write a Lick,

It certainly is true that some of us are more journaling-types that others. Yet I've found that if you can personalize your own method of journaling so that it is both meaningful and useful, you'll be more inclined to continue using it as a self-learning tool. The key is to turn it into a habit. One way to do this in the beginning is by blocking out a particular day and time each week for journaling. Another way is to share your journal entries and insights with your supervisor and/or mentor. Whatever you do, the bottom line is to make sure it works for you.

—Dr. Mac

Dear Dr. Mac,

Do you have any tips on how I can connect with my staff so that I don't have to experience the kind of turmoil that Justin went through in the story?

Don't Want to be Justin

Dear Don't Want to be Justin,

There are two things that you can do on an ongoing basis that should help. First, have informal, one-on-one meetings with each member of your staff at least twice a year. By informal I mean have the meeting over a cup of coffee somewhere outside of the office or in the company cafeteria. The purpose of these meetings should primarily be to check in with each of them on how things are going. Be sure to ask them what more you could be doing to support them at work. This not only keeps the communication channels open but gets them in the habit of giving you feedback as well.

My second suggestion would be to have some sort of teambuilding event twice a year. You need to do something for the group as a whole and teambuilding does make a difference. Keep in mind that not all teambuilding has to be off site or involve "touchy-feely" activities. There are a lot of ways to bring a group together.

—Dr. Mac

A Tribute to the *Real* Dr. Mac

KEN MCDIFFETT (ALSO KNOWN AS DR. MAC), was my graduate school professor at Miami University in Ohio. He was the best professor I ever had and I'm proud to say that he has been a mentor and friend of mine since 1980.

Dr. Mac

I decided to use Dr. Mac's name as one of the main characters for a number of reasons. First and foremost, I wanted to pay tribute to a man who has had such a tremendous impact on my own leadership development for so many years. Secondly, although he never was a management consultant or advice columnist, Dr. Mac is by far the most caring man I have ever met, and one whose personality matched up perfectly with his fictional counterpart. Thirdly, Dr. Mac is the kind of person who has tried to help everyone and anyone who has ever crossed his path without ever once expecting anything back. He represents what is missing in today's leaders—humility for oneself and compassion for others.

Lastly and probably most important, I wanted to inspire future leaders to become their own version of Dr. Mac. If anything, we need more Dr. Macs in the world right now, and perhaps this book will help make that happen.

On May 16, 2006, my friend and mentor passed away. It was the very same day that this book came out. He never saw it.

About the Author

GREG *"GEESE"* GIESEN is president of Greg Giesen & Associates, Inc., a leadership development company specializing in:

- **Keynote/Motivational Speaking**
- **Dispute Resolution**
- **Management Coaching/Consulting**
- **Team Building**
- **Executive Team Retreats**
- *Leading From Within* **Workshop**

Some of Greg's past and present clients include: Anheuser-Busch, Level 3 Communications, Children's Hospital of Denver,

CH2M-Hill, U.S. Forest Service, Fidelity Investments, American Red Cross, National Renewable Energy Laboratory, First Data Corporation, National Public Safety Telecommunications Council, Raytheon Polar Services, Republic Financial Corporation, Judicial Council of California, and the Denver Public Schools, to name a few.

Greg is also the architect and lead-facilitator for the workshop, **Leading From Within;** a highly successful leadership retreat designed to help participants achieve optimal performance as a leader in both their personal and professional lives. Now in its 14th year, Leading From Within was recently awarded the *Best Practices in Training Programs* by the American Society for Training & Development.

In addition, Greg teaches graduate courses at the University of Denver in the areas of public speaking, leadership, and team development and was recently honored with the distinction of Master Teacher. He has also written numerous books on creating authenticity in the workplace.

And finally, Greg produces and hosts the weekly Leading From Within talk radio show on Castle Rock Radio (www .castlerockradio.com). The show features powerful interviews with inspirational authors, speakers, and business leaders. Go to www.greggiesen.com to learn more.

Services Available

To inspire your present and future leaders, contact Greg Giesen about any of the services listed below.

Greg is available to speak on the following topics:
- If You Had To Deliver Your *Last Lecture,* Do You Know What You Would Say?
- Eight Simple Rules…To Mastering Conflict
- Leading From Within: Five Keys to Living a Life with Purpose and Passion
- Using *True Colors* to Improve Communication and Understanding

Macology 101 Certificate Management Program:
Based on the *Mondays at 3* book, the *Macology 101 Certificate Management Program* provides quality soft skills training through a series of eight concise and powerful half-day programs. Candidates selected from your organization or association will go through the certificate series of classes together and will be required to complete deliverables for each class. This program can be customized to fit the needs of your organization.

Leading From Within *Public & Corporate* Programs:

The *Leading From Within* public program is a nationally award-winning transformational workshop developed to help you discover your true passions and purpose in becoming the authentic leader you were meant to be in both your personal and professional life.

By participating in the *Leading From Within* workshop, you will:

- Gain a whole new self-awareness regarding your ability to lead your life with purpose, passion, and integrity.
- Develop the ability to integrate your true leadership abilities into all facets of your life.
- Learn how to lead your life as your authentic self.
- Replace unwanted patterns of your past and re-create new patterns to live and lead by.
- Create a personalized leadership vision, purpose, and balanced scorecard that will guide you to optimal performance in both your personal and professional worlds.

The corporate version of the *Leading From Within* program is designed for intact workgroups and combines leadership development with teambuilding to create a high performance team like you've never seen before.

Ask Greg about the following:
- Conflict Resolution Services
- Management Coaching Program
- Teambuilding
- True Colors Personality Profile Workshop

For additional information about Greg or his services, contact:

Greg Giesen

Greg Giesen & Associates

www.greggiesen.com

greg@greggiesen.com

(866) 322-7868

(303) 346-0183

What Others Are Saying...

Damn, it's good! It totally hooked me in. It is not just for the beginning supervisor. Even an old dog like me can be reminded on how to do this hard stuff. I will definitely be recommending this to others."
—Jo Mattoon, director, Human Resources, City of Arvada

"I finished *Mondays at 3* yesterday—It has been such a breath of fresh air for me to read this novel—The story itself is heart-warming. It touched my soul. I only wish the message on management had come my way earlier in my career. I found myself sad when I finished the book—I WANTED MORE—I laughed, I cried—I felt a gamut of emotions throughout. It's one of those books that the world should 'move it forward' with. Your book is truly awesome."
—Jaime Rosen, Timeless Wood Floors

"While I was getting my hair done yesterday, sitting under the dryer, I was reading your book and got so choked up I got teary-eyed! Good grief!"
—Jo Ellen Snell, Manager of Community and Public Relations, E-470 Public Highway Authority

"Do you know how little sleep I have gotten for the past few days? I cannot put your book down. It is really, really good.

Seriously, I can't stop reading it and I have to force myself to shut off the light and go to sleep. The book flows so well and before you know it I am learning!"
—CHRISTY THEIS, ADVENTURE CLUBS INTERNATIONAL

"I'm not a person who likes to sit and read but found myself intrigued and could not put the book down. The insight that seems to jump out at me is to take opportunities as they come along and don't be ordinary. Discover your passion and follow it. I would recommend *Mondays at 3* it to anyone."
—CARLA CAMPBELL, SENIOR TECHNICAL PROJECT MANAGER, QWEST COMMUNICATIONS

"Greg Giesen cleverly captures his audience by demonstrating how seemingly inextricable problems can be solved with basic managerial and leadership skills. This is an absolutely essential read for young managers and seasoned chiefs who want to review their managerial skills."
—THOMAS C. SCANLAN, PRESIDENT, SURPLUS RECORD MACHINERY & EQUIPMENT DIRECTORY

"*Mondays at 3* tells a really interesting story of the type of struggles we all go through. I would most definitely recommend the book for supervisory personnel as well as anyone who works in a team environment."
—STEVE CHUCKER, SYSTEM ENGINEER/BUSINESS DEVELOPMENT LEAD, THE BOEING COMPANY

"Greg, I have to thank you for this book. It is the only management type book that I have ever encountered, that I started and never sat down. I read it cover to cover in 4½ hours. I was touched and this is a book that I will be sure to keep in my personal library."
—ESTHER DAM, GRADUATE STUDENT

"The short chapters kept my interest in reading, and the characters are so realistic. The story itself was very well explained, especially the transformation of Justin from team member to manager, not to mention all the feelings and emotions that came with it. The journal entries were extremely helpful as well."
—SANTHOSH CHAVAKULA, SR. CONSULTANT, KEANE, INC.

"I am reading the book, and you are so correct: Ken comes through over and over again. I am most thankful that his influence on you has been so meaningful, and know that through you it will be carried to others. That is the kind of legacy of him that I wanted, and deep inside him, it was his."
—RUTH MCDIFFETT, WIDOW OF DR. MAC

"Justin's journey, from raw potential to becoming a successful manager, is an ideal synopsis of how effective leadership can be learned."
—JOHN J. HORAN, PRESIDENT/CEO, HORAN & MCCONATY FUNERAL SERVICE/CREMATION

"I really enjoyed reading *Mondays at 3*. Greg's writing style was easy to read and very thought provoking. I'd recommend this book for anyone in a management position."
—EHAB ABUSHMAIS, ENGINEER, IBM CORPORATION

"Leadership is a contact sport and *Mondays at 3* offers an insightful playbook to help all managers and leaders improve their game! It's a down-to-earth story that emphasizes the fundamentals of self-leadership and people management, with rich lessons for new and experienced leaders alike."
—ADAM COHEN, VICE PRESIDENT, PERFORMANCE EXCELLENCE, CH2M HILL

"Nicely done! I read it, most of it, on a round trip to Washington DC. I thought it was an easy read and is a well-crafted way of delivering messages on how to manage situations."
—IAN MASSEY, PRESIDENT, REPUBLIC FINANCIAL CORPORATION

"Using a story to teach management skills is what I love most about *Mondays at 3*. The reading was fast and easily digested. The main points of the story were exemplified in the journal entries. Well done."
—CRAIG ALBERS, iGEN3 SALES ANALYST, XEROX CORPORATION

"*Mondays at 3* is a believable story of an ambitious young exec who diligently learns the masterful art of leading others."
—CHRIS CLAGGETT, WORKFLOW COORDINATOR,
NEXTEL COMMUNICATIONS

"*Mondays at 3* is some of the finest storytelling on becoming a better leader I have seen."
—ROBERT HOTTMAN, PRINCIPAL, EKS&H

"Every new manager needs to read this book! It's a compelling story full of advice for every new leader."
—MICHELLE DILLARD, TRAINING MANAGER,
ANHEUSER-BUSCH INC.

"Whether you are new to management or a seasoned veteran, *Mondays at 3* has something to teach everyone, leaving readers yearning for a Dr. Mac of their own."
—KAREN WENZEL, EXECUTIVE DIRECTOR, ROCKY MOUNTAIN
MULTIPLE SCLEROSIS CENTER

Go to www.greggiesen.com…

- To order additional copies of *Mondays At 3*.

- To download your <u>free</u> *Mondays At 3 Study Guide*.

- To order the *Mondays At 3* audiobook.

- To order Greg's book, *Creating Authenticity: Meaningful Questions for Meaningful Moments*.

- To order Greg's book, *Creating Authenticity: Meaningful Questions for the Minds & Souls of Today's Leaders*.

- To download your <u>free</u> copy of *The Book of Readings: Inspirational Quotes for the Leader Within*.

- To sign up for Greg's weekly eBlast about upcoming guests for the Leading From Within Talk Radio Show.

- To read Greg's weekly blog.

CPSIA information can be obtained
at www.ICGtesting.com
Printed in the USA
FSOW01n1519301215
15042FS